DEVELOPMENT CENTRE STUDIES

CHINA'S ECONOMIC PERFORMANCE IN AN INTERNATIONAL PERSPECTIVE

By
Ren Ruoen

DEVELOPMENT CENTRE
OF THE ORGANISATION FOR ECONOMIC CO-OPERATION AND DEVELOPMENT

ORGANISATION FOR ECONOMIC CO-OPERATION AND DEVELOPMENT

Pursuant to Article 1 of the Convention signed in Paris on 14th December 1960, and which came into force on 30th September 1961, the Organisation for Economic Co-operation and Development (OECD) shall promote policies designed:

- to achieve the highest sustainable economic growth and employment and a rising standard of living in Member countries, while maintaining financial stability, and thus to contribute to the development of the world economy;
- to contribute to sound economic expansion in Member as well as non-member countries in the process of economic development; and
- to contribute to the expansion of world trade on a multilateral, non-discriminatory basis in accordance with international obligations.

The original Member countries of the OECD are Austria, Belgium, Canada, Denmark, France, Germany, Greece, Iceland, Ireland, Italy, Luxembourg, the Netherlands, Norway, Portugal, Spain, Sweden, Switzerland, Turkey, the United Kingdom and the United States. The following countries became Members subsequently through accession at the dates indicated hereafter: Japan (28th April 1964), Finland (28th January 1969), Australia (7th June 1971), New Zealand (29th May 1973), Mexico (18th May 1994), the Czech Republic (21st December 1995), Hungary (7th May 1996), Poland (22nd November 1996) and the Republic of Korea (12th December 1996). The Commission of the European Communities takes part in the work of the OECD (Article 13 of the OECD Convention).

The Development Centre of the Organisation for Economic Co-operation and Development was established by decision of the OECD Council on 23rd October 1962 and comprises twenty-three Member countries of the OECD: Austria, Belgium, Canada, the Czech Republic, Denmark, Finland, France, Germany, Greece, Iceland, Ireland, Italy, Japan, Korea, Luxembourg, Mexico, the Netherlands, Norway, Poland, Portugal, Spain, Sweden and Switzerland, as well as Argentina and Brazil from March 1994. The Commission of the European Communities also takes part in the Centre's Advisory Board.

The purpose of the Centre is to bring together the knowledge and experience available in Member countries of both economic development and the formulation and execution of general economic policies; to adapt such knowledge and experience to the actual needs of countries or regions in the process of development and to put the results at the disposal of the countries by appropriate means.

The Centre has a special and autonomous position within the OECD which enables it to enjoy scientific independence in the execution of its task. Nevertheless, the Centre can draw upon the experience and knowledge available in the OECD in the development field.

Publié en français sous le titre :

LES PERFORMANCES ÉCONOMIQUES DE LA CHINE DANS LE CONTEXTE INTERNATIONAL

*

* *

Foreword

This study is part of the OECD Development Centre's research programme on "Financial Systems, Allocation of Resources and Growth".

Table of Contents

* With Adam Szirmai

Acknowledgements

We would like to express our deep gratitude to Jean Bonvin and Jean-Claude Berthélemy, without whom this project would never have been possible.

Our thanks also go to Angus Maddison for his indispensable assistance, his constructive suggestions and the unstinting interest he has shown in our work throughout the project.

Amongst those who contributed to the project, we would particularly like to thank Professor Adam Szirmai for his precious co-operation, as well as Hou Jie, Chen Kai, Han Yue, Jiang Pu, Zhang Xiaobin, Zeng Zhaohui et Cheng Jun. Professor Stanley Fischer also played a key role in the course and completion of the work for which we are profoundly grateful.

We are very grateful to the following people for their comments and advice: Dirk Pilat, Bart van Ark, Nanno Mulder, Remco Kouwenhoven, Alan Heston, Dwight Perkins, Abram Bergson, James Poterba, William Wheaton, John O'Connor, Sultan Ahmad, Jong-goo Park, Boris Blásic-Metzner, Jitendra Borpujari, Yonas Biru, Harry Harding, Myron Gordon, Robert Field, Clopper Almon, Peter Harrold, Zafer Ecevit, Albert Keidel, Gyorgy Szilagyi, Gerard Adams, Thomas Rawski, Doak Barnett, Peter Havlik, Athar Hussain, Cui Shuxiang, Mao Yushi, Derek Blades, David Turnham, David O'Connor, Carliene Brenner and two anonymous reviewers for the Review of Income and Wealth.

Our thanks also go to the OECD Development Centre, the Natural Science Foundation of China, the Social Sciences Foundation of China, the Education Committee of China, the Royal Dutch Academy of Sciences, the University of Gröningen in the Netherlands, the University of Maryland, MIT, and the World Bank.

The ideas expressed in this publication are those of the author and do not necessarily reflect those of the OECD, nor of any other institution.

Preface

China has become a major actor in the world economy and will be playing a leading role in the coming decades. Yet the available information on its level of development is incomplete and difficult to interpret. The author of this book, Professor Ren Ruoen, is one of the foremost Chinese specialists in national accounting. His study clarifies the available data and puts the results achieved by China's economy since adopting a policy of openness to the world into perspective.

The author explains an extremely ambitious project to evaluate the Chinese domestic product in a way similar to the methods used by other countries. This means evaluating Chinese output at internationally comparable prices (purchasing power parities: PPPs), rather than using Chinese ones, and comparing the results. The difficulty of collecting and analysing the detailed economic data to bring the research to its conclusion is obvious. The author's calculations have been done thoroughly and provide very useful insights. The analysis reveals that the Chinese domestic product in PPP terms is much greater than indicated by official statistics in Chinese prices. The 1994 per capita output in PPP terms was between $2 200 and $2 500, which shows that China is already a major player. This evaluation clearly changes the view of China's place in the world economy. The country may be further along in the process of catching up than is indicated by official data, but is less open than generally thought, since exports only represent about 5 per cent of its domestic product in international prices, compared to the more than 20 per cent in the official figures. Professor Ren Ruoen also re-evaluates China's real growth: inflation could have been underestimated by 3 to 4 points during the 1985-94 period, meaning that growth was overestimated.

Though these results should be interpreted with reserve because of the uncertainties about the underlying data, the study makes a significant contribution to knowledge of China's economy. The Development Centre is pleased to make it available for readers interested in China's future and its place in the world economy.

Jean Bonvin
President
OECD Development Centre
July 1997

Executive Summary

China has a much larger economy than is commonly believed. Estimated on an internationally comparable scale, its aggregate Gross Domestic Product (GDP) ranks second in the world, higher than those of Germany and probably Japan. Its per capita GDP in dollars is two or three times that suggested by conversions based on exchange rates.

Nearly two decades have passed since China embarked on an economic reform programme aimed at rapid development through greatly enlarged participation in the world economy. It has performed remarkably, becoming one of the fastest-growing and most dynamic economies in the world. Although well known, however, this performance has proved elusive of measurement or comparison on generally accepted international statistical norms, in part because the reform of China's domestic statistical system, while solidly under way, remains incomplete. Experts widely agree that the official figures — and estimates based on them — both understate China's national income and overstate its economic growth rates. Alternative estimates in dollar terms have come largely from academic researchers, and they differ from one another by as much as a factor of ten.

Policy makers, investors and others with an interest in the Chinese economy need better data. Such information can not only help foster better informed and more appropriate policy choices but also permit more reliable evaluation of China's economy, living standards and markets.

This volume reports the outcome of new efforts to make more accurate and internationally comparable measures of the Chinese economy and its performance. It contains two new estimates of China's GDP and comparisons with that of the United States, using the two main methodological approaches now most favoured for this kind of research. The first, built from calculations of the *expenditure* components of GDP, follows techniques developed in the UN International Comparison Project (ICP). The second, the "industry-of-origin" approach developed in the International Comparison of Output and Productivity (ICOP) project at Groningen University, constructs the aggregates from measures of the *output* or production components. Both approaches jettison exchange rates as price converters (a major source of misleading errors) and instead use new estimates of purchasing power parities (PPPs) to achieve international comparability. The two procedures serve as checks against one another.

11

The results provide a new realism. As estimates, they lack precision and demand cautious interpretation, but they offer pragmatic orders of magnitude for China's GDP. They are keyed to 1986, the benchmark year for the ICP calculations; the ICOP work had to be benchmarked to 1985 and updated to 1986 because China's second industrial census covered 1985. In 1986, China's officially reported GDP, converted at the prevailing exchange rate, was $291.5 billion; the World Bank, which also used an exchange-rate converter, estimated it at $430 billion. This study's ICP valuation, however, placed it at $1 082 billion, and the ICOP calculation emerged as $945 billion — with both more or less centred in a group of eight other (non-Chinese) estimates that ranged from $348 billion to $3 678 billion. The per capita GDP numbers naturally tell the same story: the official figure converts to $273; the World Bank puts it at $403; the other estimates range from $347 to $3 448; and this study has yielded $1 014 (ICP) and $886 (ICOP). The new estimates thus lend strong but conservative support to the view that the official figures underestimate the size of the Chinese economy. They also demonstrate the superiority of PPPs as price converters to achieve international comparability.

International comparisons put these figures into perspective, although they too need prudent interpretation. Based on the ICP comparisons, total real expenditure in the United States in 1986 reached 6.3 times that of China when valued with Chinese price weights and 2.5 times China's with US price weights; the corresponding multiples in the ICOP comparison of total real product were 5.6 and 3.6 respectively. On a per capita basis, however, the gap grows radically. In the ICP comparison the US economy appeared 28 times (at Chinese prices) and 11 times (at US prices) as large as China's, with the analogous ICOP multiples at 25 and 16 respectively. Limited comparisons with other countries (limited because they must be on the same basis; it is nonsensical to compare PPP-based figures with those using exchange rates) suggest that China remains a low-income developing country with much lower GDP per capita than dynamic Asian countries like Thailand. At the same time, its GDP was a fraction of those in Hungary, Poland and Yugoslavia at about the time when they began their transitions to market economies — which not only implies caution when making comparisons between them and China but also hints why China chose a generally different reform strategy.

Quite aside from establishing benchmark levels of GDP, an analysis of economic growth rates also has important implications for policy and evaluation of economic performance. The study provides evidence to confirm that officially reported growth rates have been overestimated — and it does so principally with a simple change in methodology to conform with international practice, using available Chinese data. Official estimates of Chinese growth rates use a "comparable-prices" approach; they compare figures on gross product at constant prices, rather than data on gross output at current prices deflated by a price index. Adopting the "deflator" approach, applying a producer price index to reported GDP, and looking at the years of rapid economic progress from 1986 to 1994, the study finds the average growth rate to have been almost four percentage points lower than officially reported — a still enviable 6 per cent rather than the official 9.8 per cent. Extending the technique to the ICP-based dollar series produced a figure of 8.4 per cent and a similar exercise with the ICOP estimates yielded 7.3 per cent, both still below the official figure.

The ICP and ICOP estimates central to this study support several analytic extensions. One of them concerns measures of the openness of the Chinese economy: trade (measured as half the sum of exports and imports) as a percentage of GDP. Use of the exchange-rate converter shows this figure at 22.67 per cent in 1994, almost doubled from 11.40 per cent in 1985; this suggests a very open economy with high dependency on trade. Yet the same measure based on the ICP PPP converter puts the 1994 figure at a much more modest 4.33 per cent, compared with 3.54 per cent in 1985; the comparable figures based on the ICOP PPPs are 5.81 per cent and 4.31 per cent.

Since the early 1980s, China has undergone two restructuring processes: industrialisation and the transition from a centrally planned to a market economy. Its successful, trade-driven development strategy has played a central role in both. The production-side (ICOP) estimates, rich in industry-by-industry detail, make it possible to explore the competitiveness of Chinese manufacturing by looking at relative price levels (the sectoral PPPs divided by the exchange rate), sectoral comparative productivity and unit labour costs.

During the 1980s, Chinese manufacturing experienced improved price competitiveness, due largely to the depreciation of the yuan, which more than offset the effects of persistently high Chinese inflation. Relative prices for all manufacturing in 1994 stood at 37.19 per cent of the US level, well below the 49.38 per cent of 1985; absent yuan depreciation, the 1994 figure would have been 109.31 per cent. Although Chinese labour productivity in manufacturing has grown substantially, by about 50 per cent between 1980 and 1992, it no more than held even with that in the United States; relative productivity was 4.9 per cent of the US level in both years. Manufacturing labour productivity in China likely was about on the level of India's in 1985 — but while India showed a marked improvement in relative productivity between 1980 and 1986, China had no significant change over the same period. Moreover, the productivity gap between China and the leading Asian economies is growing, notwithstanding that China has a very dynamic economy. Unit labour costs in Chinese manufacturing were about 83 per cent of the US level in 1990; they had fallen dramatically from levels higher than in the United States in 1980, reached a low of about 62 per cent in 1985 and then began a strong rise.

Since the early 1980s, increases in manufacturing output may have come mainly from increases in the fraction of the population working in that sector — i.e. labour migration from agriculture to industry, including a shift of hidden agricultural unemployment to industrial employment. This would explain the apparent inconsistency between rapid increases in per capita income for the economy as a whole and the relatively slow increase in labour productivity in manufacturing, the modern part of the economy. Labour costs are low in Chinese manufacturing but rising rapidly. In the face of such increases and because further substantial yuan depreciation seems unlikely, China's manufacturers appear to have only one way to maintain their cost competitiveness, namely to improve labour productivity.

This study has a heavily empirical, statistical focus, aimed at overcoming the substantial methodological problems that estimates of China's national income on an internationally comparative basis encounter. China's statistical authorities have under way major efforts to improve the country's economic data and develop new systems for collecting and reporting economic information in accordance with international statistical conventions. These efforts can only be encouraged.

Chapter 1

Introduction

China's statistical authorities have published very high economic growth rates for the past decade and the international organisations have accepted them. Yet according to figures computed by the World Bank's Atlas approach and published in the Bank's *World Development Report* (1992*a*), the Chinese per capita GDP, in dollars, remained in the range of $300-$370 from 1980 to 1990, notwithstanding relatively slow growth of the population. These figures are inconsistent. The Bank revised upward by 34 per cent its GDP estimate in the national currency for China for the years 1978-93 and now has a new time series showing more volatility of per capita GDP in its *World Tables* (World Bank, 1995); but it still uses the exchange rate to obtain a figure in dollars, which distorts the evaluation of China's economic performance on an internationally comparable basis simply because the Chinese currency has depreciated considerably several times in the past decade.

This study evaluates China's economic performance in an international perspective, based on the findings of two research projects. One derives from work started by a group under the author's guidance five years ago and refined by him at MIT, the World Bank and the University of Maryland in the United States (Ren and Chen, 1994, 1995). This is an expenditure-based comparison of GDP between the United States and China, with 1986 as a reference date, using the purchasing power parity (PPP) approach developed by the United Nations International Comparison Project (ICP). After an introductory review of notable past efforts to estimate China's national income (Chapter 2), revised results from this ICP programme appear in the first part of Chapter 3.

The second project is a production-based bilateral comparison between the same two countries, using an industry-of-origin approach with 1985 as its benchmark year. Professor Szirmai (University of Groningen, the Netherlands) and the author undertook the first stage of this study (Szirmai and Ren, 1995). The approach itself has been developed in the International Comparison of Output and Productivity (ICOP) project at Groningen since 1983. The present study extends it from the industry sector to cover the whole economy, with the findings reported and compared with the ICP results in the second part of Chapter 3 .

Differences between the PPPs for GDP yielded by the two approaches are not significant and the two studies therefore suggest similar levels of development in the Chinese economy. Based on their results, a re-assessment of Chinese growth rates appears in Chapter 4, and Chapter 5 presents an internationally comparable GDP time series built from the basic studies of GDP levels. Together, the level estimates and the time series derived from the production-based study make it possible to explore China's macroeconomic performance as well as comparative productivity at the sectoral level. Chapter 6 discusses the staples of an exercise to examine comparative advantage and the competitiveness of Chinese manufacturing, namely the sectoral PPPs, relative price levels and comparative unit labour costs.

These kinds of studies involve difficult presentational problems because they must include lengthy and detailed methodological discussion as well as voluminous statistical and source documentation — which are essential for other researchers but excessive for policy makers and general readers.

Internationally Comparable Macro Indicators: Some Basic Considerations

Making internationally comparable estimates of any country's GDP involves two distinct stages. The first compiles GDP data in national currencies in an internationally standardised framework such as the UN System of National Accounts (SNA). Where the official compilers of national accounts use the SNA, the data become comparable in terms of the economic activities they cover but not in terms of the units (national currencies) in which they are expressed. When the compilers follow other frameworks such as the Material Product System (MPS), the data lose comparability in terms of both coverage and valuation (see Marer, 1985). The second stage converts the GDP data in national currencies into a common currency, e.g. US dollars or "international dollars", depending on the converter used. Both stages become necessary for countries which do not work within the SNA system; the second stage applies even when they do.

National accounting techniques can measure national income in three ways (Maurice, 1968):

— summing expenditures on output, with principal distinctions between consumption and investment expenditures;

— summing the outputs of industries or enterprises, essentially the sum of value added at each stage of production; and/or

— summing incomes obtained by entities involved in economic activity, broadly distinguished between labour and capital incomes.

In principle, international comparisons can use any or all of these three methods to derive PPPs from local currencies and compare national incomes. In fact, there has been no substantial work on the third technique (the income side), which explains why this study, like most others in the field, focuses on the expenditure and production approaches.

One can make the conversions from local currencies to a common unit in several ways. Exchange rates provide the simplest of these, but they reflect purchasing power mainly over tradeable items. In developing countries where wages are low, non-tradeables such as service sector outputs generally are cheaper than in developed economies; hence the exchange rates would underestimate the purchasing power of these countries' currencies and therefore their income levels. Moreover, exchange rates often are volatile and influenced by capital flows, which makes them unreliable converters even for the advanced OECD countries (see Maddison, 1995, pp. 170-172).

Changes in exchange rates as a result of either devaluations or decisions to let them float freely may produce GDP comparisons unrelated to relative real growth in the countries under comparison. For example, China and India had per capita GDPs of $130 and $110, respectively, in 1973; over the next 15-20 years, China had a much faster growth rate and its GDP (in local currency terms) grew at about 3.5 per cent per year relative to India's; yet official exchange rate conversions ($360 for China and $350 for India in 1990) would suggest that China's real per capita GDP did not increase at all relative to India's (World Bank 1989, 1991).

Comparisons between centrally planned and market economies encounter greater difficulty than those between market economies. This happens not only because the two kinds of economies have different institutional structures, pricing regimes, taxation policies and subsidy systems, but also — and especially — because they have different statistical systems which give different economic meanings to macro measurements (Marer, 1985). For these reasons, and because China has a much lower income level than the United States, a bilateral comparison between the two presents many unusual methodological problems. This study contains some discussion of first-stage work to harmonise the national accounts, but it concerns itself mainly with the second-stage effort to convert the macro indicators into a common valuation.

Chapter 2

Estimates of China's National Income and Growth: An Overview

Estimates of National Income in Local Currency

Reliable measurement of China's national income in its own currency forms the basis for a time series of GDP on an internationally comparable scale. Western scholars have produced since the 1950s a considerable literature on estimating Chinese real income, but Chinese economists gave us the earliest estimates. Ou and his associates published *China's National Income, 1933* in Chinese in 1947 (Ou *et al.*, 1947). Although an English version did not appear, they published two papers based on their work in the *Economic Journal* and *Journal of Political Economy* (Ou, 1946 and Ou *et al.*, 1946), and Ou incorporated the findings of the Chinese version in his Harvard Ph.D. thesis (1948). In the same period, Liu, Ta-chung published *China's National Income, 1931-36: An Exploratory Study* (Liu, 1946). Simon Kuznets undertook a critical examination of these two studies of pre-war Chinese national income during his trip to China in 1946 (Liu and Yeh, 1965).

China computed the national income figures it began to publish in the 1950s according to the "Eastern National Income Accounts System", which used the Material Product System (MPS) methodology. This interested many economists in estimating China's GDP to accord with international statistical definitions and practices. The incompatibility of the two systems arises from the distinction between productive and unproductive labour in Chinese statistical practice. China's State Statistical Bureau (SSB) has published time series for GDP as well as net material product (NMP) since 1978, but for preceding years the construction of GDP estimates has depended on academics.

Three studies using different approaches provided estimates of GDP for China for the 1950s. Hollister based his calculations for 1950-57 on final expenditure, in both constant and current prices (Hollister, 1958). Liu and Yeh relied on the product and expenditure accounts for a time series covering 1952-57 (Liu, 1959). Eckstein combined the value-added approach for agriculture with the factor shares method for all other sectors to offer an estimate only for 1952 (Eckstein, 1961); Perkins (1975) extended the same format for 1952-57. These estimates were not completely independent of economic data provided by the Chinese statistical authorities (Dernberger, 1980). The main data source was *Ten Great Years* (SSB, 1960).

The ongoing lack of data on China's macroeconomic performance in the 1960s and 1970s continued to stimulate efforts to derive estimates of the major indicators of China's economy (Liu, 1968; Swamy, 1973; Liu and Yeh, 1965, 1973; Eckstein, 1973; Perkins, 1975). Recently Wu (1993) attempted ingeniously to bridge the gap between the SNA concept of GDP and the MPS concept. Based on the official data available since 1978, he calculated regression equations relating GDP to NMP in agriculture, industry and services. He applied the results to transform NMP data into GDP estimates for 1952-78. Wu's estimates took a step long awaited towards an extended series for Chinese GDP. Yet because he based them on official GDP figures after 1978, the problems of undercoverage, distorted price weights and inadequate deflators discussed by the World Bank (1992*b*) and Keidel (1992) remain to be solved. Finally, a joint project on multi-factor productivity analysis by a team under Li Jingwen from China, Kuroda from Japan and Jorgenson from the United States built a Chinese GDP time series for 1952-77 — but documentation on the procedure adopted and data sources used is very brief and the reliability of the time series is therefore hard to evaluate (Li *et al.*, 1993).

Table 2.1 pulls together all of the estimates cited above (adjusted where necessary to a current price basis) for part or all of the long period from 1952 through 1977. Two benchmark years have special importance. Many studies took 1952 as the starting point of China's modern economic development, and scholars usually chose 1957 to benchmark later years because most agreed that the official economic data for 1957 were the best before 1978. No great discrepancies appear among the various estimates (including those from recent studies in the 1990s) for 1952, while the estimates for 1957 differ only somewhat more. The recent estimate for 1957 derived from Li *et al.* (1993) is very close to previous calculations. Wu's figure is slightly higher than the others, except for Hollister's. For the longer period after 1957, judgements on the various estimates become much more difficult. In a long perspective, both Wu's and Li's time series suggest similar levels and trends.

To facilitate comparisons of growth rates, Table 2.2 presents (in index form) calculations of China's GDP in constant prices. It includes those from Table 2.1 which originally appeared in constant prices or as indexes, as well as three others. Starting in 1967 and during the 1970s and 1980s, the Joint Economic Committee (JEC) of the US Congress issued a series of studies on the size and growth of the Chinese economy. The first of them reported Liu's estimate (Liu, 1968) with a slight revision. The second (Ashbrook, 1972) contained Ashbrook's work on estimates of China's GNP in 1970 dollars; it provided a much longer time series (1949-73) and implied that China's economy grew faster than suggested by other series prepared in the 1970s but more slowly than indicated by the later work of Wu and Li *et al.* (see Dernberger, 1980).

Table 2.1. **Estimates of China's GDP in Current Prices, 1952-77**
(billion yuan)

Year	Eckstein	Perkins	Liu and Yeh	Hollister	Wu	Li et al.
1952	71.25	70.5	67.86	68.10	70.5	
1953				82.38	85.0	81.46
1954				88.99	89.7	85.91
1955				92.10	94.5	90.58
1956				106.43	105.8	101.37
1957	104.68	104.68	108.80	114.45	109.0	104.36
1958	126.29				134.3	128.54
1959	130.59				146.9	140.34
1960	123.08				146.7	140.12
1961			125.99		119.6	116.42
1962		128.78	122.93		110.9	108.01
1963	126.69		131.73		120.1	116.89
1964			144.25		140.1	136.34
1965		178.3	155.17		166.8	162.18
1966	161.27		166.87		190.9	185.45
1967	153.59		160.87		178.9	173.88
1968			154.67		170.2	165.44
1969			155.21		194.7	191.00
1970	196.01	224.58	170.94		232.1	225.19
1971					250.4	246.63
1972					257.5	254.63
1973					279.6	276.36
1974		296.49			283.2	279.95
1975					302.0	298.38
1976					292.8	289.40
1977					319.1	315.28

Note: Li *et al.* (1993) included a time series (1952-90) for the GDP deflator; this was used to convert some constant-price figures in the original sources to current prices.

Sources: Eckstein's estimates for 1952 from Eckstein (1961); for other years from Eckstein (1973); Hollister (1958); Liu and Yeh (1973); Perkins (1980); Wu (1993); Li *et al.* (1993, in Chinese).

Swamy (1973) tried to assess China's economic development from a different angle. His quite complex methodology converted net value added in each sector into Indian PPP equivalents, at rates which he estimated. He used data for 1952-57 (his or others' calculations) to make estimates for 1958-70 independent from the official figures. The results from this methodology gave the official data after 1957 a poor rating for quality.

Underestimation in Official National Income Figures

After economic reform and opening to the world economy started in the early 1980s, China's statistical authorities began to calculate GDP using methods closer to standard international methodology. In 1992, the SSB implemented a new national income accounts system that is to conform with the basic definitions and methodology of the *United Nations System of National Accounts* (SNA) (United Nations, 1968).

Table 2.2. **Estimates of China's GDP in Constant Prices, 1952-77**
(1957 = 100)

Year	Eckstein 1952 yuan	Perkins 1957 yuan	Liu 1952 yuan	Liu &Yeh 1952 yuan	Hollister 1952 yuan	Ashbrook 1973 $	Swamy rupees	Wu 1980 yuan	Li et al. 1978 yuan
1952					66.3			71.8	65.8
1953					75.3			78.0	74.5
1954					80.0			81.1	78.8
1955					83.4			87.1	83.9
1956					95.0			96.1	95.7
1957	100.0	100.0	100.0	100.0	100.0	100.0	100.0	100.0	100.0
1958	119.6		113.3			120.1	110.4	113.9	122.1
1959	122.4		109.5			114.2	107.7	113.1	131.9
1960	113.9		100.6			113.3	90.7	105.9	129.5
1961			96.7	98.2		87.3	98.9	82.3	93.1
1962		102.1	98.6	98.0		99.4	103.8	82.7	87.0
1963	104.1		102.9	105.0		109.8	112.2	89.4	96.3
1964			109.3	113.0		124.6	121.7	103.8	112.3
1965		140.5	113.4	124.4		142.7	123.9	119.2	131.3
1966	133.2			132.3		154.0		136.4	153.6
1967	125.5			125.3		149.5		130.3	142.5
1968						151.1		123.6	133.2
1969						166.8		139.8	159.0
1970	170.0	189.9		142.8		190.5	125.3	164.6	195.9
1971		202.0				202.8		175.7	213.8
1972						210.2		179.9	219.9
1973						230.8		195.7	238.1
1974						237.8		199.0	240.9
1975								214.9	260.9
1976								209.1	254.0
1977								223.1	274.8

Note: To facilitate comparisons, data for Hollister (1952 base), Wu (1978 base) and Li et al. (1978 base) have been recalculated on the 1957 base common to the rest of the table (ed.).

Sources: Eckstein's estimates for 1952 from Eckstein (1961) and for other years from Eckstein (1973); Hollister (1958); Liu (1968); Liu and Yeh (1973); Perkins (1980); Wu (1993); Li et al. (1993, in Chinese); Ashbrook (1972); Swamy (1973).

Nevertheless, and although SSB has published GDP time series since 1978, studies of the Chinese national accounts (World Bank, 1992b; Keidel, 1992; Wu, 1993; Perkins, 1988) reflect a consensus that official figures underestimate the level of national income in Chinese currency. They offer several reasons:

— *Concepts.* Until recently, Chinese national accounting still used material product concepts to some extent. Material product accounting systems (MPS) report only material output and output in service sectors that make a direct contribution to the production of physical commodities. They do not regard health care, education, passenger transport, government administration and residential housing as related to production and do not measure output in these sectors. The Chinese national accounts still remain a hybrid between MPS and SNA; adjustments are made for services output, but the official statistics on service sectors may be too weak.

— *Incomplete coverage.* The system of data collection is an administrative one, rooted in a planned economy. Enterprises still within the planning system provide statistical agencies with very detailed data, but coverage is weaker in the booming private and semi-private sector of township and village enterprises, and in rural services. Despite recent moves in the direction of sample surveys, administrative reporting remains the basis of data collection.

— *Low valuation of output due to pricing and subsidy conventions.* Even after liberalisation in the 1980s and early 1990s, some prices are still fixed at low levels and do not reflect scarcity relationships. Chinese statistical practice emphasizes quantities rather than prices and values.

— *Provision of free or low-cost services to employees by firms.* Low valuation or failure to account for such services leads to underestimation of value added.

— *Understatement of agricultural value added,* due to the lower valuation of grain products and vegetables produced for farmers' own consumption.

— *Lack of knowledge or underestimation of the informal economy.*

Keidel (1992) estimated China's 1987 GNP as 55 per cent higher than reported in official statistics. He based this figure on adjustments made in three cumulative steps:

1) *Consistency corrections* to the original input-output table to improve valuation consistency and sector assignments of economic activities, especially in real estate activities; they increase GDP by 6 per cent;

2) *Scope and coverage adjustments* in agriculture and housing; they raise GDP by an additional 21 per cent;

3) *Valuation adjustments* result from revaluing prices in sectoral flows so that the net operating surplus in each sector has a reasonable relationship to the value of its productive assets; GDP rises by a further 21 per cent with these corrections.

Keidel found by far the largest discrepancies between official and adjusted data and between MPS and SNA in the service sector. The adjustments in the industry sector (including mining) added up to zero because they cancelled each other out (see Keidel, 1992, Table 1.1). In some sub-sectors of manufacturing Keidel made negative revisions to value added, derived from higher valuations of intermediate service inputs. For example, downward adjustments were 14 per cent for textiles and 41 per cent for consumer manufactures. The most controversial component of Keidel's methodology was his revaluation of sectoral flows with prices that gave sector profits a more uniform relationship to the value of productive assets. This correction is inconsistent with accepted statistical practice in most countries. The World Bank therefore did not incorporate this correction in its revised yuan estimate of GNP for China which raised the figure for GNP by 34 per cent (World Bank, 1994). The SSB recently undertook a census of China's tertiary industry and published a new GDP time series for 1978 onward in its 1995 *Yearbook* (SSB, 1995); it revises upward previous estimates of GDP for all years by 5 to 10 per cent. The revisions affect only tertiary industry and the figures for primary and secondary industries remain unchanged. Considering that the Chinese statistical system is in transition and that some conjectural assumptions underlie Keidel's corrections, the World Bank and SSB adjustments probably furnish a range within which plausible estimates of China's GDP in local currency should tend to fall.

Estimates of National Income in Dollars

Hollister (1958) made the earliest effort to undertake bilateral comparisons between China and the United States in an expenditure framework for three categories of national income: consumption, investment and government purchases. His first estimates covered 1952, whence he derived a comparison for China's GNP in 1955 at 1955 US prices by adjusting for price trends in each country by major categories. Tables 2.3 and 2.4 summarise the two in a standard International Comparison Project (ICP) format.

Eckstein (1961) repriced China's agricultural output in 1952 in Indian and US prices, following the international comparison procedure. His findings revealed exchange rate conversions of China's output in agriculture as grossly misleading. Table 2.5 shows his results, indicating PPPs well below the exchange rate.

Chao (1963) made another effort to estimate the PPPs of the Chinese yuan in 1952. He collected a relatively large sample of prices and weights and gave full documentation on the data and methods. His methodology, however, followed neither the expenditure-based nor the production-based approach because he had prices for both final use and intermediate inputs in the sample, and his breakdowns of GDP did not match the classifications of expenditure or industry of origin. He estimated PPPs much higher than those of Hollister and Eckstein. Building on his earlier work for the JEC, Ashbrook (JEC, 1975) presented estimates for China's GNP in 1949-73, valued in 1973 dollars. He obtained them by converting an estimate of China's GNP in 1955, valued in 1955 dollars, into a 1973 dollar value for China's GNP in 1955 by means of the US GNP price deflator, and then using his index of China's GNP during 1949-73 to obtain values for all the other years.

Over the past decade, the quality and scope of China's economic statistics have improved significantly. Despite more accurate and detailed data, however, the debate over dollar estimates of China's GDP has continued, as researchers deal with such persistent and standard estimation problems as how to account for quality differences between Chinese products and similar US goods, and relative price distortions caused

Table 2.3. **Hollister's Comparison of Chinese and US GNP: 1952**

	Per capita expenditure		Purchasing Power Parity Yuan/$			Per capita values (US value = 100)		
	China (Yuan)	United States ($)	US weights	China weights	Geometric Mean	US weights	China weights	Geometric Mean
Consumption	88.32	1 386.33	3.45	0.94	1.80	6.78	1.85	3.54
Government purchases	13.78	489.87	3.03	0.61	1.36	4.61	0.93	2.07
Gross domestic investment	17.55	321.54	3.61	2.00	2.69	2.73	1.51	2.03
Net foreign investment	-1.60	-1.02						
GNP	118.05	2 196.72	3.38	0.95	1.79	5.66	1.59	3.00

Note: The official exchange rate based on the cross rate with the HK$ was 2.10 yuan to $1.
Source: Hollister (1958)

Table 2.4. **Hollister's Comparison of Chinese and US GNP: 1955**

	Per capita expenditure		Purchasing Power Parity (Yuan/$)			Per capita values (US value = 100)		
	China (Yuan)	United States $	US weights	China weights	Geometric Mean	US weights	China weights	Geometric Mean
Consumption	109.43	1 530.58	3.71	1.02	1.95	7.01	1.93	3.68
Government purchases	17.40	462.84	2.96	0.70	1.44	5.37	1.27	2.61
Gross domestic investment	24.24	364.97	3.07	1.95	2.45	3.41	2.16	2.71
Net foreign investment	-1.75	-2.83						
GNP	149.31	2 355.56	3.46	1.04	1.90	6.09	1.83	3.34

Note: The official exchange rate based on the cross rate with the £ was 2.46 yuan to $1.
Source: Hollister (1958)

Table 2.5. **Eckstein's Comparison of Chinese and US Agricultural Output, 1952**

	Output values (million)		Purchasing Power Parity Yuan/$			Value of Chinese output ($ million)		
	China (yuan)	United States ($)	US weights	China weights	Geometric Mean	US weights	China weights	Geometric Mean
Crops	28 610.8	18 135.9	1.729	0.912	1.2558	31 365.1	16 548.6	22 782.7
Livestock	6 717.6	18 882.0	1.008	1.096	1.0509	6 129.1	6 667.2	6 392.5
Total	35 328.4	37 017.9	0.942	1.361	1.1324	25 958.3	37 494.2	31 197.5

Source: Eckstein (1961)

by state controls. The range of existing dollar measures of GDP by different methods reflects the difficulty of estimating the size of a centrally planned economy undergoing market-oriented reform, and complicates the task of estimating China's productive potential. The most often used methods include the World Bank Atlas approach (World Bank, 1991), the reduced information method (Ahmad, 1980), the ICP technique (Kravis et al., 1975, 1978, 1982), and a production-based PPP approach (Taylor, 1991). Table 2.6 describes nine different studies that used these techniques. Table 2.7 contains the results of five of them (details on the others will appear shortly) and shows why the debate and intensive research continue: efforts to calculate a dollar value of China's GDP by different methods have produced estimates that vary by as much as a factor of ten.

Because of the inadequacy of official exchange rates for converting estimates in national currencies to a common basis of valuation (in most cases, dollars), and the arbitrariness of the physical-indicators method for the same task, the PPP method formulated by the ICP has gained favour as an alternative method. Marer reached this conclusion in his assessment of different methods of computing per capita dollar GNP levels and growth rates for centrally planned economies. The three-year research project which included his work produced a main report on methodology, studies on eight countries, and two background papers (Marer, 1985; Brabant, 1985; Campbell, 1985; Collier, 1985; Fallenbuchl, 1985; Havlik and Levcik, 1985; Hewett, 1985; Jackson, 1985; Mesa-Lago, 1985; Singh and Park, 1985; Wolf, 1985). China was not included in this project. The ICP has been under way for over two decades and has produced benchmark surveys for 90 countries (Kravis et al., 1975, 1978, 1982). The results have been extrapolated to other countries and years in five versions of the Penn World Tables (Summers and Heston, 1984, 1988, 1991). China first appeared in the 1984 Penn World Table (Mark Three).

The Penn World Table (Mark Five) estimates, when applied to the published growth rates, imply excessively high income levels for China. The World Bank (1989) reports a per capita annual growth rate of 5. 5 per cent from 1965 to 1988, which would entail a doubling every 13 years. Kravis (1981) initially published an estimate of China's real GDP per capita in 1975 as 12.3 per cent that of the US (India was 6.6 per cent). That figure, coupled with China's growth rate during the last decade, would have put China at well over 20 per cent of the US per capita GDP in 1988, which most experts on China's economic development believe is too high. Summers and Heston (1991) estimate China's per capita GDP at almost three times India's, but their best guess puts it at only somewhat over twice India's. The latest Penn World Table (version 5.6a) substantially revised the estimates for China (see Table 2.6).

Aside from the Kravis estimates, several other studies in the 1980's compared China's prices with foreign prices to construct PPPs and estimate China's real income in dollars. An annex to the World Bank report entitled *China: Long-Term Development Issues and Options* (World Bank, 1985), contained an input-output Table for 1981 based on a variety of published data. To identify "real" structural differences and similarities between China and other countries, members of the Bank's mission to

Table 2.6. **Comparisons of Nine Studies Estimating China's GNP/GDP in Dollars**

Name of study	Description and comments
US Bureau of the Census PPP Study (J.R. Taylor)	A production-side estimate, which differs from both the ICP and the standard "industry of origin" approaches. Taylor estimated dollar GNP at constant 1981 prices, using average sectoral dollar/yuan price ratios derived from a sample covering mainly the industrial sector. Service sector purchasing power parities (PPPs) were generated from PPPs for manufacturing sectors based on an input-output framework by resort to a general equilibrium model for price formation; the IMF used these estimates for revised weights for China in its *World Economic Outlook* (IMF, 1993). The Taylor study differed from the "industry of origin" approach by using only China's gross values of output, rather than both US and Chinese values, as weights to derive sectoral PPPs. Such one-way weighting seems inappropriate, given that PPPs for a sector or an entire economy should represent aggregated price ratios. (Taylor, 1986, 1991)
Kravis	A "reduced information" exercise which used the ICP approach to approximate China's real per capita GDP in $ for 1975. The estimates reflect price structures and economic conditions before the start of both China's economic reforms and the opening of the economy in the early 1980s. Price data were collected in October 1979 on visits to five cities and rural areas adjacent to three of them. (Kravis, 1981)
Penn World Tables	Five successive versions of these tables have extrapolated benchmark surveys done in the ICP framework. China first appeared in the 1984 Penn World Table (Mark Three), where $ per capita GDP figures for 1950-80 were extrapolations of the Kravis estimates. The 1988 version (Mark Four) made revisions, providing 1980 and 1985 figures in 1980 international prices; Mark Five in 1991 estimated China's per capita GDP at $2 368 for 1988, in 1985 international prices; both were again extrapolations from Kravis. The latest version (Mark 5.6a) substantially revised the estimates for China, for three reasons: (1) a reassessment of constant-price growth rates measured in yuan; (2) an upward revision in GDP (in yuan) by the World Bank in its *World Tables, 1994*; and (3) a new conversion factor derived principally from the present author's expenditure-side PPP estimates for a 1986 benchmark. (Summers and Heston, 1984, 1988, 1991; Penn World Table Mark 5.6a diskette; Ren and Chen, 1994, 1995)

28

Table 2.6. (continued and concluded)

Name of Study	Description and Comments
US Arms Control and Disarmament Agency (ACDA)	Based on World Bank estimates in yuan, with final results in 1987 US dollars. The conversion rate was based on a 1981 PPP (2.23 yuan/dollar) from Taylor, which had its basis in Han's calculation of the ratio of China's total trade (exports plus imports) in yuan at domestic prices to the same at world prices in dollars, using sources from 1979 and 1980. The PPP was shifted to 1987 by the ratio of the Chinese implicit price deflator in yuan to that in dollars. Note that Han's original PPP reflects only the relative price differentials for goods traded between China and the world market; they should be smaller than for non-tradeables, as many studies have demonstrated. (ACDA, 1988; Taylor, 1986; Han, 1982)
World Bank	Based on the World Bank Atlas conversion factor: the average of the official exchange rate for each year and the same rates for the two preceding years, after adjustment for differences in relative inflation between the country concerned and the United States. (World Bank, 1991; upward revision in World Bank, 1994)
Ahmad	Estimated real per capita GDP for 1981 based on retail-price yuan/dollar ratios constructed from a comparison, in a standardised format, of the structure of Chinese prices with those of other countries. (Ahmad, 1983)
Gordon, et al.	Constructed PPPs between the yuan and the Canadian dollar, by economic sector, based on some strong assumptions; estimated China's GDP prices in 1987 at about one-sixth of Canada's. (Gordon et al., 1990; see also comments by Summers and Heston in Penn World Tables, version 5.6)
Wharton Economic Forecasting Associates (WEFA)	Constructed retail price PPPs to estimate the Chinese net material product in dollars (1981 benchmark). (WEFA, 1984)
Ma and Garnaut	Based on strong assumptions, including that of a stable relation between food consumption and national income across countries, the analysis compares Chinese per capita food consumption with that of other Asian economies (e.g. Chinese Taipei, Hong Kong, Singapore, Korea and Japan) and suggests that Chinese official GNP figures should be revised upward by a factor of three. (Ma and Garnaut, 1992)

Table 2.7. **Estimates of China's Per Capita GDP**
(1986 $)

Year	Census PPP Study (Taylor)	Penn World Table (Mark 4)	Penn World Table (Mark 5)	ACDA	World Bank	Growth rates from yuan data (per cent)
1978	442			217	347	9.5
1979	469			230	377	6.8
1980	488	2 152		241	399	5.9
1981	506			249	388	5.7
1982	544			268	365	4.9
1983	592			294	351	7.8
1984	670			332	338	13.0
1985	737	3 248		466	339	11.3
1986	785			391	310	6.8
1987	853			422	300	9.3
1988	918		2 368		310	9.6
1989	939					2.8

Source: Originally from US CIA (1991) ; the figures are based on GDP in Chinese currency before upward revisions made in the 1995 Chinese Yearbook (SSB 1995). The aggregates have been converted to per capita numbers in constant 1986 dollars by the relevant price index and population figures. The growth rates in the last column were calculated by this author, based on data for China's GDP index and the population growth rate, from the 1994 *Chinese Yearbook* (SSB, 1994).

China attempted, on the very limited information available, to explore price differences between China and other countries. They estimated price-adjustment coefficients in each sector and used them to modify the input-output table. In principle, each price-adjustment coefficient should be the ratio of the average price of gross output in the sector in question in a typical low-income country to its average price in China, suitably corrected for differences in commodity composition within the sector. Table 2.8 shows that large discrepancies persist among the purchasing power parity studies themselves. The table includes the two estimates of PPP for GDP ("Ren ICP" and "Ren ICOP"; see Chapter 3), which have been the major objective and comprise the principal findings of the current study. Per capita GDP estimates for China based on the PPP approach cannot be compared with those for other developing countries based on the World Bank Atlas approach; different estimates by different methods imply very different positions of China relative to other countries. Table 2.9 presents comparative estimates of GDP for China and the United States, again including the estimates developed in this study.

As Tables 2.8 and 2.9 indicate, the two calculations of China's 1986 per capita dollar GDP developed in this study differ substantially from the other estimates cited. Several reasons explain the discrepancies. The World Bank's estimate ($403) used the Atlas approach, a method based on exchange rates. This study's results should be expected considerably to exceed it, given the findings in ICP and other theoretical studies on the relationship between PPPs and exchange rates in low-income countries, using the productivity differential or factor proportion differential model (Kravis, Heston and Summers 1982; Kravis and Lipsey 1983; Bhagwati 1984). WEFA's estimate ($327) raises questions because it falls even lower than the World Bank figure, although it claims to follow the PPP methodology (Taylor, 1986). Taylor's alternative estimate ($788) derives from a production-based approach that differs from the ICOP methodology discussed in Chapter 3. He also has generated PPPs for missing sectors producing many non-tradeables (e.g. services) using PPPs for manufacturing sectors which include mostly tradeable goods, based on an input-output table. This procedure is difficult to justify in light of ICP and related theoretical studies in the past several decades and the impossibility of using a general equilibrium model to simulate price formation in China in 1981 (the benchmark of Taylor's study). Gordon ($1 663) applied the PPP concept in general but has poor statistical support and strong assumptions, which weaken the comparability of his estimate.

Table 2.8. **Estimates of Yuan/$ PPPs and Chinese Per Capita GDP in Dollars,**
1986

Benchmark year	Author	Yuan/$ PPP in 1986	Per capita GDP 1986
1975	Kravis	0.34	2 813
1981	Ahmad	0.8998	1 063
1981	Taylor	1.2134	788
1981	WEFA	2.9464	327
1986	Ren (ICP)	0.9432	1 014
1985	Ren (ICOP)	1.0793	886
1987	Gordon	0.5752	1 663

Note: The PPPs are extrapolated by deflating PPPs originally derived for the benchmark years of these studies (column 1). Per capita figures are based on the yuan estimate of 1986 per capita GDP from the 1995 *Statistical Yearbook* (SSB, 1995) and the extrapolated PPPs. Population figures are from the same source and adjusted to a mid-year basis.

Sources: See Table 2.6 and Chapter 3. Consumer price indexes from SSB (1995) and SSB (1987a) for China and US Department of Commerce (1992) for the United States were used as deflators for PPPs — except for deflation of Taylor's PPP which is based on producer price indexes from the same sources.

The Penn World Table results ($3 448 in Mark 4 and $2 513 in Mark 5) were extrapolated from Kravis ($2 813) which followed the ICP methodology. In fact, only Kravis's estimates and the present study take the same methodological approach. The higher Kravis figures may result from two possible causes. First, Kravis calculated the PPPs from a sample of prices with limited coverage. Second, several adjustments in the housing and service sectors made in the present study lead to much higher PPPs for these categories than those revealed by the actual prices.

Table 2.9. **Comparisons of Chinese and US GDP**
Based on Various Estimates of PPP, 1986

Country	Source	Aggregate GDP		Per capita GDP	
		(million)	(US = 100)	($)	(US = 100)
United States		4 268 600	100.00	17 735	100.00
China	Penn (Mark 4)	3 677 815	86.16	3 448	19.44
	Penn (Mark 5)	2 681 225	62.81	2 513	14.77
	Kravis	3 000 520	70.29	2 813	15.86
	Gordon	1 773 866	41.56	1 663	9.38
	Ahmad	1 134 199	26.57	1 063	5.99
	Ren (ICP)	1 081 660	25.34	1 014	5.71
	Ren (ICOP)	945 250	22.14	886	5.00
	Taylor	840 705	19.70	788	4.44
	ACDA	442 929	10.38	415	2.34
	World Bank	430 028	10.07	403	2.27
	WEFA	348 323	8.16	327	1.84

Sources: The Penn, ACDA and World Bank per capita GDPs from Table 2.7; the others from Table 2.8. The Chinese population (1.06679 billion) from SSB (1995), adjusted to a mid-year basis. Data for the United States from US Dept. of Commerce (1992) (the population figure is 240.68 million).

Concluding Remarks

The estimation of Chinese income in Chinese currency according to the SNA guidelines has always been central to studies of Chinese economic development in western literature. As the Chinese statistical system has moved towards the SNA concept of national accounting, more scholars use the official data in their research, although problems of understated output remain significant. As the Chinese statistical transition proceeds, the reliability of the macro-indicators issued by SSB will improve. While this result must come primarily from SSB's own work, experience accumulated in the international community can be very helpful. Estimates of Chinese GDP in an international common unit also are in high demand because of their usefulness for analysis, especially for international comparisons; these have their place alongside but distinct from the important analytic and policy uses for accurate and improved national accounts in local currency.

The growth rate, another important indicator for evaluating economic performance, presents a puzzle because on the one hand China's dynamic economy has grown very fast, while on the other the official growth rate is too high to be accepted. Methodology comprises the key factor in this anomaly. Chinese statistical convention uses the comparable-prices approach to estimate growth rates. A switch to the use of deflators would greatly improve the estimates. An exploratory exercise developed in this study provides evidence for this.

Chapter 3

New Estimates of China's GDP Level

This chapter presents the principal findings of the study: new estimates of China's GDP and comparisons with that of the United States, using the two main methodological approaches most often applied in this kind of research. The first, built from calculations of the *expenditure* components of GDP, follows techniques developed in the ICP programme. The second (ICOP) constructs the aggregates from measures of the *output* or production components. In an ideal world with perfectly accurate and comparable data, the two should match. The absence of such ideal conditions has spawned the massive, detailed methodological and statistical research which the topic has attracted over the decades.

Estimate of China's GDP in the ICP Framework

A significant advance in international national income comparisons occurred at the Organisation for European Economic Co-operation (OEEC) in the 1950s (Gilbert and Kravis, 1954; Gilbert and Associates, 1958; Paige and Bombach, 1959). All subsequent international comparison studies follow either the production approach of Paige and Bombach or the expenditure methodology now associated with the ICP programme. The ICP has been under way for over two decades, producing benchmark surveys for 90 countries at one time or another. Techniques for providing multilateral measures at The Progress with and Prospects for Reform in Non-Member Countries "international" prices by Geary-Khamis (Geary, 1958; Khamis, 1970; 1972; 1984) or other approaches were developed in the ICP, which also pioneered the bilateral comparison methodology. The methodological research reports on the first three phases of ICP for 1967, 1970 and 1975 (Kravis, *et al.* 1975, 1978, 1982), published the three binary PPP variants — the Paasche PPP (with own-country weights); the Laspeyres PPP (with quantity weights of the numerary country, the United States); and the Fisher geometric mean of the Laspeyres and Paasche measures. China has not fully participated in the ICP surveys, and its PPPs and GDP in "international" prices by multilateral comparison methods remain unavailable. A bilateral comparison between China and the United States in the ICP framework, such as that provided here, thus retains a top priority.

Outline of the ICP Bilateral Comparison Methods

This methodology has been described in detail in many publications (see Kravis et al. 1975, 1978, 1982 and Kravis, 1984), so only an outline is needed here. The actual work of bilateral comparisons from the expenditure side includes two main steps: first, to choose a sample of items and match their qualities and prices for the two countries being compared, within the Classification System of the ICP; and second, to aggregate the quantities being compared.

The GDP of each country represents a set of final purchases of commodities and services. Some of these are common to both countries, while others appear only in the set of one country or the other. In principle, an international price comparison should be based on a representative sample of the price ratios for the goods and services found in the overlapping set. The process of choosing price ratios for China and the United States involved an attempt to match quality as closely as possible, subject to resource constraints and data availability. The basic information for a benchmark year consists of two sets of data for each country:

— expenditures in domestic currencies for all detailed commodity categories and services defined by the ICP approach. These expenditures add up to GDP;

— a sample of price ratios that provide at least one such ratio between China and the United States for each category. Some detailed categories have empty boxes.

The ICP approach operates through price comparisons for about 150 detailed categories. The methods chosen for the bilateral comparisons should satisfy the following three requirements:

— *Characteristicity*: The sample of prices or quantities and the weights used in an international comparison conform closely to a representative sample of items and to the weights of each of the countries included in the comparison. This means that a comparison between any two countries is influenced only by the commodities, prices, and weights of the two countries. Data associated with all other countries are ignored. When the purpose is to compare a pair of countries, a bilateral comparison is the best choice (see Kravis, *et al.* 1978, pp. 5, 70, 255).

— *The country-reversal test*: In a given bilateral comparison, it should not matter which country is used as the base country. According to index number theory, this means that if $I_{j/k}$ represents the price index for countries j and k with the base country in the denominator, then the following identity should hold:

$$I_{j/k} \times I_{k/j} = 1 \qquad\qquad (3.1)$$

— *The factor-reversal test:* The product of the price and quantity ratios should equal the expenditure ratio, and both the price and quantity indexes must be computed independently.

The first calculation is carried out within each detailed category. Because the expenditure data used as the weights are not available at the detailed category level for both China and the United States, an unweighted geometric mean of those price ratios is used for that category if more than one price ratio is available for a detailed category. For example, for category I:

$$(PPP)_i = \left[\prod_{\alpha=1}^{A} \left(\frac{P_{\alpha c}}{P_{\alpha u}} \right) \right]^{1/A} \tag{3.2}$$

where $(PPP)_i$ is the purchasing power parity (PPP) of the *ith* detailed category; $P_{\alpha c}$ is the price of the αth item in China; $P_{\alpha u}$ is the price of the αth item in the United States (the prices are expressed in the local currencies); and A is the number of items within the category. In ICP-type international comparisons, the geometric mean is preferable to the arithmetic mean because it satisfies the country-reversal test. The necessary use of an unweighted mean departs slightly from common statistical practice; for discussion on this topic, see Kravis *et al.* (1975).

Averaging within each detailed category yields the PPP for each of about 150 detailed categories (Kravis, *et al,* 1975). Laspeyres, Paasche, and Fisher index-number formulas were used to estimate the PPPs for GDP and other aggregates. The PPPs for the detailed categories were aggregated using first the US expenditure weights and then the Chinese expenditure weights. The formulas for these weighted indexes are:

$$I_u = \sum_{i=1}^{m} \left(\frac{P_c}{P_u} \right) \times w_{iu} \tag{3.3}$$

$$I_c = \frac{1}{\sum_{i=1}^{m} \left(\frac{P_u}{P_c} \right)_i \times w_{ic}} \tag{3.4}$$

where the index i runs over the categories, u is the subscript for the United States and c is that for China. The weights are:

$$w_{iu} = \frac{e_{iu}}{\sum_{i=1}^{m} e_{iu}} \tag{3.5}$$

$$w_{ic} = \frac{e_{ic}}{\sum_{i=1}^{m} e_{ic}}$$

(3.6)

where e is per capita expenditures in local currency.

The Fisher index, the geometric mean of the China-weighted and US-weighted index numbers, was then calculated for each sector. This is also called an ideal index number because it meets criteria set by Irving Fisher as necessary conditions for an ideal index (Fisher, 1922).

These aggregation methods suggested by ICP have a very intuitive interpretation, especially because the international comparisons can be regarded as the counterpart to single-country, intertemporal comparisons in a certain sense. See Hill (1982) and Diewert (1986) for excellent discussions of this issue.

After selecting the sample of prices and specifying each item in the sample, careful comparisons tried to ensure that qualities were equivalent between China and the United States. For some goods, such as foods, quality can be assumed to be the same; while for others, no brief specification can define the product with sufficient precision to ensure quality matching. Each specification still covers a variety of different goods. A useful way of coping with this problem is to consult engineering experts. Sometimes, they can give the price ratios for products whose qualities are matched; or they can provide specifications for matched products. These clues yield more price ratios for the sample. This approach was used for aircraft, ships and boats, and metalworking machinery.

The criteria used in the matching process were:

— *physical identity:* The preferred method is to find physically identical goods in both countries. This is possible where the same goods of a given brand or trademark are sold. Many durable consumer goods and other goods fell into this group, because imported goods were selected for the specifications;

— *equivalence in quality:* In some cases, exactly identical commodities cannot be found, but products in both countries conform with the same general specifications, with slight and relatively unimportant differences in design or composition. If such differences are unlikely to affect the price ratios, it is safe to ignore them and include the items in the comparison;

— *replication of products:* In principle, the end product is regarded as the standard in assessing equivalence in quality, and different prices are compared for equivalent goods even though different means of production are used in the two countries;

— *equivalence in use:* In some cases products not physically identical clearly serve the same needs or uses. The most obvious example is the light bulb. The United States uses 120-volt bulbs whereas China uses 220-volt bulbs, and no differences exist in either their utility or their costs of production under similar conditions in the same country. Hence they qualify for treatment as equivalent products;

— *taste equivalence:* In a few cases, one variant of a product was cheaper than another in one country, but the reverse occurred in the other country. These instances were regarded as attributable to taste differences, and a direct price comparison was made between the cheaper variants in each country.

Results of the ICP Bilateral Comparison

Table 3.1 contains a summary of the purchasing power parities (PPPs) and the principal aggregates in the bilateral comparison. More complete sectoral results appear in Table 3.A.11.

Table 3.1. **A Summary of ICP Expenditure Comparisons: China and the United States, 1986**

	Consumption	Capital formation	Government	GDP
Purchasing Power Parities (Yuan/$)				
US weights	1.1158	2.8417	0.5403	1.5091
China weights	0.5840	0.9634	0.2099	0.5895
Geometric Mean	0.8072	1.6546	0.3368	0.9432
Per capita expenditure in China				
(US = 100)				
US weights	9.13	6.88	14.29	9.15
China weights	4.78	2.33	5.55	3.57
Geometric Mean	6.60	4.00	8.90	5.72
Expenditure (billion)				
China				
$	1 019.79	329.81	309.10	1 730.66
Yuan	637.60	317.74	64.88	1 020.22
United States				
Yuan	3 011.13	3 074.43	263.71	6 441.74
$	2 698.63	1 081.90	488.07	4 268.60
Per capita expenditure				
China				
$ (at China-weighted PPPs)	1 023.42	309.17	289.76	1 622.31
Yuan	597.68	297.85	60.82	956.35
United States				
Yuan (at US-weighted PPPs)	12 510.93	12 773.92	1 095.67	26 764.76
$	11 212.52	4 495.17	2 027.89	17 735.58

Sources: Annex Table 3.A.11.

37

These results revise earlier estimates by Ren and Chen (1994, 1995). Based on data from the *Statistical Yearbook of China, 1995* (SSB, 1995), the per capita GDP of China was 956.35 yuan in 1986, which converts to $1 622 using the China-weighted PPPs. More significantly, however, use of the Fisher PPP (the geometric mean) of 0.9432 derived in this study produces an estimated per capita GDP for China in 1986 of $1 014, somewhat lower than the $1 098 obtained using the Fisher PPP of 0.8709 derived from the earlier study. Both results still considerably exceed the value obtained by converting at the official exchange rate and show about an 8 per cent difference. The main revisions which produced the difference between the present estimate and the previous one are:

— a quality adjustment in the housing comparison;

— a higher estimate of Chinese housing expenditure and an effort to match the shadow prices for Chinese housing in estimating the PPP for the category;

— the comparison of government now includes expenditure on commodities as well as compensation of employees;

— some revisions in expenditure weights used in the aggregation of PPPs; and

— the expenditure weights for consumption, investment and government of the United States in the final aggregation of PPPs, from the Penn World Table version 5.6, differ slightly from those used in the previous calculation.

The Paasche-Laspeyres spread (PLS) derived as the ratio of the per capita GDP of China with US price weights to that with Chinese price weights — which is the same as the yuan/dollar PPP in US quantities divided by the same PPP in Chinese quantities — provides one way to analyse the plausibility of estimates. This study has a PLS of 2.56, compared with the 3.18 calculated from the earlier study. This lower PLS suggests an improvement in the estimates.

Analysis of Errors

An international comparison concerning China encounters many unusual methodological problems because China has a much lower income and very different institutions. This study should therefore be considered very preliminary — an attempt not to give an accurate estimate, but only to suggest possible orders of magnitude within which China's US dollar per capita GDP might lie. In this perspective, it becomes very important to analyse the sources of errors.

The ICP work shows that deleting some sub-aggregates will affect the final results. To analyse the effects of errors in the comparisons of gross capital formation, the results of the comparisons after deleting one to five sub-aggregates from the original seven were calculated and compared. Errors increased as the number of deleted sub-aggregates increased.

During the collection and processing of data, because national average prices were not available in some categories for China, an average of prices collected in ten cities was substituted. Limitations of time and resources prevented incorporation of price information from rural areas in the calculations. Because rural areas account for the lion's share of both population and territory, this must have distorted the final results; more information is needed to judge the direction and extent of the errors.

This study has made an effort to estimate some prices where markets still did not clear or even did not exist in the benchmark year in China, as in the cases of rent, health services, education and government. These adjustments probably are insufficient and an upward bias may still exist in estimating Chinese real income.

Another source of errors arises from the use of prices of some imported or luxury goods in the survey. Some categories have no comparable domestic goods, so imported goods were taken as representative. Domestic import substitutes do exist for some other categories. The original purpose for taking these prices was to obtain better quality matching, but two kinds of error intrude. First, the selection of the prices of imported and luxury goods does not meet the *characteristicity* requirement because these goods account for only a small share of actual consumption of such goods. Second, the price differentials between imported and domestic goods reflect quality differentials only partially. Imported goods can be more expensive both because their quality exceeds that of similar domestic products and because they are simply overpriced. The inclusion of these prices in the sample generally would lead to an upward bias in the estimates of real income in the former case and a downward bias in the latter one.

An assumption of no international productivity differential between professional personnel was made in comparison-resistant categories. Several issues relate to this assumption. Many ICOP studies have shown that productivity gaps between countries can vary greatly among industries (van Ark, 1993a, van Ark and Pilat, 1993); a country very advanced in some industries may not have the same position in others. Theoretical studies related to empirical work on international comparisons have shown that the service sectors in low income countries have relatively higher productivity than the manufacturing sectors (Bhagwati, 1984). An industry-specific study would be needed for the adjustment of productivity in any industry in the international comparisons. Many unresolved questions persist in the measurement of service sectors in the national accounts and in international comparisons (see Kravis *et al.,* 1982). For example, what is output in these comparison-resistant sectors? If it cannot be defined and therefore measured accurately, how can an adjustment of the international productivity differential be made?

Phase III of the ICP introduced the number of pupils as a further dimension of output in the education sector and the results showed that low-income countries have higher quantity indexes because they have larger class sizes than higher-income countries. This certainly would be the case in China if numbers of pupils were adopted as the indicator to measure educational output. An alternative approach takes educational achievement as the output indicator. Some international comparisons (Kravis, *et al.*, 1982, Pilat, 1994) have used international test scores for several subjects across countries. The International Association for the Evaluation of Education Achievement has conducted comparative international studies of educational achievement for a large sample of countries. China has participated only in the Second International Science Study, contributing data for several cities (Postlethwaite and Wiley, 1992). These results certainly are not representative for this study, but if more complete data become available this approach would be worth using to make an alternative assumption on the productivity differential.

This study made a quality adjustment only for the housing category and it is tentative. If such desirable quality adjustments could be made for other Chinese goods and services, the PPP for GDP would be higher and the real income level would be lower.

Concluding Remarks on the ICP Estimates

This comparison has the basic goal of estimating a conversion factor which can be used to convert macroeconomic indicators from local currency to dollars for China based on ICP methodology. Because it is a cross-system comparison, many adjustments have been made to take into account the institutional differences between the two countries, especially in service sectors. Further research would almost certainly improve this estimate. A new survey of prices supported by the official statistical authorities will provide more information on the dollar/yuan price ratios for all sectors and the economy. This may correct some biases in this study due to lack of information — the price differential between urban and rural areas, for example, and the allocation of imported and domestic goods in some categories.

Estimate of China's GDP in the ICOP Framework

Data from censuses of industry permit a detailed and reliable estimate of PPP for each industry in manufacturing by the "industry-of-origin" approach, with results useful for economic analysis and the formulation of economic policy. This section presents an alternative bilateral comparison between China and the United States for 1985 using such a production-based method. China's second industrial census in 1986 (the first since 1950), which produced data for 1985, dictated the choice of the benchmark year. This work has three main objectives:

The new estimate of real GDP offers a cross-check on the results obtained from the expenditure-based approach and permits an attempt to reconcile the two estimates. The reconciliation provides new insights into the problems involved in the estimation of real income in an internationally comparable framework for developing countries and countries in transition from centrally planned to market economies.

Comparisons between the PPPs at different levels of aggregation (industry, branch, sector, economy as a whole) obtained by the two methods help to highlight the specific characteristics of the Chinese economy; in many cases, the differences relate to transport costs, distribution margins, subsidisation and taxation systems and so on.

The industry-of-origin method yields additional information on productivity differentials. Hence it can provide fresh perspectives on Chinese economic performance at the sectoral level in an international context and highlight comparative advantages in Chinese manufacturing.

The industry-of-origin approach to compare real output by sector derives originally from Rostas (1948), Paige and Bombach (1959) and Maddison (1970). The Paige and Bombach study pioneered sectoral comparisons for the economy as a whole and contrasted with the aggregate results obtained in the expenditure study by Gilbert and Kravis (1954). Other investigations of the ICOP type have covered agriculture (van Ooststroom and Maddison, 1984; Maddison and Van Ooststroom, 1993); mining (Wieringa and Maddison, 1985, Houben, 1990); transport and communication (Mulder, 1994a, 1994c, 1995a); distribution (Mulder and Maddison, 1993, Mulder, 1994b); and manufacturing (30 binary comparisons, see van Ark, 1993a). Pilat (1994) completed the first international ICOP comparisons covering the total economy for Japan, South Korea and the United States. He used ICOP techniques for goods-producing sectors (agriculture, mining, manufacturing, utilities, transport and communications), and the quantity-indicator approach for education, finance, insurance, and real estate. For comparison-resistant services (distribution, health, other private services, government) and construction, Pilat used existing ICP estimates of PPPs or proxy PPPs derived from them. Meanwhile work has continued within the ICOP project on the further development and refinement of the methodology for comparisons in service sectors along lines set out in Mulder and Maddison (1993) and Mulder (1995b, 1995c, 1995d, 1995e, 1995f).

Outline of the ICOP Bilateral Comparison Methods

The ICOP technique has extensive description in the literature (see van Ark, 1993a; Maddison and van Ark, 1988, 1994a, 1994b; Szirmai and Pilat, 1990). Because it is well adapted — and has been widely used — for level comparisons in manufacturing, this brief outline will focus on that sector to show the essence of the ICOP method. The primary data sources used in the comparison of those sectors for which a standard ICOP method can be applied are the censuses of manufactures, agriculture, and other sources on the US side and the industrial census, national accounts and input-output table for China. These sources provide information on product quantities and gross output values, making it possible to derive unit values for large numbers of products.

The basic approach involves matching comparable products or product groups from the two countries and calculating unit-value ratios based on the ex-factory prices of products for each of the matches. The unit-value ratios are used to calculate PPPs in a number of steps. First, all the ratios are aggregated for sample industries for which the ex-factory prices of the main products can be compared, using output quantities of either country as weights:

$$
PPP_j^{XU(X)} = \frac{\sum_{i=1}^{s}(Q_{ij}^X * P_{ij}^X)}{\sum_{i=1}^{s}(Q_{ij}^X * P_{ij}^U)} \qquad PPP_j^{XU(U)} = \frac{\sum_{i=1}^{s}(Q_{ij}^U * P_{ij}^X)}{\sum_{i=1}^{s}(Q_{ij}^U * P_{ij}^U)} \qquad (3.7)
$$

where:

$PPP^{XU(X)}$ is the purchasing-power parity of the Chinese yuan against the dollar in sample industry or sector j, with Chinese quantity weights;

$PPP^{XU(U)}$ is the purchasing-power parity of the yuan against the dollar in sample industry or sector j, with US quantity weights; and

$i = 1...s$ is the sample of matched items.

Next, the sample industry or sector PPPs are aggregated at the branch level in manufacturing or in other sectors producing commodities, such as agriculture, mining, transport and communications, by taking the weighted average of sample-industry or detailed-sector PPPs, using gross value added weights:

$$
PPP_k^{XU(U)} = \frac{\sum_{j=1}^{o}[GVA_j^{U(U)} * PPP_j^{XU(U)}]}{\sum_{j=1}^{o}GVA_j^{U(U)}} \qquad PPP_k^{XU(X)} = \frac{\sum_{j=1}^{o}GVA_j^{X(X)}}{\sum_{j=1}^{o}[GVA_j^{X(X)} / PPP_j^{XU(X)}]} \qquad (3.8)
$$

where:

$GVA^{U(U)}$ is gross value added in US sample industry or detailed sector j in dollars;

$GVA^{X(X)}$ is gross value added in Chinese sample industry or detailed sector j in yuan;

k is the branch or sector of industry; and

$j = 1...o$ is the sample of industries belonging to k.

Finally, the branch PPPs are aggregated into PPPs for total manufacturing or other sectors such as agriculture, transport and communications, using branch value added weights. The rationale behind these weighting procedures is to ensure that unit-value ratios in large sample industries and branches receive larger weights than in small ones (see van Ark, 1993a, 1993b).

At each level of aggregation — sample industry, branch and total manufacturing — the PPPs serve to convert value added into the currency of the other country for real value added comparisons. Because insufficient information exists on quantities and values of inputs, ICOP studies have generally applied output PPPs to value added, although theory calls for double-deflated comparisons based on PPPs for both inputs and outputs. In bilateral comparisons one gets two PPPs at every level of aggregation, one at quantity weights of country X, the other at quantity weights of country U. If the production structures are very different, as is often the case in a comparison of a low-income country with an advanced economy, the PPPs may differ quite substantially. This study uses the Fisher geometric average of the two PPPs as a summary measure.

Because each sector on the production side of an economy has its own characteristics, the comparisons involved for each sector fall into four categories of methods used.

— In the agriculture, mining, manufacturing, public utilities and transport and communications sectors, a standard ICOP method was applied based on the direct product matches.

— The distribution sector (wholesale trade and retail trade) will not support application of the ICOP method based on matches of products because this sector intermediates between producers and consumers and does not produce any physical product (see Pilat (1994) on this issue). The PPPs from the expenditure-based study were reweighted and used in the comparison for this sector.

— For finance, insurance and real estate, the PPPs were calculated from quantity indicators. The quantity-indicator approach and the standard ICOP method have both similarities and differences.

— In construction, education, health services, other services and government, the PPPs from the expenditure-based study served as proxy PPPs. For construction, this approach is valid because construction output is only for final use. For other sectors in this category, conceptual difficulties or lack of information made it impossible to derive PPPs by the ICOP approach.

International comparisons for two countries from expenditure-side and production-side calculations should in theory show no difference between the PPPs for aggregate GDP. In practice, both they and PPPs for each sector can differ simply because of the heterogeneity of primary sources. For the sectoral PPPs, moreover, differences which arise between the estimates relate to two dimensions that matter:

—   While the PPPs in an expenditure-side study derive from market prices, the unit-value ratios in an industry-of-origin analysis use ex-factory prices. The latter omit the transport-cost, commercial-margin and indirect-tax components of prices.

—   The production and expenditure classifications inevitably mismatch because the expenditure side has no intermediate products; all goods and service are for final use. The production side includes intermediate products used in other sectors as inputs. Moreover, the expenditure comparison does not include exports because they are not for final use inside the country, while the production comparison has no imports because they are not domestically produced.

The ICOP Estimates and a Comparison with those in the ICP Framework

Table 3.2 summarises the main findings of the ICOP study and Table 3.3 provides a comparison with the principal results of the ICP study presented above.

The ICOP approach yields a per capita GDP for China of about $800 in 1985 at 1985 US prices. If the Fisher PPP (the geometric mean) from the ICOP study is updated from 1985 to 1986 by the deflators for both countries, the estimate for China in 1986 at 1986 US prices becomes $886. The production study indices (Table 3.3) indicate that the United States had a total real product in 1985 about 600 per cent of that of China when valued at Chinese prices, and about 384 per cent using US price weights. The percentages were slightly lower in 1986 because China's economy grew faster. The corresponding per capita quantities are about 2 644 per cent and 1 694 per cent in 1985, and 2 500 per cent and 1 602 per cent in 1986.

Since the Paasche-Laspeyres spread (PLS) derived from the production study is narrower than that from the expenditure study (1.56 against 2.56), the latter implies that China had a lower real income valued at Chinese prices (by about 9 per cent) and higher real income (about 33 per cent) in American prices. This pattern differs from that provided by the OEEC comparisons between the United Kingdom and the United States by both methods in the 1950s.

The expenditure study shows a greater divergence from the official exchange rate than does the production study at Chinese quantity weights and on a Fisher basis, but not at US quantity weights.

The PPPs within the manufacturing sector reveal several additional details. As shown in Table 3.5, they fall far below the exchange rate of 2.9 yuan to the dollar. The PPP for total manufacturing is 1.45, indicating a relative price level (PPP/exchange rate) of 0.5. The lowest PPPs occurred in tobacco products, followed by leather products, electrical machinery and beverages. The highest (2.3) appeared for machinery and transport equipment and even it was well below the exchange rate. Most PPPs with US quantity weights exceed those with Chinese quantity weights — an expected result in binary comparisons between rich and poor countries. Differences in both

44

Table 3.2. A Summary of ICOP Calculations for China and the United States, 1985

Industries	Purchasing Power Parities			China: Sectoral GDP (value added) at market prices				US sectoral GDP in $ at market prices (million)
	US weights	Chinese weights	Geometric Mean	Amount ($ million)	% of total $	Amount (million yuan)	% of total (yuan)	
Agriculture	2.2785	1.8572	2.0571	126 024.08	14.93	259 243.20	28.92	84 300
Mining	1.0850	1.1298	1.1072	30 561.01	3.62	33 836.34	3.77	130 600
Manufacturing	1.8400	1.1500	1.4546	198 046.55	23.47	288 087.96	32.14	798 500
Electricity	0.8139	0.9340	0.8719	20 487.23	2.43	17 862.50	1.99	129 400
Construction	1.0886	0.8472	0.9603	43 515.63	5.16	41 790.00	4.66	179 200
Transport	1.2357	0.7524	0.9643	38 852.93	4.60	37 463.18	4.18	136 000
Communications	2.0611	1.6812	1.8615	1 733.47	0.21	3 226.82	0.36	112 600
Wholesale trade	2.7050	1.0823	1.7110	25 275.14	2.99	43 246.50	4.82	276 600
Retail trade	1.3303	0.5464	0.8526	52 304.78	6.20	44 593.50	4.97	390 900
Finance	2.9094	1.1365	1.8184	18 296.67	2.17	33 270.43	3.71	160 800
Insurance	3.0175	1.5804	2.1838	405.61	0.05	885.75	0.10	61 300
Rear estate	0.6721	0.6721	0.6721	16 810.06	1.99	11 298.04	1.26	459 700
Education	0.1601	0.2203	0.1878	125 205.34	14.84	25 513.96	2.62	25 900
Health	0.6092	0.1107	0.2597	29 704.56	3.52	7 713.95	0.86	186 200
Other services	0.6576	0.4215	0.5265	60 027.67	7.11	31 603.21	3.53	438 800
Government	0.5321	0.2067	0.3316	56 702.06	6.72	18 804.67	2.10	481 800
Total	1.3315	0.8531	1.0658	843 952.77	100.00	896 440.01	100.00	4 052 600

Sources: Sectoral GDPs for China are this author calculations based on official GDP figures. Sectoral GDPs for the United States are from US Dept. of Commerce (BEA) (1993), p. 51. Sectoral PPPs for China are from Annex Tables 3.A.17, 18, 23, 24, 25, 26, 27 and 28, and from Table 3.5 in the text.

Table 3.3. **Total and Per Capita GDP: China and the United States, 1985 and 1986**
(China = 100)

	Total			Per capita		
	At Chinese prices	At US prices	Geometric Mean	At Chinese prices	At US prices	Geometric Mean
1985						
ICOP Method	600	384	480	2 644	1 694	2 116
ICP Method	657	257	411	2 897	1 132	1 810
1986						
ICOP Method	564	361	452	2 500	1 602	2 002
ICP Method	631	247	395	2 799	1 093	1 749

Sources: The PPPs applied under the two approaches are from Tables 3.2 and 3.A.11., respectively. Population for China is from SSB *(1995)*, p. 59, adjusted to a mid year basis; and GDP is from the same source, p. 2. US population figures are from US Dept. of Commerce (1992), p. 8 and the US GDPs are from US Dept. of Commerce (BEA) (1993).

production structures and consumer preferences tend to make products relatively cheap and common in the United States expensive and rare in a low income country like China, and vice versa. Product matches with high unit-value ratios will receive high weights in the United States and low ones in China, while those with low unit-value ratios will tend to receive low US weights and high Chinese weights.

PPPs lower than the exchange rate may result in part from unrecognised quality differences for identical products, and a comparative predominance of low-quality items in the Chinese product mix. If the PPPs have a downward bias, productivity is biased upward; hence the productivity estimates for China in Chapter 6 — low as they are — represent an upper bound. Low PPPs also in part reflect fixed administrative prices and subsidy conventions in China. To the extent that they really bespeak lower price levels in China, they point to a tremendous export potential as the economy turns outward. This has happened in countries like Indonesia in the past ten years. An ICOP study for Indonesia (Szirmai, 1993), also found a similar pattern of PPPs well under the exchange rate.

Comparative Sectoral Productivity between China and the United States

The PPPs derived in the ICOP framework for each sector of the economy make it possible to compare labour productivity between the two countries at the sectoral level. The procedure involves applying these PPPs to the Chinese sectoral value added figures to obtain value added for each sector in dollars, then using sectoral input information for productivity calculations. Table 3.6 shows the figures for China and makes the comparisons with the United States.

Table 3.4. **PPPs and the Exchange Rate Deviation Index by the Two Methods,**
1985 and 1986

(Deviation index = Exchange rate/PPP)

	Chinese quantity weights		US quantity weights		Geometric Mean	
	PPP	Deviation index	PPP	Deviation index	PPP	Deviation index
1985 exchange rate:						
2.9 yuan = $1						
Expenditure method	0.57	5.09	1.4593	1.99	0.9121	3.18
Production method	0.8531	3.40	1.3315	2.18	1.0658	2.72
1986 exchange rate:						
3.5 yuan = $1						
Expenditure method	0.5895	5.94	1.5091	2.32	0.9432	3.71
Production method	0.8639	4.05	1.3484	2.60	1.0793	3.24

Concluding Remarks

In the benchmark years for these two studies, China had more or less dominant central planning operations in all aspects of the economy. Payments for factors of production did not necessarily reflect the relative costs of resources used in producing goods and services. The gap between ex-factory prices that enterprises received and market prices that consumers paid actually consists of subsidies and turnover taxes. The PPP estimates derived from the two studies can be used to explore subsidies. For example, consumer subsidies tend to keep the prices established by government for agricultural products and basic consumer needs in China lower than those for industrial durables. The government purchases agricultural products from farmers at high prices designed to cover their cost of production, and the distribution outlets [which appear as an industry in the Input-Output Table of China, 1987 (SSB, 1991)] sell these goods at much lower prices to city dwellers. This makes the distribution sector a big loss-maker, wholly dependent on subsidies.

This incomparability carries over to the comparisons between China and the United States from the expenditure side because that approach derives PPPs from market prices. It does not affect the derivation of PPPs for agricultural products from the production side because they are based on ex-farm prices which reflect or at least approximate the actual costs involved. The production-side study yielded a PPP for agriculture of 2.0499 yuan per dollar in 1985; the PPP for the food category in the expenditure-based study in 1986 is 1.2943 yuan per dollar. If, as seems reasonable, the PPP from the expenditure study is underestimated, real income is overestimated.

Table 3.5. **Purchasing Power Parities and Relative Price Levels by Major Manufacturing Branches, China/United States,** 1985

	PPPs (yuan/$)			Relative
	At US quantity weights	At Chinese quantity weights	Geometric Mean	Price Level (US = 100)
Food and beverages	1.62	1.43	1.52	52.5
Food manufacturing (a)	1.77	1.53	1.64	56.7
Beverages	0.91	0.91	0.91	31.3
Tobacco products	0.39	0.37	0.38	13.0
Textile mill products	1.49	1.44	1.47	50.5
Wearing apparel (b)	1.37	1.39	1.38	47.5
Leather products and footwear	0.84	0.84	0.84	29.1
Wood products, furniture and fixtures	1.73	1.73	1.73	59.7
Paper products, printing and publishing	1.97	1.58	1.76	60.8
Chemical products (including oil)	1.63	1.16	1.37	47.3
Rubber and plastic products	3.65	0.81	1.72	59.4
Non-metallic mineral products	1.14	0.52	0.77	26.6
Basic and fabricated metal products	0.66	1.49	0.99	34.2
Machinery and transport equipment	2.85	1.92	2.34	80.6
Electrical machinery and equipment	0.96	0.77	0.86	29.7
Other manufacturing	1.81	1.17	1.45	50.1
Total manufacturing, with branch value-added weights (c)	1.84	1.15	1.45	50.1
(Exchange rate)	(2.9)	(2.9)	(2.9)	

(a)   For the sample industry dairy products only a Paasche PPP at Chinese quantity weights could be calculated. A derived proxy Laspeyres PPP for this sample industry applies the average Laspeyres to Paasche ratio for all sample industry PPPs.

(b)   Products and No sample industries in this branch. The PPP for wearing apparel is the weighted average of the PPPs for textiles and leather footwear.

(c)   The PPPs for total manufacturing are the weighted averages of the PPPs of all manufacturing branches, weighted with census value-added weights. The PPP for food manufacturing is the weighted average of the sample industry PPPs for meat products, dairy products [see note (a)], fats and oils, grain mill products, sugar and sugar factories, and confectionery products, with gross value added by sample industry serving as weights; the PPP for leather products and footwear is the PPP for leather footwear; the PPP for chemicals products is the weighted average for agricultural fertilizers, soap and detergents and oil refining; the PPP for rubber and plastic products is the weighted average for tires and tubes and rubber and plastic footwear; the PPP for non-metallic mineral products is the weighted average for bricks and cement; the PPP for basic and fabricated metal products is the PPP for iron and steel; the PPP for machinery and transport equipment is the PPP for motor vehicles and equipment; the PPP for electrical machinery and equipment is the weighted average for radio and TV receivers, lamps and bulbs; and the PPP for other manufacturing is the weighted average of all product unit value ratios.

Sources :   See Annex to this chapter.

Table 3.6. Comparative Labour Productivity: China and the United States, 1985

Sectors	China GDP at factor cost (million yuan)	PPP Geometric Mean (yuan/$)	GDP at factor cost ($ million)	Value Added as % of total	Persons engaged (thousands)	GDP per person engaged ($)	United States GDP at factor cost ($ million)	Persons engaged (thousands)	GDP per person engaged ($)	Fisher Productivity Ratios: China to US (%)
Agriculture, forestry and fisheries	255 038.20	2.0571	123 979.49	15.58	310 672	399.07	86 599.01	3 242	26 711.60	1.49
Mining	32 054.17	1.1072	28 950.66	3.64	7 128	4 061.54	111 012.29	947	117 225.23	3.46
Manufacturing	247 563.63	1.4546	170 193.61	21.39	72 205	2 357.09	757 622.86	19 700	38 458.01	6.13
Electricity, gas and water	12 583.76	0.8718	14 432.57	1.81	1 380	10 458.39	109 493.80	914	119 796.28	8.73
Construction	39 505.00	0.9604	41 133.90	5.17	18 475	2 226.46	175 071.55	6 186	28 289.02	7.87
Transport and Communications										
Transport	32 713.83	0.9643	33 924.95	4.26	11 045	3 071.52	129 960.81	3 371	38 552.60	7.97
Communications	3 105.81	1.8615	1 668.44	0.21	960	1 737.96	101 098.43	1 332	75 899.72	2.29
Wholesale and retail trade										
Wholesale trade	42 651.65	1.7110	24 927.91	3.13	7 310	3 410.11	228 591.67	6 112	37 400.47	9.12
Retail trade	43 974.37	0.8526	51 576.79	6.48	14 190	3 634.73	325 412.37	19 465	16 717.82	21.74
Finance, insurance and real estate										
Finance	29 307.35	1.8184	16 117.11	2.03	1 299	12 407.32	138 448.81	2 906	47 642.40	26.04
Insurance	792.17	2.1838	362.75	0.05	27	13 435.13	56 653.84	2 045	27 703.59	48.50
Real estate	11 282.48	0.6721	16 786.91	2.11	360	46 630.30	382 289.18	1 802	212 147.16	21.98
Services and government										
Education	23 513.96	0.1878	125 207.45	15.74	11 288	11 092.08	196 875.84	9 305	21 158.07	52.42
Health	7 713.95	0.2597	29 703.31	3.73	4 338	6 847.24	184 469.82	6 828	27 016.67	25.34
Other services	31 603.22	0.5265	60 025.11	7.54	21 964	2 732.89	426 750.51	19 130	22 307.92	12.25
Government	18 804.67	0.3316	56 708.90	7.13	7 710	7 355.24	315 714.43	13 247	23 832.90	30.86
Total economy	832 208.22		795 699.86	100.00	490 351	1 622.71	3 726 045.00	116 532	31 974.44	5.08

Sources: Annex Table 3.A.14.

Since the matching of quality is always the main concern in international comparisons between countries with huge income gaps and because only a few quality adjustments were feasible here, these two studies may have overstated China's performance to some extent. Many of the quality matches relied heavily on the concept of "equivalence in use" because the large income disparities between the countries — and hence differences in consumption habits and the characteristics of goods produced for similar uses — made rigorous quality matching in the sense of "physical identity" impossible.

The ICP and ICOP approaches have different strengths and weaknesses. In China's case, preference might be given to the ICOP estimate over the ICP estimate of total GDP for the following reasons:

— theoretical discussion has concluded that, "From the standpoint of reliability, the choice of method for any pair of countries must depend largely on whether the industry or the final product data for manufactured goods are better" (Gilbert and Beckerman, 1961). Chinese data for manufactured goods from the industrial census are much better than the expenditure data for the final product. Moreover, the production-side study, done later, incorporated some intervening improvements in the Chinese data available.

— the expenditure approach based its estimates on a sample of prices and the breakdowns of GDP from the expenditure side. The price sample, however, cannot be characterised as containing the most representative items, both because the price structure in China is so complicated and because only limited resources could be devoted to the sampling. The breakdowns of GDP in the expenditure categories were based on the author's estimates for each category, which involved some compromises due to the lack of data. On the other hand, the breakdown of GDP by industry of origin was based on the 1987 input-output table which constitutes a solid foundation.

50

Methodological Discussion and Statistical Documentation

The Expenditure-Side Study

Data Collection and Processing

The basic data for binary comparison include prices of goods and services and relevant expenditure in accordance with the Classification System of the ICP. In ICP practice, the quantity comparison is derived by dividing the expenditure ratio by the price ratio, which requires that the price used for each specification corresponds to the price embedded in the expenditure figure (Kravis, 1981). The following two tables show the distribution of the samples and the items in the samples.

Sources of the price data for goods and services in China include *Price Statistics Yearbook of China* (State Statistical Bureau, 1987*a*), local price information in some provinces, *The Price Handbook in Heavy, Machinery and Transportation Industries* (processed), newspapers, magazines, and other sources. Where national average prices were not available, the project research team conducted market surveys through field observation and correspondence in ten Chinese cities: Beijing, Shanghai, Shenyang, Taiyuan, Xian, Chengdu, Nanjing, Wuhan, Kunming, and Guangzhou. The average of prices in these cities was taken as the national average price. Some price data for other years were converted to 1986 prices by relevant price index numbers. If prices for some goods were obtained in only one city, they were converted to national averages using the regional differences issued by the State Price Management Authorities.

Because multiple prices exist for many items in China, it is very difficult to judge whether the prices used in this study matched the prices used by the compiler of GDP, except in some cases such as the mixed average prices provided in the *Price*

Table 3.A.1. **The Distribution of Samples Used in the ICP-Based Bilateral Comparison**

Code number	Main categories	Sub-sample size
–	GDP	314
0	Final consumption expenditure of the population	210
01.000	Food, beverages and tobacco	72
02.000	Clothing and footwear	24
03.000	Gross rent, fuel and power	6
04.000	Furniture, furnishings, household equipment and operations	35
05.000	Medical care and health expenses	11
06.000	Transport and communications	18
07.000	Recreation, entertainment, education and cultural services	27
08.000	Other goods and services	17
1	Gross capital formation	103
10.000	Residential building	1
11.000	Non-residential building	6
12.000	Other construction	0
13.000	Land improvements; plantation and orchard development	0
14.000	Transport equipment	19
15.000	Non-electrical machinery and equipment	38
16.000	Electrical machinery and equipment	31
17.000	Other durable furnishings and equipment	8
18.000	Increase in stocks	0
19.000	Exports less imports of goods and services	0
2	Public final consumption expenditure	1
20.000	Compensation of employees	1
21.000	Expenditure on commodities	

Statistics Yearbook of China and prices in the *Price Handbook in Heavy, Machinery and Transportation Industries*. If the two types of prices had not been matched this would have caused errors in the PPP for the basic headings and the final results.

Sources of price data on the US side include the *Statistical Abstract of the United States* (US Dept. of Commerce, 1987, 1988,1989), *CPI Detailed Report* (US Dept. of Labor, 1986*b*), *Producer Prices and Price Indexes Data* (US Dept. of Labor, 1984), *Producer Price Indexes Data* (US Dept. of Labor, 1985, 1986*a*), advertisements in such newspapers as *The New York Times*, the price lists of several supermarkets, the Chinese versions of market survey reports by consulting firms in the United States, and interviews with ten Chinese scholars who lived in different cities in the United States in 1986 and had more than one year's residence. Some price data were estimated from quantity and expenditure data.

Quality Matching

In tobacco (01.400), the three American brands of cigarettes most popular in China were selected to guarantee quality matching. In clothing and footwear (02.000), we consulted experts in these industries and then decided on the selection of goods. After the author arrived in the United States, he re-examined quality matching in these categories and found it reasonably satisfactory.

Table 3.A.2. **List of Items in the Samples of Price Relatives**

Code number	Detailed category
0	Final consumption expenditure of the population
01.000	Food, beverages and tobacco
01.100	Food
01.100	Bread and cereals: rice flour, wheat flour, maize flour, bread, biscuits, powdered milk, starch, macaroni, noodles
01.110	Fresh beef, fresh lamb, fresh pork, chicken, chicken breasts, chicken legs, turkey, duck, ham, knuckle, sausages
01.120	Cod, frozen shrimp, canned fish
01.130	Fresh milk, cheese, eggs
01.140	Butter, edible oils, peanut butter, margarine, lard
01.150	Bananas, oranges, apples, pears, strawberries, lettuce, tomatoes, peas, cabbage, celery, cucumber, mushrooms, onions, carrots
01.160	Orange juice, Coca-Cola, vegetable juices
01.170	Potatoes, sweet potatoes
01.180	Sweeteners, sugar
01.190	Coffee, tea, cocoa
01.200	Other food: jam, chocolate, confectionary, ice cream, salt, vinegar, sauces
01.300	Beverages
01.310	Mineral water, soft drinks
01.320	Brandy, cider, beer
01.400	Tobacco
01.410	Cigarettes: Marlboro, Hilton, Kent
01.420	Tobacco
02.000	Clothing and footwear
02.100	Clothing other than footwear, including repairs
02.110	Woolen material, cotton material, silk
02.120	Suits (men's), jackets, suits (womens), overcoats, boys' and girls' wear
02.130	Men's underwear, men's nightwear, men's hosiery, women's underwear, women's nightwear, women's hosiery
02.150	Gloves, smocks, swim-suits, tiepins, hairpins
02.160	Rental of wedding suits
02.200	Footwear, including repairs
02.210	Men's footwear, women's footwear, children's footwear
02.220	Repairs to footwear
03.000	Gross rent, fuel and power
03.100	Gross rent (a suite)
03.200	Fuel and power
03.210	Electricity (civil)
03.220	Gas, liquefied gasses
03.230	Kerosene
03.240	Water
04.000	Furniture, furnishings, household equipment and operation
04.100	Furniture, fixtures, carpets and other floor covering
04.110	Beds (for two persons), folding chairs, desks, sofas (for three persons)
04.120	Woolen carpets
04.200	Household textiles and other furnishings
04.300	Heating and cooking appliances, major household appliances
04.310	Refrigerators, freezers, room air conditioners, fans
04.320	Washing machines
04.330	Microwaves, electric cooking stoves, high pressure stoves
04.340	Electric irons
04.350	Vacuum cleaners

Table 3.A.2.(continued)

Code number	Detailed category
04.360	Sewing machines, knitting machines, power-driven lawnmowers
04.400	Glassware, tableware and household utensils, cutlery, thermos bottles, flashlights, cups
04.500	Household operation
04.510	Household paper products, household soap, matches, insecticides, screws, clothes hangers
04.520	Baby-sitters
04.530	Laundering
05.000	Medical care and health expenses
05.100	Medical and pharmaceutical products
05.110	Pain relieving medicines, vitamin C
05.120	Blood pressure meters, stethoscopes, rubber gloves, trauma medicines, medical massage equipment
05.200	Therapeutic appliances and equipment, artificial limbs
05.300	Services of physicians, dentists, midwives, etc.
05.310	Physicians
05.320	Dentists
05.330	Nurses, physiotherapists, technicians, midwives, etc.
06.000	Transport and Communications
06.100	Personal transport equipment
06.110	Passenger cars
06.120	Motorcycles, bicycles
06.200	Operation of personal transport equipment
02.210	Tires
06.220	Repair charges
06.230	Gasoline
06.240	Parking, road tolls
06.300	Purchased transport services
06.310	Local transport: train fares, bus fares, taxi fares
06.320	Long-distance transport: rail, bus, air
06.400	Communications
06.410	Postage (domestic)
06.420	Telephone and telegraph
07.000	Recreation, entertainment, education and cultural services
07.100	Equipment and accessories
07.110	Radios, television sets (black and white), television sets (color), recorders
07.120	Cameras, pianos, typewriters, telescopes
07.130	Records, films, electronic instruments
07.200	Entertainment, religion, recreational and cultural services
07.210	Expenditures on: cinemas, zoological gardens
07.220	Expenditures on: film developing, boats
07.300	Books, newspapers, magazines and stationery
07.310	Books, newspapers, magazines
07.320	Pens, typewriter ribbons, calculators
07.400	Education
07.410	Compensation of employees: primary and secondary school teachers, college and university teachers
07.420	Desks, swivel chairs
07.430	Penholders, notebooks
08.000	Other goods and services
08.100	Services of barbers and beauty shops, baths and the like, barbers (men), permanent waves (women)
08.200	Goods for personal care
08.210	Makeup boxes, razors, electric hair dryers, combs

Table 3.A.2. (concluded)

Code number	Detailed category
08.220	Watches, umbrellas, lighters, sunglasses, clocks, bracelets, necklaces
08.300	Expenditures in restaurants, cafes and hotels
08.310	Restaurants, cafes
08.320	Hotels
08.400	Other services: payments for copies of marriage certificates
1	Gross capital formation
10.000	Residential building
10.100	Buildings of one and two dwellings
11.000	Non-residential buildings
11.200	Industrial buildings
11.300	Commercial buildings
11.400	Office buildings
11.500	Educational buildings
11.600	Hospital and institutional buildings
11.800	Other buildings
14.000	Transport equipment
14.200	Passenger cars (expensive, common), complete passenger automobiles
14.300	Trucks, buses and trailers: trucks, trailers, jeeps
14.400	Aircraft: fighters, specific transport planes, regional transport planes, airplanes
14.500	Ships and boats: freighters (14 000 tons), freighters (7 000 tons), freighters (3 000 tons), tugboats (4 000 HP), tugboats (2 000 HP)
14.600	Other transport machinery: motorcycles, bicycles
15.000	Non-electrical machinery and equipment
15.200	Agricultural machinery: tractors
15.300	Office machines: computers, printers, duplicators, facsimile machines
15.400	Metalworking machinery: lathes (common), vertical lathes, millers, planers, horizontal grinders, multi-function grinders, borers
15.600	Special industrial machinery: wheat rollers, multi-function cutters, ovens, sewing machines
15.700	General industrial machinery: pumps, bearings, refrigerators
15.800	Service industry machinery: washing machines, stoves
16.000	Electrical machinery and equipment
16.100	Electrical transmission, distribution and industrial apparatus; electric motors (micro)
16.200	Communications equipment: wireless telephones, wire telephones, megaphones, gramophones, smoke alarms, public address systems, pickup cameras for burglar alarms, tape, magnetic tape, slide projectors
16.300	Other electrical equipment: wire (plastic covered), cable, daylight lamps, emergency lamps, batteries, sockets, switches
6.400	Instruments: liquid crystal all-purpose meters, liquid crystal current meters, audio amplifiers
17.000	Other durable furnishings and equipment
17.100	Furniture and fixtures: terminal desks, high-back revolving chairs, low-back revolving chairs, drawing desks, I-type desks, document shelving
17.200	Other durable goods: screwdrivers, pincers
2	Public final consumption expenditures
20.000	Compensation of employees in government

In furniture, furnishings, household equipment and operations (04.000), different approaches for dealing with quality matching were employed in various detailed categories. The choice of goods in category 04.100 (furniture, fixtures, carpets and other floor covering), for example, followed the principle of equivalence in use; goods very often imported or considered as luxury goods by Chinese standards were selected. In heating and cooking appliances, and major household appliances (04.300), the criterion of equivalence in quality was used. As China's economic reforms progressed in the 1980s, more and more durable consumer goods made in other countries, especially Japan, could be bought in China while Chinese factories produced more products at international quality standards; many of these factories either are joint-ventures or have imported assembly lines. The same approach applied to transport and communications (06.000), with selection of goods either imported or produced on imported assembly lines. Consultations with experts in transport and communications ensured that quality was matched. The issue of quality matching in the main aggregates of gross capital formation will be discussed in detail later.

Some Topics in the Bilateral Comparison

Gross Rent

The ICP specifies measuring market prices for housing services only for rented dwellings. This is far more difficult than comparisons for other consumer commodities and services, given the limited possibilities for substitution among houses in different places and the variety of dwellings with respect to structure, condition, size, facilities and location. A much greater dispersion of rents around the national average exists for each given type of dwelling than for most other commodities and services. Housing is one of the categories in which differences between countries with high and low incomes are quite substantial. As a result, the types of housing in China and the United States overlap much less than for most other commodities and services.

People obtain housing in very different ways in China, depending mostly on where they live (urban or rural) and on what kinds of jobs they have (government; institutions in education and research; large, medium or small factories and so on). In rural areas, people usually have their own houses constructed; some estimates show that more than 80 per cent of the rural population lives in owner-occupied houses. In some sense, a rural housing market exists, there are no subsidies, and one could impute rents based on construction costs, corresponding to imputed rent in a market economy. In urban areas, people working in state-owned sectors, especially in large organisations (in terms of employment) or higher-level institutions (in terms of the location in the hierarchy) can obtain housing at very low, heavily subsidised rents. The urban housing administration departments also provide at low prices dwellings which are often in short supply. These two categories account for a small proportion of the population. Nevertheless, housing expenditures per person in rural areas were much higher than in urban locations in 1985 (see SSB, 1995), a strange phenomenon given the income differential between farmers and city dwellers; it probably reflects the subsidy for

56

housing in urban areas. People who have no access to subsidised housing because of their job status and cannot build their own houses because they live in cities usually live in permanently cramped quarters.

In this complicated situation, if the very low house rents actually charged in China (i.e. rents in subsidised houses) had been compared with rents in the United States, the requirement of *characteristicity* would not have been satisfied because it calls for comparison based on the best sample of representative items that can be obtained for the two countries. Real housing expenditure and the PPP in this category in China would have been underestimated. Hence, this study undertook to revalue housing costs, following Kravis (1981). He attempted to assess "the full social cost of housing", using an estimation of the "average rent" based on the overall costs of housing construction. This procedure tries to ascertain what lodgers would pay if housing were not subsidised. The costs of land, insurance and profits were not included in the calculation because data were not available, although these items are incorporated in rent in the United States; the inclusion of the cost of land in the estimation of imputed rents in China would raise the parity. Table 3.A.3 documents the estimation procedure. Average rent represents the "space" rent required by the ICP. The estimated rent can represent the national average because construction cost, the base of the estimate, is a national average figure. This revaluation of housing requires adjustment of the cost of living of government employees and professional personnel in education and medical services, which in turn warrants a revaluation of these sectors' output. In the estimates for these sectors presented below, "the full social cost of housing" is incorporated as a step in that direction.

Table 3.A.3. **Estimates of Average Rents in China**

Category	Explanation of method (a)	Value (Yuan/square metre)
(1) Construction cost		447.27 (b)
(2) Scrap value	4.966 per cent	22.21
(3) Service life	50 years	
(4) Depreciation	Rows [(1) - (2)/(3)]	8.50
(5) Maintenance	1.91 per cent of construction cost	8.54
(6) Management	0.40 per cent of construction cost	1.78
(7) Interest	8.64 per cent of construction cost (c)	38.64
(8) Taxes	10.33 per cent of row (9) (d)	2.17
(9) Rent (building area)	Rows (4) + (5) + (6) + (7) + (8)	59.64
(10) Rent (living area) (e)		91.76
(11) Rent per month	Row (10)/12	7.65

(a) The formula is from the *Regulation of Housing* issued by the Management Bureau of Housing in Beijing.
(b) The construction cost is an average of data from several sources. In 1988, it varied from 175 yuan/sq.m. to 651 yuan/sq. m.
(c) Interest is that specified for loans for land improvement and construction.
(d) If rent (building areas) is X, then [X = rows (4) + (5) + (6) + (7) + 0.1033X].
(e) Building area rent based on construction cost was adjusted by the ratio: living area = 0.65 building area.

In the United States, market mechanisms largely determine rents. Some rent controls still existed in 1986, however, in 200 communities in New York, New Jersey, Massachusetts, Connecticut, and California. Low-income households also have access to housing vouchers which provide cash assistance to help pay rent for otherwise unaffordable, minimum-standard dwelling units. In 1974, Section 8 of the Housing and Community Development Act created a housing program under which, with other forms of Section 8 assistance, an estimated 2 139 000 lower-income households received payments in 1985. This study has not taken these two rent subsidies into account because detailed rent control and voucher data were not available.

Rents in the United States were calculated with a regression equation estimated by a sample containing about 10 000 dwellings selected in 1975 (Kravis, *et al.*, 1982). The dependent variable is the natural logarithm of rent of a dwelling; the characteristics of dwellings are the explanatory variables included in the equation as a set of dummy variables. The procedure is rooted in the hedonic index approach (Griliches, 1971). Average US rent estimated by the regression equation was adjusted to the benchmark year. The detailed procedure is shown in Table 3.A.4.

Table 3.A.4. **Estimates of Rents in the United States**

Independent variable	Regression coefficients and adjustments	Results (in $)
Dwelling with electricity, water and flush toilet, built in 1945-59, 35 square metres		52.17
Bath and central heating	1.932	100.79
Built in 1970-75	1.232	124.18
60 square metres (1970)	1.114	138.34
Standard rent (1986)	(1986/1970) = 3 (price index)	415.02

Note: The standard rent in 1970 was brought forward by means of a price index to obtain the standard rent in 1986.

The parity of rents between the two countries was based on the above estimations. Rent in China was calculated by assuming 60 square metres per dwelling and then multiplying by the rent per square metre shown in Table 3.A.3. To deal in the rent comparison with the substantial difference in housing quality between the two countries, a tentative, obviously subjective 30 per cent downward adjustment was made for China. A better method would have been to compare the basic characteristics of houses for both countries and use the hedonic index approach to estimate an average rent for American houses equivalent in quality with their Chinese counterparts. Housing expenditure for China was estimated from actual expenditure in rural areas.

Rent in the United States is for 60-square-meter dwellings built in 1986 with electricity, water, flush toilet, bath and central heating. The US rent obtained from the equation is an estimate of the median rent rather than the mean. The shadow rent in China is the mean, so the median needs to be converted by an adjustment factor of 1.04 (Kravis, *et al.,* 1975). The mean standard rent thus becomes $ 431.62. The weights in both countries refer to the weights for category 03.000: gross rents, fuel and power. For comparison, the American Housing Survey in 1987, conducted by the Office of Policy Development and Research, Bureau of the Census, US Department of Commerce, reports that the median monthly rent was $399, computed from a sample containing 32 724 occupied units.

Medical Services

ICP practice makes no direct price comparisons of service outputs for three sectors (which include ten detailed categories): health care, education, and government services. This reflects the great difficulty in defining satisfactory measures of outputs in these sectors, and in collecting data on such measures if they could be defined. Because these comparison-resistant services of physicians, dentists, nurses, teachers and government employees account for a quite large share of all service expenditures in GNP, an approach needs to be developed to make valid comparisons between the two countries, taking institutional differences into account.

For medical care comparisons, two procedures exist — comparing either specific services or average annual earnings of medical professionals. Although the second cannot avoid the problem of quality matching, it does have two advantages. It can result in more comprehensive price comparisons than looking at a limited number of specific services; and it does not involve the problem which arises when differences in services and social security regulations between the two countries cause a difference in the costs of the services. This study employed the second approach.

The use of inputs as output indicators in international comparisons for the comparison-resistant service sectors involves an underlying assumption about the productivity differential between professional personnel working in these sectors of the two countries. Kravis, *et al.* (1982) considered this issue in general in their report on Phase III of the ICP, and Gordon, *et al.* (1990) discussed medical care service comparisons between China and the United States in particular, suggesting as well that the statistics in the UNDP's *Human Development Report 1990* (UNDP, 1990) on life expectancy, infant mortality rates, inoculation against disease and other indicators of health could be taken as evidence of the high quantity and quality of care provided by China's 4.97 million health care workers to its population of over 1 billion people. Differences between the two countries in the length and quality of medical training, however, suggest that the average quality of service could be quite different between the two countries. At this stage an assumption has to be made of no differences in quality and productivity between the medical professionals of the two countries.

The items of comparison include earnings of physicians, dentists, nurses, physiotherapists, technicians, midwives, pharmacists and other medical personnel. All estimated earnings cover disposable income because they are below the minimum liable to pay tax under the Chinese income tax law implemented in 1986. Conceptually, they correspond to after-tax income in the United States. They can be estimated by direct and indirect approaches in order to include extra income and transfers from government.

Direct Estimation

All components of earnings need consideration, including the base and duty salaries of doctors and other allowances such as bonuses, housing allowances, and benefits and labour insurance (including medical care insurance and fringe benefits for birth control, death, care for dependants, poverty, entertainment, bathing and haircuts). The base and duty salaries differ for various levels of medical professionals, but the allowances are the same. Table 3.A.5 presents the estimates.

Table 3.A.5. **Earnings of Medical Professionals, Computed by the Direct Approach**
(yuan per year)

Category	Base and duty salary	Bonuses, benefits and allowances				Total earnings
		Bonuses	Benefits and labour insurance	Housing allowances	Total	
Physicians	1 615.56	432.30	236.41	1 050.92	1719.63	3335.19
Dentists	1 615.56	432.30	236.41	1 050.92	1719.63	3335.19
Nurses, etc.	787.68	432.30	236.41	1 050.92	1719.63	2507.31

Notes: In China dentistry and medicine are not considered as different professions. Earnings of physicians and dentists are a geometric mean of earnings at the various levels. Earnings of nurses etc. are a geometric mean of earnings of various types of non-doctor medical professionals. Benefits and labour insurance are computed by dividing total expenditures on benefits and labour insurance by the number of employees. Housing allowances are computed by the shadow rents estimated in this paper. The formula is: Housing Allowance = 7.65 yuan/sq.m./month x 6.36 sq.m. (average housing floor area per person in an urban region) x 1.8 (1 + dependency ratio) x 12 months.

Indirect Estimation

This approach, which the study rejected in favour of the direct approach, involves estimating the average annual earnings of medical professionals from the proportion of medical professionals' salaries in national health expenditures and the number of medical professionals, using data from the Ministry of Public Health and some information derived from the direct estimates. The health-expenditures budget for institutions affiliated with the Ministry of Public Health shows a ratio of wage costs to total costs of 18.05 per cent. The direct estimates suggest that the ratio of doctors' to other medical professionals' earnings is 1.026. Assuming that the distribution of health expenditure nationwide is similar to the distribution in the Ministry of Public Health institutions, earnings can be calculated as shown in Table 3.A.6.

Table 3.A.6. **Earnings of Medical Professionals, Computed by the Indirect Approach**
(yuan per year)

Category	Salary	Housing allowance	Other allowances	Total earnings
Physicians	1 750	1 050.92	300.50	3 101.42
Dentists	1 750	1 050.92	300.50	3 101.42
Nurses, etc.	1 312	1 050.92	300.50	2 663.42

Notes: Earnings equal total wage cost divided by the number of professionals. Allowances were calculated from the proportions and average wages in the medical services industry.

Data on the numbers of medical professionals and national health care expenditures for the United States came from the *Statistical Abstract of the United States, 1987* (US Dept. of Commerce, 1987). After deducting personal income taxes from the US figures and adopting the direct estimates for China, the comparison for medical services between China and the United States emerged as shown in Table 3.A.7.

Table 3.A.7. **Bilateral Comparison of Medical Services**

Category	China (yuan)	$	Parity
Services of physicians	3 335.19	103 771.84	0.0321
Services of dentists	3 335.19	102 518.99	0.0265
Services of nurses, etc.	2 507.31	23 593.22	0.1062

Education

Because an "output" of qualified students is very difficult to quantify, the approach in this sector resembled that of medical services, with the direct chosen over the indirect approach to estimating earnings in China. UNESCO's definitions classify teachers on three levels: primary-school teachers, secondary-school teachers and college and university professors. Because primary and secondary teachers educated at the same level receive similar salaries, the ICP education comparisons use two categories of earnings by collapsing the first two UNESCO categories into one. Table 3.A.8 shows the two estimates for China and Table 3.A.9 gives the bilateral comparison, where the US figures are after-tax figures from the *Statistical Abstract of the United States, 1988* (US Dept. of Commerce, 1988).

Table 3.A.8. **Earnings of Teachers in China, Computed by the Direct and Indirect Approaches**
(yuan per year)

Category	Salary	Allowances	Total earnings
Direct Approach:			
Primary and secondary teachers	1 064.35	1 590.48	2 654.83
College and university professors	1 539.48	1 590.48	3 129.96
Indirect Approach:			
Primary and secondary teachers	1 716.24	1 050.92	2 767.16
College and university professors	2 394.20	1 050.92	3 445.12

Notes: In the direct approach, salaries are base salaries and housing is included in allowances. In the indirect approach, salaries include all allowances except housing, which is the only value in the allowances column.

Table 3.A.9. **Bilateral Comparison of Education Services**

Category	Yuan	$	Parity
Earnings of primary and secondary school teachers	2 654.83	18 169.18	0.1461
Earnings of college and university professors	3 129.96	21 080.77	0.1485

Gross Capital Formation

The difficulties of quality matching and the general lack of published price data on producer durables in the United States made the gross capital formation comparison the most intractable. The absence of relevant data forced deletion from the study of the sub-aggregates for land improvement and plantation and orchard development (13.000); increase in stocks (18.000); and net export of goods and services (19.000). For practical reasons the product comparisons followed the principle of quality matching in an economic sense, emphasizing equivalence in some key properties, rather than in a technical sense requiring full coincidence in specification.

In some categories, goods with the same specifications are used in both China and the United States, because the imported goods are dominant in China's market. In office machines (15.300), for example, China now imports many exemplars of the items selected for comparison — computers, printers, duplicators and facsimile machines — so that the matching of quality was good. For other goods, because the specification for one product in one country matched the specifications for two or more in the other country, the average price in the latter country was used for comparison. Thus, for example, the comparison contained one Chinese 25-horsepower electric motor whose price was P_c; the US sample had three similar motors, each varying slightly in horsepower, rotational speed or weight, at prices P_{u1}, P_{u2}, and P_{u3}. In this case, the parity should be:

$$R(parity) = \frac{P_c}{\sqrt[3]{P_{u1} \times P_{u2} \times P_{u3}}}$$

(3.A.1)

When a category has price ratios available for some products but not for others, the ICP approach allows estimating the others from the available ones. Thus, if the price ratios for locomotives (14.110) (R_1), passenger cars (14.200) (R_2), and Trucks, buses, and trailers (14.300) (R_3) are known, but those for aircraft (14.400) (R_4) and ships and boats (14.500) (R_5) are unknown, R_4 and R_5 can be estimated using formula (2) below. This approach was used for railway vehicles (14.100); engines and turbines (15.100); construction, mining, and oil-field machinery (15.500); and electrical transmission, distribution, and industrial apparatus (16.100).

(3.A.2)

$$R_4 = R_5 = \sqrt[3]{R_1 \times R_2 \times R_3}$$

Sometimes items equivalent in specification, type or function could not be found. Therefore, the character of the items having the strongest influence on the price of the goods was selected as the basis for quality matching. If this character was matched, the goods were considered as satisfying the requirement of quality matching.

Dwellings could be sold in China only recently and basic information on residential buildings covers only the period from 1988 to 1990, which had to be extrapolated backward to 1986. Prices of non-residential buildings were estimated based on the costs of those buildings. Prices in the United States can be estimated by selling prices and floor space from the *Statistical Abstract of the United States, 1988* (US Dept. of Commerce, 1988). Table 3.A.10 presents the bilateral comparisons for construction.

Table 3.A.10. **Bilateral Comparisons for Construction**
(prices per square metre)

Types of construction	Yuan	$	Parity
Residential houses	773.27	621.35	1.244
Industrial buildings	442.03	493.90	0.895
Commercial buildings	452.76	354.65	1.277
Office buildings	639.19	1 153.29	0.554
Educational buildings	784.89	1 150.59	0.682
Hospital and institutional buildings	743.56	1 094.09	0.680
Other buildings	760.69	881.34	0.862

Notes: The selling price of residential buildings in China is the geometric mean of selling prices ranging from 426 to 1 800 yuan/sq.m. in eight districts of China. The price of non-residential buildings is the cost according to the construction standard of China. For the United States, all prices were based on data in Section 26, "Construction and Housing" of the *Statistical Abstract of the United States, 1988* (US Dept. of Commerce, 1988).

Public Final Consumption Expenditure

The comparison of government services in the ICP consists of two categories: one includes inputs, measured as the compensation of government employees; the other relates to expenditures on commodities used in government activities. The compensation comparison, as in other service sectors, assumed employees educated at the same level to have the same productivity in the two countries. Based on the definition of government given by the ICP, the average annual income of government employees in China was 2 554.04 yuan; that for the United States was $21 018.96; and the parity was 0.1215. For commodities, the PPPs for "House furnishings" were used as proxies because the data on detailed expenditures by the Chinese government were not available.

Results of the Bilateral Comparison

Table 3.A.11 on the following pages brings together all of the results of the bilateral comparisons for GNP and its components.

The Production-Side Study

Data Sources

An industry-of-origin study requires detailed information on output quantities and corresponding output values. This information forms the basis for the calculation of unit-value ratios and PPPs, which are subsequently used to convert output values into the currency of another country. In order to make the study as transparent as possible, the data used have been confined to the published sources. Data for the United States are discussed extensively by Pilat (1994). For the industry-of-origin estimate of real income for the Chinese economy as a whole, the main sources of data were:

— *Industrial Census of China, 1985* (Office of Leading Group of the National Industrial Census under the State Council, PRC, 1987-88);

— *Input-Output Tables of China, 1987* (State Statistical Bureau, 1991);

— *Statistical Yearbook of China, 1986, 1994, 1995* (State Statistical Bureau, 1986, 1994, 1995);

— *Industrial Statistical Yearbook of China, 1988, 1993* (State Statistical Bureau, 1988, 1993*a*).

Table 3.A.11.a. A Summary of the ICP Expenditure Comparisons, China and the United States, 1986

Category		PPA (yuan/$)			Quantity per capita (US = 100)		
		US weight	China weight	Fisher mean	US weight	China weight	Fischer mean
0	Consumption	1.1158	0.5840	0.8072	9.13	4.78	6.60
01.000	Food beverages and tobacco	1.6579	1.1292	1.3682	15.97	10.88	13.18
01.100	Food	1.5903	1.0532	1.2942	16.72	11.08	13.61
01.100	Bread, cereals	0.8990	0.8990	0.8990	48.41	48.41	48.41
01.110	Meat	1.2250	1.2250	1.2250	18.79	18.79	18.79
01.120	Fish	1.6670	1.6670	1.6670	26.83	26.83	26.83
01.130	Milk, cheese, eggs	2.0820	2.0820	2.0820	4.70	4.70	4.70
01.140	Oils, fats	2.2150	2.2150	2.2150	13.56	13.46	13.46
01.150	Fruits, vegetables	0.8940	0.8940	0.8940	31.69	31.69	31.69
01.160	Fruits, vegetables other than fresh	1.7720	1.7720	1.7720	5.04	5.04	5.04
01.170	Potatoes, manioc, tubers	2.2780	2.2780	2.2780	46.02	46.02	46.02
01.180	Sugar	1.1810	1.1810	1.1810	5.24	5.24	5.24
01.190	Coffee, tea, cocoa	2.2300	2.2300	2.2300	0.14	0.14	0.14
01.200	Other foods	0.7520	0.7520	0.7520	42.06	42.06	42.06
01.300	Beverages	2.2624	1.6722	1.9450	18.07	13.36	15.54
01.400	Tobacco	1.9272	2.5753	2.2278	4.52	6.04	5.22
02.000	Clothing, footwear	0.4466	0.3852	0.4148	17.95	15.48	16.67
02.100	Clothing	0.4809	0.4967	0.4887	12.52	12.94	12.73
02.200	Footwear	0.2097	0.2111	0.2104	55.48	55.85	55.67
03.000	Gross rent, fuel	1.6258	1.1674	1.3777	2.39	1.71	2.02
03.100	Gross rent	1.3819	1.3819	1.3819	2.10	2.10	2.10
03.200	Fuel and power	2.0262	0.9088	1.3570	2.86	1.28	1.91
04.000	House furnishings, operations	1.3717	0.7202	0.9939	11.80	6.19	8.55
04.100	Furniture	1.0531	0.8425	0.9419	6.59	5.27	5.89
04.200	Household textile	0.6562	0.6562	0.6562	5.16	5.16	5.16
04.300	Heating and cooking appliances	2.8600	4.2034	3.4672	4.66	6.84	5.64
04.400	Household utensils	0.5471	0.5471	0.5471	14.00	14.00	14.00
04.500	Household operation	1.1967	0.1550	0.4307	22.49	2.91	8.09
05.000	Medical care	0.6262	0.1138	0.2669	32.18	5.85	13.72

Table 3.A.11.b.

| Category | | Expenditure (billion) | | | | Per capita expenditure | | | |
| | | China | | United States | | China | | United States | |
		$	yuan	$	yuan	$	yuan	$	yuan
0	Consumption	1 091.79	637.60	2 698.63	3 011.13	1 023.42	597.68	11 212.52	12 510.93
01.000	Food beverages and tobacco	303.29	342.47	428.48	710.38	284.30	321.03	1 780.29	2 951.54
01.100	Food	274.70	289.31	370.60	589.36	257.50	271.20	1 539.80	2 448.74
01.100	Bread, cereals	75.89	68.22	35.37	31.80	71.15	63.96	146.97	132.13
01.110	Meat	50.23	61.54	60.33	73.90	47.09	57.68	250.65	307.05
01.120	Fish	9.80	16.33	8.23	13.73	9.18	15.30	34.21	57.03
01.130	Milk, cheese, eggs	7.50	15.61	36.02	74.98	7.03	14.64	149.64	311.55
01.140	Oils, fats	3.92	8.68	6.56	14.53	3.67	8.13	27.26	60.36
01.150	Fruits, vegetables	57.83	51.70	41.16	36.80	54.21	48.46	171.03	152.90
01.160	Fruits, vegetables other than fresh	4.71	8.35	21.10	37.38	4.42	7.83	87.65	155.32
01.170	Potatoes, manioc, tubers	5.29	12.04	2.59	5.90	4.95	11.28	10.76	24.51
01.180	Sugar	2.19	2.59	9.45	11.16	2.06	2.43	39.27	46.38
01.190	Coffee, tea, cocoa	0.76	1.70	119.43	266.33	0.71	1.59	496.22	1 106.57
01.200	Other foods	56.58	42.55	30.36	22.83	53.05	39.89	126.13	94.85
01.300	Beverages	22.67	37.91	28.30	64.02	21.25	35.53	117.57	265.99
01.400	Tobacco	5.92	15.26	29.58	57.02	5.55	14.30	122.92	236.89
02.000	Clothing, footwear	138.60	53.39	174.17	77.78	129.91	50.04	723.66	323.19
02.100	Clothing	84.48	41.96	152.16	73.18	79.18	39.33	632.22	304.03
02.200	Footwear	54.14	11.43	22.01	4.62	50.73	10.71	91.44	19.17
03.000	Gross rent, fuel	37.59	43.88	355.56	578.07	35.24	41.14	1 477.31	2 401.81
03.100	Gross rent	20.55	28.39	220.99	305.38	19.26	26.62	918.18	1 268.83
03.200	Fuel and power	17.05	15.49	134.57	272.67	15.98	14.52	559.13	1 132.91
04.000	House furnishings, operations	104.27	75.09	199.37	273.48	97.74	70.39	828.38	1 136.29
04.100	Furniture	13.48	11.35	46.18	48.63	12.64	10.65	191.86	202.05
04.200	Household textile	3.10	2.03	13.50	8.86	2.90	1.90	56.11	36.82
04.300	Heating and cooking appliances	9.39	39.49	45.53	130.22	8.81	37.02	189.18	541.05
04.400	Household utensils	25.70	14.06	41.42	22.66	24.09	13.18	172.10	94.16
04.500	Household operation	52.57	8.15	52.74	63.11	49.29	7.64	219.13	262.23
05.000	Medical care	276.80	31.50	194.06	121.52	259.49	29.53	806.28	504.89

Table 3.A.11.c.

Category		PPA (yuan/$)			Quantity per capita (US = 100)		
		US weight	China weight	Fisher mean	US weight	China weight	Fisher mean
06.000	Transport and communications	1.5150	1.2059	1.3516	0.47	0.38	0.42
06.100	Equipment	1.9618	2.1860	2.0709	0.38	0.43	0.40
06.200	Operation costs	1.4312	1.4920	1.4613	0.00	0.00	0.00
06.300	Purchased transport	0.7791	0.7270	0.7526	34.74	32.42	33.56
06.400	Communications	0.6554	0.8639	0.7525	0.17	0.23	0.20
07.000	Recreation, education	1.3120	0.3824	0.7083	12.39	3.61	6.69
07.100	Equipment and accessories	2.8620	2.7586	2.8098	2.38	2.30	2.34
07.200	Entertainment and religious services	0.1427	0.0468	0.0817	21.75	7.13	12.46
07.300	Books, newspapers, magazines	0.9082	0.3740	0.5828	17.54	7.22	11.26
07.400	Education	0.1626	0.2237	0.1907	18.37	25.27	21.54
08.000	Other expenditures	0.3140	0.3140	0.3140	2.79	2.79	2.79
1	Capital formation	2.8417	0.9634	1.6546	6.88	2.33	4.00
	Construction	1.0794	0.8401	0.9533	14.86	11.56	13.09
10.000	Residential	1.2445	1.2445	1.2445	0.95	0.95	0.95
11.000	Non-residential	0.8579	0.8260	0.8418	44.92	43.25	44.08
12.000	Other construction	0.7950	0.7950	0.7950	7.70	7.70	7.70
	Producer durables	4.0252	1.8590	2.7355	1.40	0.65	0.95
14.000	Transport equipment	1.7259	2.1099	1.9083	1.14	1.40	1.26
15.000	Non-electrical machinery	5.5316	1.4233	2.8059	1.12	0.29	0.57
16.000	Electrical machinery	3.8922	2.5833	3.1709	1.39	0.92	1.13
17.000	Other durables	1.0981	0.9886	1.0419	9.34	8.41	8.87
2	Government	0.5403	0.2099	0.3368	14.29	5.55	8.90
20.000	Compensation	0.1215	0.1215	0.1215	24.69	24.69	24.69
21.000	Commodities	0.9941	0.9941	0.9941	3.02	3.02	3.02
Gross Domestic Product		**1.5091**	**0.5895**	**0.9432**	**9.15**	**3.57**	**5.72**

Table 3.A.11.d.

Category	Expenditure (billion)				Per capita expenditure			
	China		US		China		US	
	yuan	$	yuan	$	yuan	$	yuan	$
06.000 Transport and communications	11.80	9.79	709.59	468.38	11.06	9.17	2 948.28	1 946.06
06.100 Equipment	6.90	3.16	364.64	185.87	6.47	2.96	1 515.04	772.27
06.200 Operation costs	0.00	0.00	293.93	205.37	0.00	0.00	1 221.24	853.30
06.300 Purchased transport	4.42	6.08	3.07	3.94	4.14	5.69	12.77	16.39
06.400 Communications	0.47	0.55	47.97	73.19	0.45	0.52	199.30	304.09
07.000 Recreation, Education	55.63	145.49	347.57	264.92	52.15	136.38	1 444.13	1 100.71
07.100 Equipment and accessories	31.54	11.43	309.61	108.16	29.57	10.72	1 286.38	449.47
07.200 Entertainment and religious services	2.12	45.25	6.68	46.81	1.98	42.31	27.76	194.51
07.300 Books, newspapers, magazines	5.25	14.03	16.36	18.01	4.91	13.13	67.96	74.83
07.400 Education	16.74	74.83	14.95	91.92	15.69	70.14	62.10	381.91
08.000 Other expenditures	23.83	75.91	192.70	613.70	22.34	71.15	800.65	2 549.84
1 Capital formation	317.74	329.81	3 074.43	1 081.90	297.85	309.17	12 773.92	4 495.17
Construction	243.51	289.86	475.08	440.13	228.27	271.72	1 973.91	1 828.71
10.000 Residential	13.63	10.95	323.64	260.05	12.78	10.27	1 344.67	1 080.49
11.000 Non-residential	216.79	262.46	113.08	131.81	203.22	246.03	469.85	547.67
12.000 Other construction	13.08	16.46	38.37	48.27	12.27	15.43	159.44	200.55
Producer durables	74.23	39.93	2 583.23	641.76	69.58	37.43	10 733.03	2 666.46
14.000 Transport equipment	15.10	7.16	243.95	141.35	14.16	6.71	1 013.59	587.28
15.000 Non-electrical machinery	19.32	13.57	1 515.95	274.05	18.11	12.72	6 298.61	1 138.66
16.000 Electrical machinery	33.74	13.06	823.35	211.54	31.63	12.24	3 420.93	878.92
17.000 Other durables	6.07	6.14	16.28	14.83	5.69	5.76	67.64	61.60
2 Government	64.88	309.10	263.71	488.07	60.82	289.76	1 095.67	2 027.89
20.000 Compensation	33.74	277.66	30.84	253.80	31.63	260.33	128.12	1 054.50
21.000 Commodities	31.13	31.32	232.89	234.28	29.19	29.36	967.65	973.39
Gross Domestic Product	**1 020.22**	**1 730.66**	**6 441.74**	**4 268.60**	**956.35**	**1 622.31**	**26 764.76**	**17 735.58**

Note: The "Fisher" mean is the geometric mean.

Sources: The population of China in 1986 was 1.06679 billion, from *Statistical Yearbook of China, 1994* (SSB,1994), p. 59, adjusted to a mid-year basis; GDP came from the same source, p. 32. The US population (0.24068 billion) and GDP are from US Dept. of Commerce (1992), p. 8 et 428, respectively.

The study followed the ICOP framework and approach used by Pilat and others. It chose 1985 as the benchmark year because an ICOP-type US/China comparison for manufacturing had already been completed based on *Industrial Census of China, 1985* (Szirmai and Ren, 1995). The data issued by SSB improve in quality each year, with revisions to historical data occurring from time to time. The present study has tried to use the most recent sources and to cross-check discrepancies between early and later sources.

Table 3.A.12. **The Classification System for GDP and Employment in the** *Statistical Yearbook of China, 1994*

Gross Domestic Product
Primary Industry : Agriculture, Forestry & Fisheries
Secondary Industry:
    Industry:
        Mining: Coal mining, Petroleum and natural Gas, Ferrous metals, Non-ferrous metals, Non-metallic minerals, Other minerals, Logging and transport of timber and bamboo
        Manufacturing: Food processing and production, Beverages, Tobacco, Textiles, Clothing & other, Leather, Timber processing, Furniture, Paper, Printing, Cultural, educational and sport activities, Petroleum and coke, Chemical products, Medical products, Chemical fibres, Rubber, Plastics, Non-metallic mineral products, Processing of ferrous and Non-ferrous metals, Metal products, Machinery, Transport equipment, Electric equipment, Electronic and Telecommunications equipment, Instruments, Other manufacturing
    Electricity, Gas & Water:
        Electric power, steam and hot water
        Gas
        Public water supply system
    Construction
Tertiary Industry:
        Geological Prospecting & Water Conservancy
        Transport, Storage and Communications
        Wholesale and Retail trade (including restaurants)
        Finance and Insurance
        Real Estate Management
        Social Services
        Health Care, Sports and Social Welfare
        Education, Culture and Art (including radio, film and television)
        Scientific Research and Polytechnic Services
        Government (including other social organisations)
        Other

Since the Chinese official statistical system is in transition, it lacks consistency in the classification systems used in statistical publications. Table 3.A.12 describes the classification system used in the *Statistical Yearbook of China, 1994*.

This classification is consistent with the *International Standard Industrial Classification of All Economic Activities* (ISIC) (UN, 1968*b*) except for logging which ISIC classifies in forestry. The *Input-Output Table of China, 1987* (SSB,1991), *Industrial Census of China, 1985* (OLG, 1987-88) and the *Industrial Statistical Yearbook of China, 1988, 1993* (SSB 1988, 1993*a*), formerly classified urban water supply in mining, but have now merged this industry with electricity, gas and water. A forage industry listing in all sources has been put into the food industry in the present study. Other adjustments (described at various points below) for differences in the classifications used in the different sources have been made where necessary.

The ICOP framework divides the economy into several sectors (agriculture, mining, construction, manufacturing, and so on). The manufacturing sector has 16 branches, which can be further disaggregated to individual industries. The study sometimes made aggregations to 6 major branches for analysis; it also chose some individual industries as samples for the product matches. It kept the terminology used consistent with all ICOP studies in manufacturing. For all other sectors, it made the comparisons either at sector level (e.g. agriculture, mining) or at branch level (e.g. wholesale and retail trade).

An economically meaningful comparison of labour productivity at the sectoral level — regarded as the strength of the ICOP approach — must observe two key criteria. First, the data for output and labour input should have matched classifications. Here, this point applies only to the Chinese side because the US data used in the labour productivity comparison had been discussed extensively in Pilat (1994). Second, the concepts of output and labour input of the countries being compared must be consistent.

Chinese Sectoral Value Added in Chinese Currency

This study required a breakdown of Chinese GDP consistent with the ICOP classifications, with detailed information on employment for each sector organised according to the breakdown of GDP. It was important to use the latest information — to capture improvements in the Chinese data in terms of transparency, better definitions and matching of the classification system with international conventions — and to ensure that figures for both GDP and employment came from the same source.

The *Input-Output Table of China, 1987* (SSB, 1991) provides the most detailed information on value added for each industry according to the standard international classification. The biggest matrix in the table has 117 industries. On the other hand, the 1994 *Statistical Yearbook* (SSB, 1994) provides the most detailed and relatively well organised data for employment. Calculating the sectoral GDPs thus required using aggregated GDPs from the *Yearbook* and breaking them down on the basis of information provided in the input-output table. This procedure involved an assumption

70

of underlying structural similarity of GDP in 1985 and 1987. Moreover, previous ICOP studies have shown that there can be considerable discrepancies between different sources which can affect the productivity measures, especially those in the manufacturing sector (see e.g. Maddison and van Ark, 1988; Szirmai and Pilat, 1990). This called for a reconciliation of the data from the two sources before making the breakdowns of GDP. The reconciliation (Table 3.A.13) covered 1987, the benchmark year for the input-output table. In fact, the discrepancy for GDP between the two sources is not significant. The discrepancies in the major sectors also are not large except in tertiary industry, where they arise from revisions made in the 1995 *Yearbook*.

Table 3.A.13. **Reconciliation of the Chinese National Accounts and Input-Output Table, 1987**

	National accounts data		Input-output table	
	Gross value added at market prices (million yuan)	Value added as percentage of total	Gross value added at market prices (million yuan)	Value added as percentage of total
GDP	1 196 250.00		1 142 407.18	
Agriculture, forestry and fisheries	320 430.00	26.79	320 203.01	28.03
Secondary activity	525 160.00	43.90	535 694.52	46.89
Industry	458 580.00	38.33	466 154.01	40.80
Construction	66 580.00	5.57	69 540.51	6.09
Tertiary activity	350 660.00	29.31	280 061.26	24.52
Transport and Communications	54 490.00	4.56	56 245.05	4.92
Wholesale and retail trade	115 930.00	9.69	59 339.23	5.19

Sources: National accounts data from *Statistical Yearbook of China, 1994* (SSB, 1994). Input-output data from the author's calculations based on *Input-Output Table of China, 1987* (SSB, 1991).

Before the study broke down GDP into its components, the following adjustments were made:

— logging was moved from mining to agriculture;

— water supply was moved from mining to electricity, gas and water;

— gas supply was moved from manufacturing to electricity, gas and water;

— storage was moved from commerce to transport.

The procedure used in the breakdown involved two steps. The first derived a distribution of sectoral value added from the biggest matrix in the input-output table, after some classification adjustments. The second step applied this distribution of sectoral value added to the GDP and its components to obtain the sectoral GDP at market prices in 1985 in the ICOP format (column 7 of Table 3.2).

Chinese Sectoral Value Added at Factor Cost

In the ICOP framework, labour productivity comparisons usually are made on a factor cost basis to assure that differences in the fiscal systems between the countries under comparison do not affect the comparative results. The contribution made by each industry to GDP is defined as value added of that industry, the difference between its gross output and its intermediate inputs; it has four components, which together define value added at market prices:

— compensation of employees;

— operating surplus;

— the consumption of fixed capital;

— the excess of indirect taxes over subsidies.

Value added at factor cost emerges after net indirect taxes are deducted from value added at market prices (see EC Commission *et al.* 1993). Except for agriculture and construction, for which tax figures appeared in the 1994 *Yearbook* (SSB, 1994) and could be used directly, the tax data are not available in the statistical sources used for this study. For these sectors, adjustments for taxes were made in three steps. The first, using supplementary information from various sources, estimated the share of taxes in figures on profits and taxes together given for each industry in the input-output table. The second used these shares to calculate the ratios of taxes to value added at market prices for each sector in 1987. The third step made adjustments based on these ratios for sectoral value added in 1985.

These three steps yielded value added at factor cost for all sectors except distribution and public utilities, which needed further adjustment for subsidies. From 1979 to 1986, six price reform programmes affected the price structure and subsidy channels. In agriculture, the government raised official purchasing prices for farm output and related "sideline" products. It kept the sales prices for staple foods unchanged, however, although it hiked prices for eight non-staple foods by 30 per cent in the cities. In staples, the official distribution mechanism had big losses and the government subsidised it considerably, while for non-staples it subsidised city dwellers with direct payments.The Input-Output table for 1987 (SSB, 1991) shows a negative figure of 18.34 billion yuan for profits and taxes in "trade of grain and cooking oils", the main distribution channel providing food for city dwellers. The government subsidised these losses. According to the *Statistical Yearbook of China, 1995* (SSB, 1995), it transferred 19.87 billion yuan as a subsidy to the supply of grain, cotton and edible oil in 1985, which provided the upward adjustment necessary for value added at factor cost in distribution. In the same table, another negative figure for "manufacture of gas and coal products", provided the adjustment for subsidies to public utilities. Other sectors may also have received government subsidies but a lack of relevant information made adjustments impossible.

The Employment Figures

The *Statistical Yearbook of China, 1994* (SSB, 1994) provided figures for employment for relatively more aggregated sectors not well matched with the breakdowns of GDP. The same source also gave more disaggregated numbers for 1993 for "staff and workers" — a narrower concept than employment because it excludes private enterprises, urban self-employment and social workers, but the figures allowed the calculation of ratios where necessary to allocate the overall employment data. Other specific adjustments made to improve consistency between the GDP and employment data included the following.

— Employment in logging (including felling and rough cutting of trees; hewing or rough shaping of poles, blocks, bolts and other wood materials; and transportation of logs) was added to agriculture based on the 1982 population census.

— Water supply from the 1994 *Yearbook* was merged into the "electricity, gas and water" sector.

— The 1994 *Yearbook* gives employment in the transport, storage and communications sectors together in 1985. The 1986 *Yearbook* (SSB, 1986), however, has separate figures for transport and communications in 1982, based on the 1982 population census, which included the storage industry in commerce. Ratios based on the 1982 data furnished the adjustment which separated these components for 1985.

— The 1994 *Yearbook* provided employment data for wholesale trade, retail trade and food service in 1985; storage was lumped with transport and communications (see previous point); and social service was a separate industry. The 1986 *Yearbook* gave figures for retail trade and storage, and placed social services in the commerce sector. The figures finally used applied the ratio of retail trade, after deducting storage and social services data from the 1982 population census, to the total in 1985 in order to get the breakdown.

— The 1994 *Yearbook* gives consolidated 1985 data for finance and insurance. The 1986 *Yearbook* provides figures for "staff and workers" in finance and insurance, respectively, in the same year. The figures presented here applied the relative proportions of "staff and workers" to total employment.

— Education in the 1994 *Yearbook* includes culture, art, radio, film and television. The 1982 population census yields a ratio between employment in education and that in the cultural activities of 0.9114; it was used to extract a figure for the broad cultural employment component in education, which went into the "other services" sector.

— Health employment in the 1994 *Yearbook* includes sports and social welfare. Based on the 1982 population census, the ratio of health services employment to the total was 0.961966, which furnished the adjustment for 1985.

Table 3.A.14 summarises sectoral employment and GDP (value added) at factor cost for both countries. It also provides for China a comparable series on GDP at market prices, to highlight the structural effects of indirect taxes and subsidies discussed above.

Agriculture, Forestry and Fisheries

Industrial activity in China's rural areas has a long history. Since the early 1980s it has increased rapidly and played a more important role in the whole economy. Its statistical treatment has changed considerably. Before 1984, the national accounts treated it separately according to ownership of enterprises; they registered the output of units administered by townships as part of the gross value of industrial output, but reported that of enterprises administered by villages and production brigades in the gross value of agricultural output. Since 1985, however, all of the rural industrial sector has been counted as part of industry. The SSB in 1987 and 1988 adjusted data after 1970 by separating all industrial activities from agriculture. No further adjustment for the 1950s and 1960s has been reported. As rural industrial activities at production-brigade level and below were not negligible in the 1950s and 1960s, this change resulted in inconsistencies of data for the agricultural sector over time (see a processed paper in Chinese, issued by SSB in 1986, and Wu, 1993). Time series on gross value of agricultural output clearly show that the reported proportion of sideline activities changed dramatically from 8.7 per cent to 2.7 per cent between 1970 and 1971 (Ministry of Agriculture Planning Bureau, 1989).

The PPP for the agricultural sector as a whole is quite simple to derive. The sector was divided into the three ICOP sub-sectors: agriculture (crops and animal husbandry), forestry and fisheries, with the breakdowns for China based on the 1987 input-output table. Pilat (1994) broke down US agricultural GDP for 1985. Sideline activity remained included in crops and animal husbandry in the breakdown for China. Because data on the value of output in agriculture for China were not available, the prices received by farmers (purchasing or procurement prices in Chinese statistical publications) were regarded as unit values for China's agricultural products. The values of output for China's agricultural goods are therefore the products of quantity and price.

Data for prices received by Chinese farmers came from the *Price Statistics Yearbook of China, 1988* (SSB, 1988*b*). Most prices referred to 1986, but had already been backdated to 1985 by the price index. Agricultural output data came from the *Statistical Yearbook of China, 1986, 1994* (SSB, 1986, 1994). These sources, however, made possible an ICOP comparison with only a relatively low coverage ratio. The UN Food and Agriculture Organization (FAO) database provided prices and quantities for other Chinese products, many of them estimates of FAO. The extra information added some important items to the product matches and increased the coverage ratio. (See Table 3.A.15)

Table 3.A.14. **Basic Information on GDP at Market Prices and at Factor Cost for China, and Comparisons of GDP at Factor Cost and Employment for China and the United States, 1985**

Sector	China						United States			
	GDP at market prices (million yuan)	Value added as % of total	GDP at factor cost (million yuan)	Value added as % of total	Persons engaged (x 1 000)	Persons engaged as % of total	GDP at factor cost ($ million)	Value added as % of total	Persons engaged (x 1 000)	Persons engaged as % of total
Agriculture, forestry and fisheries	259 243.20	28.92	255 038.20	30.65	310 672	63.36	86 599.01	2.32	3 242	2.78
Mining	33 836.34	3.77	32 054.17	3.85	7 128	1.45	111 012.29	2.98	947	0.81
Manufacturing	288 087.96	32.14	247 563.63	29.75	72 205	14.73	757 622.86	20.33	19 700	16.91
Electricity, gas, water	17 862.50	1.99	12 583.63	1.51	1 380	0.28	109 493.80	2.94	914	0.78
Construction	41 790.00	4.66	39 505	4.75	18 475	3.77	175 051.50	4.70	6 186	5.31
Transport and Storage	37 463.18	4.18	32 713.83	3.93	11 045	2.25	129 960.81	3.49	3 371	2.89
Communications	3 226.82	0.36	3 105.81	0.37	960	0.20	101 098.42	2.71	1 332	1.14
Wholesale trade	43 246.50	4.82	42 651.65	5.13	7 310	1.49	228 591.69	6.13	6 112	5.24
Retail trade	44 593.50	4.97	43 974.37	5.28	14 190	2.89	325 412.33	8.73	19 465	16.70
Finance	33 270.43	3.71	29 307.35	3.52	1 299	0.26	138 448.80	3.72	2 906	2.49
Insurance	885.75	0.10	792.17	0.10	27	0.01	56 653.85	1.52	2 045	1.75
Real estate	11 298.04	1.26	11 282.48	1.36	360	0.07	382 289.18	10.26	1 802	1.55
Education	23 513.96	2.62	23 513.96	2.83	11 288	2.30	196 875.86	5.28	9 305	7.98
Health	7 713.95	0.86	7 713.95	0.93	4 338	0.88	184 469.85	4.95	6 828	5.86
Other services	31 603.21	3.53	31 603.22	3.80	21 964	4.48	426 750.57	11.45	19 130	16.42
Government	18 804.67	2.10	18 804.67	2.26	7 710	1.57	315 714.35	8.47	13 247	11.37
Statistical Discrepancy							(13 900)			
Total	**896 440.01**	**100.00**	**832 208.22**	**100.00**	**490 351**	**100.00**	**3 726 044.82**	**100.00**	**116 532**	**100.00**

Note: "Other Services" for China includes geological prospecting, social services, scientific research and others, and the "Government" figure includes data for other social organisations.

Sources: GDPs at market prices are from Table 3.2. For GDPs at factor cost: Data (including employment data) for the United States are from Pilat (1994), *The American Almanac, 1992*, and the *Survey of Current Business* (US Dept. of Commerce, May 1993); the sectoral figures for China are the author's estimates based on official data in the *Statistical Yearbook of China* (SSB, 1995); the Chinese employment figures, after adjustment by the author, are from the same source.

75

Table 3.A.15. Matched Agricultural Products, China and the United States, 1985

(Quantities in thousands of metric tons (MT); values in million yuan and $ million; unit values in yuan per MT or $ per MT)

	Quantities produced China	Quantities produced United States	Values of output China	Values of output United States	Unit values China	Unit values United States	PPP At Chinese quantity weights	PPP At US quantity weights	US Quantities at Chinese prices	Chinese Quantities at US prices
Wheat	85 805.00	61 597.84	35 719.55	7 648.00	416.29	124.16	3.3528	3.3528	25 642.41	10 653.57
Rice	168 569.00	6 174.40	54 942.14	893.00	325.93	144.63	2.2536	2.2536	2 012.44	24 380.04
Maize	63 826.00	225 486.19	20 373.21	21 029.00	319.20	93.26	3.4227	3.4227	71 975.03	5 952.46
Sorghum	5 609.00	28 499.31	2 108.86	2 538.00	375.98	89.21	4.2145	4.2145	10 696.32	500.39
Soybeans	10 500.00	53 317.06	7 625.16	10 571.00	726.21	198.27	3.6628	3.6628	38 719.15	2 081.80
Potatoes	26 750.00	18 325.04	4 280.00	1 563.00	160.00	85.29	1.8759	1.8759	2 932.01	2 281.59
Sweet potatoes	103 430.00	796.80	14 480.20	142.90	140.00	179.34	0.7806	0.7806	111.55	18 549.32
Eggplants	3 800.00	34.00	988.00	13.60	260.00	400.00	0.6500	0.6500	8.84	1 520.00
Cabbages	6 100.00	1 400.00	1 098.00	196.00	180.00	140.00	1.2857	1.2857	252.00	854.00
Tomatoes	6 000.00	7 859.93	1 560.00	1 194.71	260.00	152.00	1.7105	1.7105	2 043.58	912.00
Tobacco	2 425.00	666.45	4489.52	2 487.00	1 851.35	3 623.00	0.5110	0.5110	1 270.85	8 785.77
Sugarcane	51 549.00	28 200.00	3 334.94	752.00	64.69	26.67	2.4260	2.4260	1 824.39	1 374.64
Sugar beets	8 919.00	22 500.00	773.60	761.00	86.74	33.82	2.5645	2.5645	1 951.57	301.66
Cotton	4 147.00	2 920.13	14 159.40	3 645.00	3 414.37	1 248.23	2.7354	2.7354	9 970.40	5 176.42
Apples	3 614.11	3 556.64	3 002.12	916.00	830.67	257.55	3.2253	3.2253	2 954.38	930.80
Oranges	1 808.35	13 972.50	1 851.58	1 508.00	1 023.90	107.93	9.4871	9.4871	14 306.51	195.17
Pears	2 136.77	747.00	1 281.04	201.00	599.52	269.08	2.2281	2.2281	447.84	574.95
Pork	16 547.00	6 719.20	29 333.32	10 567.20	1 772.73	1 572.69	1.1272	1.1272	11 911.31	26 023.26
Beef	467.00	10 986.80	1 422.90	30 685.60	3 046.89	2 792.95	1.0909	1.0909	33 475.57	1 304.31
Mutton	593.00	319.62	1 372.70	434.00	2 314.83	1 357.88	1.7047	1.7047	739.86	805.22
Eggs	5 347.00	4 282.50	12 082.50	3 268.00	2 259.68	763.11	2.9612	2.9612	9 677.07	4 080.33
Cows' milk	2 499.00	64 869.01	1 124.55	18 228.19	450.00	281.00	1.6014	1.6014	29 191.06	702.22
Honey	155.00	68.00	290.47	102.00	1 874.00	1 500.00	1.2493	1.2493	127.43	232.50
Total matched output			217 693.77	119 344.20			1.8422	2.2811	272 241.58	118 172.41
Total output (crops/animal husbandry)			330 470.00	136 300.00						
Ratio of matched to total output			65.87%	87.56%						
Geometric mean of PPPs								2.0499		

Notes: The unit values for China are prices received by farmers., originally for 1986 but backdated to 1985 by the relevant price indices. Output values are these prices multiplied by the quantities of output. The total output figures for China are gross value of output; those for the United States cover farm output (crops, livestock and farm products consumed on farms).

Sources: *Statistical Yearbook of China, 1986, 1988, 1994* (SSB, 1986, 1989, 1994); *Statistical Abstract of the United States, 1987* and *National Income and Product Accounts of the United States, Vol. 2, 1959-88* (US Dept. of Commerce, 1987, US Dept. of Commerce (BEA), 1992); and data on China kindly provided by Professor Prasada Rao from FAO files.

The separate comparison for fisheries followed Pilat (1994), basing relative output on the total quantity of fish caught (see Table 3.A.16). The PPPs for agriculture and fisheries were weighted by their respective GDP figures to derive a PPP for agriculture and fisheries combined. This PPP was also used for forestry in the final aggregation of PPPs for the whole sector (Table 3.A.17). Dividing the values of output by the quantities produced gave the unit values for US products, the data for which came from the *Statistical Abstract of the United States, 1987*, (US Dept. of Commerce, 1987). Quantities originally expressed in US measurement units were converted to metric equivalents. The ratios of matched output in total output for both countries are based on gross value of output for China and on farm output including crops, livestock and farm products consumed on farms for the United States.

The unit-value ratios provided the basis for deriving the PPPs weighted by Chinese and US quantities, respectively. The Fisher index (geometric mean) of these two indices is 2.0571 yuan/dollar. Chinese agricultural GDP in dollar terms was computed from GDP in local currency and the PPP for the sector. The FAO's Economic and Social Development Paper, *International Comparisons of Agricultural Output and Productivity* (Prasada Rao, 1993), presented estimates of real income, PPP and productivity in Chinese agriculture for several benchmark years (1970, 1975, 1980, 1985, and 1990); its PPP for 1985 of 2.447 applied only to agriculture because the study excluded forestry and fisheries due to lack of comparable data.

Table 3.A.16. **Production of Fishery Products, China and the United States, 1985**

	China	United States	China as percentage of United States
Quantity of catch (1 000 MT)	7 051.50	2 841.00	248.20
Value of catch			
million yuan	12 611.00	5 080.88	248.20
$ million	5 773.24	2 326.00	248.20
PPP for fisheries (yuan/dollar)			
at Chinese quantity weights			2.1844
at US quantity weights			1.1844
Geometric mean			2.1844

Source: See text.

Pilat's comparison between Japan and the United States in 1985 (Pilat, 1994). His original data source is the *Minerals Yearbook, 1985*, (US Bureau of Mines, 1987). Both China and the United States produce a very wide range of minerals and are the leading producers in some products. The spread between the PPPs by China and US weights is very small and the geometric mean is around unity (Table 3.A.18).

Table 3.A.17. **Output and PPPs for Agriculture, Forestry and Fisheries: China and the United States, 1985**

	China	United States	China as percentage of United States
GDP in crops and livestock			
million yuan	232 358.72	164 327.16	141.40
$ million	126 133.10	72 037.10	175.09
GDP in fisheries			
million yuan	12 697.29	4 463.49	284.47
$ million	5 812.75	2 043.36	284.47
GDP in crops, livestock and fisheries			
million yuan	245 056.01	168 790.64	145.18
$ million	131 945.85	74 080.46	178.11
PPPs for crops, livestock and fisheries			
at Chinese quantity weights			1.8572
at US quantity weights			2.2785
Geometric mean			2.0571
GDP in forestry			
million yuan	14 187.19	23 285.50	60.93
$ million	7 638.83	10 219.54	74.75
GDP in agriculture			
million yuan	259 243.20	192 075.64	134.97
$ million	139 584.68	84 300.00	165.58
PPPs for the agriculture sector			
at Chinese quantity weights			1.8572
at US quantity weights			2.2785
Geometric mean			2.0571

Source: See text.

Manufacturing

Szirmai and Ren (1995) made a comparison between Chinese and US manufacturing for fifteen branches based on the *Industrial Census of China, 1985* (OLG 1987-88) and the *1987 Census of Manufacturing* (US Dept. of Commerce, 1990). These sources provide information on product quantities and gross output values, making it possible to derive unit values for large numbers of products. The paper examined the various issues concerning the feasibility of the application of ICOP methods to Chinese census data and the several conceptual problems involved in the comparisons.

78

Table 3.A.18. **Matched Products in Mining, China and the United States, 1985**
(Quantities in thousands of MT; values in million yuan and $ million;
unit values in yuan per MT or $ per MT)

	Quantities produced		Values of output		Unit values		Purchasing Power Parities at quantity weights of:		US quantities at Chinese prices	Chinese quantities at US prices
	United States	China	United States	China	United States	China	United States	China		
Non-Energy Products										
Copper ores	1 106.00	225.37	1 633	758.84	1 476.49	3 367.12	2.2805	2.2805	3 724.03	332.75
Lead and zinc ores	641.00	521.66	376	742.62	586.58	1 432.56	2.4269	2.4269	912.50	306.00
Iron ore	50 200.00	40 040.00	2 077	1 469.81	41.37	36.71	0.8872	0.8872	1842.77	1 656.64
Bauxite	674.00	490.87	13	8.86	19.29	18.05	0.9358	0.9358	12.17	9.47
Boron minerals	1 151.24	337.42	405	32.71	351.62	96.94	0.2757	0.2757	111.60	118.64
Phosphate rock	50 800	6 222.43	1 236	186.00	24.33	29.89	1.2286	1.2286	1 518.51	151.40
Bentonite	2 898.00	24 014.40	102	244.20	35.20	10.17	0.2889	0.2889	29.47	845.23
Asbestos	57.00	168.12	21	206.04	359.65	1 225.55	3.4076	3.4076	69.86	60.46
Gypsum	13 063.68	5 373.49	112	102.77	8.57	19.13	2.2308	2.2308	249.85	46.07
Salt	36 378.72	14 047.42	740	1 854.16	20.34	131.99	6.4888	6.4888	4 801.73	285.75
Energy products										
Coal and lignite	801 788.00	716 970.00	22 240	22 275.12	27.74	31.07	1.1201	1.1201	24 910.28	19 887.32
Natural gas (a)	464 400.00	13 283.29	42 580	1 130.31	91.69	85.09	0.9281	0.9281	39 517.01	1 217.92
Crude petroleum (b)	520 468.00	124 770.00	78 430	20 380.78	150.69	163.35	1.0840	1.0840	85 016.78	18 801.75
Total matched output			149 964	43 392.22			1.0850	1.1298	162 716.56	43 719.40
Total output			168 154	54 420.17						
Matched as % of total output			89.18	90.76						
Geometric mean of PPPs								1.1072		

Notes: (a) Quantity in millions of cubic meters; (b) Quantity in millions of litres.
Sources: See Annex text.

It presented the results derived at different levels of aggregation and discussed the economic implications of the comparative estimates. Part of that paper has been incorporated in the present study to arrive at a PPP-based GDP in dollar terms for the economy as a whole. The geometric mean of purchasing power parities at US and Chinese quantity weights found for total manufacturing is 1.45 yuan to the dollar, half the 1985 exchange rate of 2.9 yuan to the dollar.

Some Methodological Issues

The basic approach matches comparable products or product groups and calculates unit-value ratios for each of the matches, which cover 23 comparable "sample industries". On the US side these consist of one or several industries at the four-digit level. The Chinese census does not classify by industry codes, but it is possible to identify industries similar to those in the US census on the basis of product descriptions.

The unit-value ratios then are used to calculate PPPs in three steps. *First*, they all are aggregated at sample industry level using output quantities of either country as weights (see equation seven in text). The initial sample-industry PPPs were based on 1987 US unit values and 1985 Chinese unit values; the use of sample-industry price deflators for the United States put them on a 1985 basis. *Second*, the sample-industry PPPs are aggregated at branch level by taking the weighted average of sample industry PPPs using sample-industry gross value added as weights (see equation eight). Manufacturing branches in this study consisted of one or more ISIC three-digit major sectors. In three instances, wood products, paper products and non-metallic mineral products, a branch coincided with a two-digit ISIC division. *Third*, the branch PPPs are aggregated into PPPs for total manufacturing, using branch value added weights according to equation eight.

At this stage, 67 product matches in 23 sample industries had been made, representing 13 out of a total of 15 branches of manufacturing. Table 3.A.19 shows the coverage ratios at branch and sample industry levels, which represented 39.7 per cent of the total gross value of output in China and 18.9 per cent in the United States. With the exception of food manufacturing and chemical products, the number of matches per branch remained limited, due to the lack of detailed value information in the Chinese census.

Data Sources

China held its first industrial census in 1950. This study used data from the second national industrial census held in the first quarter of 1986 for the calendar year 1985. The census aimed at complete coverage of all enterprises producing both single and multiple products. The basic reporting unit was the "independent accounting industrial enterprise", whose characteristics the compiler of the census defined as:

— possession of an independent administrative organisation;

— ability to account independently for profit and loss; and

— empowerment to sign contracts with other units.

Besides information on manufacturing proper, the industrial census also provided information on mining and logging, normally categorised as primary activities; and on electricity, gas and water supply, usually classified as public utilities. The complete results are reported in a ten-volume Chinese publication (OLG, 1987-88). Results for large and medium sized enterprises are reported in English in OLG (1988)[1].

The Chinese edition of the census provides detailed lists of quantities produced (Vol. 10), including some 4 800 products (excluding mining, logging and utilities) in 56 manufacturing industries[2]. Closer inspection, however, shows considerable double counting: the same products are subcategorised in various ways and subtotals seldom add up to totals. The product list can be used only after very detailed screening. Moreover, the tables with product quantities unfortunately contain no information on the gross value of output Such information exists only for a much shorter list of product categories (about 600, see Vol. 3), although the number of reporting enterprises can differ substantially between volumes ten and three. The detailed products from volume 10 have been combined to correspond with the product categories of Vol. 3.

Only very rough unit values can be calculated for larger product categories. At a later stage it might well be necessary to supplement census information on value of output with value or price information from other published or unpublished sources, such as yearbooks of administrative prices compiled by the State Statistical Bureau. Sometimes price ratios from other sources such as the *Statistical Yearbook of China* can be applied to average prices for product categories to derive more detailed unit values. This study derived the data on gross value of output and gross value added by branch of industry in Table 3.A.20 basically from a table in Vol. 3 of the industrial census. This table provides information on gross value of output and "net industrial output" at market prices. Deducting an estimate of indirect taxes, calculated by applying the ratio of indirect taxes to sale values (Census, Vol. 3) to gross value of output at market prices, served to adjust output and value added to factor cost.

The concept of "net industrial output" in Chinese statistical convention has roughly similar coverage in most cases to the US census concept of "net value added". It excludes depreciation, considered as part of intermediate inputs in Chinese national accounts and in the industrial census. Net value added has been adjusted to gross value added (both at factor cost) by adding figures on depreciation given in Vol. 3 of the census. As service inputs from outside manufacturing are not included in intermediate input in the Chinese census, the Chinese figures for gross value added are broadly consistent with the US census concept of value added. A table in Vol. 8 provided the employment figures.

Table 3.A.19. **Coverage Ratios in Manufacturing: Gross Value of Output**
of Matched Industries

as per cent of total gross value of output in sample industries

Branches (numbered) and sample industries within them	China: 1985	United States: 1987	Number of matches
1.	57.14	30.67	22
Meat products	51.48	75.35	5
Dairy products	100.00	61.96	7
Fats and oils	34.07	72.43	3
Grain mill products	94.33	39.26	4
Sugar and sugar factories	95.89	68.08	2
Confectionary products	100.00	27.84	1
2.	13.04	27.49	1
Malt and malt beverages	100.00	91.94	1
3.	10.61	15.21	3
Tobacco and tobacco products	10.61	15.21	3
4.	69.80	53.09	7
Textile yarn and cloth	80.16	88.57	7
5.	0.00	0.00	0
Men's and women's clothing	0.00	0.00	0
6.	42.87	43.68	1
Leather footwear	100.00	91.89	1
7.	39.97	19.73	2
Sawmills, planing, other wood mills	78.27	45.20	2
8.	63.96	11.93	4
Pulp and paper	100.00	38.56	4
9.	30.62	25.47	10
Agricultural fertilizers	99.73	86.44	3
Soap and detergents	100.00	33.88	2
Petroleum refining	63.65	70.95	5
10.	30.67	3.20	4
Tires and inner tubes	34.56	20.98	2
Rubber and plastic footwear	100.00	16.92	2
11.	56.90	7.84	3
Bricks	79.79	72.23	2
Cement	100.00	65.85	1
12.	48.52	14.69	2
Iron and steel	88.51	70.79	2
13.	10.79	20.79	4
Motor vehicles and equipment	67.22	52.81	4
14.	20.09	5.06	4
Radio and TV receivers	98.23	88.04	2
15.	0.00	0.00	0
Other manufacturing	0.00	0.00	0

Table 3.A.20. Basic Data on Output, Employment and Productivity in Chinese Manufacturing, 1985

	Gross value of output at factor cost (a) (million yuan)	Gross value added at factor cost (million yuan) (b)	Gross value added at factor cost (% of total)	Employment (persons) Total	Employment (persons) Net (c)	Number of enterprises	Gross value added per person employed (yuan) Total	Gross value added per person employed (yuan) Net (c)
Food manufacturing	63 386.04	8 544.56	4.70	3 028 400	2 771 812	41 841	2 821.5	3 082.7
Beverages	12 856.36	3 217.06	1.77	975 300	907 777	13 197	3 298.5	3 543.9
Tobacco products	8 954.44	488 50	0.27	225 400	204 142	313	2 167.3	2 393.0
Textile mill products	97 532.64	18 737.74	10.31	6 830 400	6 194 181	18 846	2 743.3	3 025.1
Wearing apparel	16 380.64	4 391.93	2.39	1 997 800	1 890 600	18 196	2 173.4	2 296.6
Leather products and footwear	7 982.67	1 931.13	1.06	825 600	774 140	1 079	2 339.1	2 494.6
Wood products, furniture and fixtures	9 917.57	2 907.7	1.60	1 434 800	1 316 469	19 736	2 026.5	2 208.7
Paper products, printing, publishing	22 092.6	6 249.9	3.44	2 124 400	1 963 345	17 756	2 942.0	3 183.3
Chemical products (a)	92 887.2	25 141.4	13.83	4 622 400	4 034 258	17 654	5 439.0	6 232.0
Rubber and plastic products	25 385.9	6 485.5	3.57	1 875 500	1 726 289	13 982	3 458.0	3 756.9
Non-metallic mineral products	37 525.7	15 148.9	8.33	6 598 600	6 159 593	48 291	2 295.8	2 459.4
Basic and fabricated metal products (b,d)	89 090.4	24 095.4	13.25	5 816 300	5 076 180	29 615	4 142.7	4 746.8
Machinery and transport equipment	124 288.9	41 505.5	22.83	11 606 600	10 207 956	53 265	3 576.0	4 066.0
Electrical machinery and equipment (d)	56 100.7	16 316.6	8.97	3 534 200	3 170 020	14 901	4 616.8	5 147.2
Other manufacturing	20 186.6	6 702.2	3.69	2 353 500	2 184 678	17 683	2 847.8	3 067.8
Total manufacturing	**684 568.3**	**181 814.1**	**100.0**	**53 849 200**	**48 581 439**	**326 175**	**3 376.4**	**3 742.2**

Notes: (a) Includes petroleum refining. The proportion of gross value of output (GVO) at factor cost to GVO at market prices from *Census*, vol. 3, p. 596 ff. was applied to GVO at market prices from *Census*, vol. 3, p. 90 ff. (b) The US census concept of value added: gross value added = net value added + depreciation. (c) Employment excluding workers producing auxiliary services such as health care, education and housing. For end-of-year employment, data excluding such services are in *Census*, vol. 8 p.18 ff. Figures in the table applied the year-end ratio of employment (excl. services) to total employment to total average employment to obtain an estimate of average employment excluding services.
(d) There is a small discrepancy between the calculated and published totals.

Sources: RC, *Industrial Census*, (OLG, 1987-88), vol. 3. GVO at market prices from p. 90 ff. GVO at market prices, p. 90 ff., adjusted to factor cost by subtracting indirect taxes calculated from p. 596 ff. Net value added at market prices from p. 90 ff., adjusted to gross value added by adding depreciation from p. 564 ff. The table, "Fixed Capital and Flow of Funds for Total Industry" was adjusted to factor cost by subtracting the estimate for indirect taxes. Number of enterprises from p. 90 ff. Also PRC, *Industrial Census*, vol. 8. Annual average employment from p. 2 ff. Auxiliary service employees from p.18 ff.

It is not clear whether the Chinese information by industry is based on a commodity classification (irrespective of whether goods produced are primary or secondary products) or on an industry classification including both primary and the secondary products. On the one hand, data collection occurs on an enterprise basis with enterprises often producing many products belonging to different industries. On the other hand, the census classification seems to follow a commodity classification. This question needs further examination.

For the United States the basic source was the *1987 Census of Manufacturing* (US Dept. of Commerce, 1990), which lists approximately 11 000 products. For most products the US census provides both quantity and value information for 1987. 1987 unit values were put on a 1985 basis using information from the *US Industrial Outlook 1989* (US Dept. of Commerce, 1989 *b*) and figures from the *Annual Survey of Manufactures*, which are reproduced in the 1987 census. The data on gross value of output (value of shipments), gross value added and employment by branch of industry in 1985 also derive from the 1987 census. It provides information on gross output, gross value added and employment by industry for years prior to 1987 including the benchmark year 1985. These data originally derive from the *Annual Survey of Manufactures.*

The US census reports industry data on gross output value, value added and employment on an establishment basis, including both production primary to the industry in question and secondary production. It arranges listings by products, irrespective of whether they are primary products of some industries or secondary products of other industries. Therefore the industry gross output totals differ from the gross output totals calculated from the product listings. Table 3.A.21 contains the basic US data used in this study.

Concepts, Adjustments and Outstanding Problems

Thirteen key conceptual and methodological issues become involved in comparisons of output and productivity in manufacturing based on industrial census data of China and the United States. Most of them focus on the Chinese data; US sources have had extensive discussion in recent ICOP publications (e.g. Szirmai and Pilat, 1990; Maddison and van Ark, 1994*b*; van Ark and Pilat, 1993).

i) The Chinese census provides information on "net industrial output" which is analogous to "net value added". China still took its 1985 industrial census within a Material Product System (MPS) conceptual framework, but because the output concept in the manufacturing sector refers to the value of physical production, conceptual discrepancies between MPS and SNA in this sector are far less troublesome than for services. Chinese statistical convention takes two basically different approaches to the measurement of net industrial output (net value added), as recommended by SSB in its guidelines in the *Explanation to the Industrial Economic Indicators* (SSB, 1987*b*; see also *Census* Vol. 1). A production-based approach derives net industrial output by

Table 3.A.21. **Basic Data on Output, Employment and Productivity in US Manufacturing, 1985**

	Gross value of output (GVO) ($ million)	GVA	GVA as % of total	Employment (a) (persons)	Employment as % of total	GVA per person engaged ($)
Food manufacturing	258 318.2	84 853.3	8.48	1 331 725	7.1	63 716.8
Beverages	43 243.8	19 292.7	1.93	197 109	1.0	97 878.3
Tobacco products	18 506.8	11 893.7	1.19	69 893	0.4	170 171.0
Textile mill products	53 276.5	20 693.3	2.07	684 756	3.6	30 220.0
Wearing apparel	56 993.1	27 728.4	2.77	1 091 743	5.8	25 398.3
Leather products and footwear	8 567.2	4 107.5	0.41	154 319	0.8	26 616.9
Wood products, furniture and fixtures	85 478.9	37 544.3	3.75	1 108 444	5.9	33 871.2
Paper products, printing and publishing	205 277.9	113 476.6	11.35	2 082 718	11.1	54 484.9
Chemicals, incl. petroleum refining	376 446.2	112 369.1	11.24	1 212 252	6.4	92 694.5
Rubber and plastic products	71 324.0	35 708.3	3.57	770 989	4.1	46 314.9
Non-metallic mineral products	55 112.0	28 877.7	2.89	550 384	2.9	52 468.3
Basic and fabricated metal products	250 110.7	107 400.0	10.74	2 291 459	12.2	46 869.7
Machinery and transport equipment	516 624.7	231 388.6	23.14	4 059 265	21.6	57 002.6
Electrical machinery and equipment (b)	154 898.3	85 708.5	8.57	1 728 419	9.2	49 587.8
Other manufacturing industries (b)	126 005.5	79 100.0	7.91	1 462 926	7.8	54 069.7
Total manufacturing (c)	**2 280 183.8**	**1 000142.0**	**100.0**	**18 796 400**	**100.0**	**53 209.2**

Notes:(a) Includes head office employment and employment in auxiliaries (some 8 per cent of the total). For 1985 no such data were available, but the figures were estimated from the ratio of data net of such employment to the total in 1987. (b) The 1987 census included no *Annual Survey of Manufactures* (ASM) data because the 1987 revision of the US Standard Industrial Classiciaation (SIC) substantially re-categorised activities in these branches. The original ASM data for 1985, based on the 1972 SIC, are not useful. The estimates here of GVO, GVA and employment came from subtracting the 1985 summed totals for all other branches from the 1985 total for manufacturing and applying 1987 proportions to distribute GVO, GVA and employment over the branches to which this note applies. (c) Total employment (column 4) includes an auxiliary component (1 288 100) from 1985 ASM data.

Sources: Census of Manufacturing, 1987, General Summary, (US Dept of Commerce 1990), Tables II.1 and II.6 (Original source for 1985 was the *Annual Survey of Manufactures*).

subtracting intermediate inputs from gross value of output, which comprises the value of finished goods, processing work, maintenance and semi-finished goods (*Census*, Vol. 1). This approach suggests using "Production Cost Table" data to calculate the intermediate inputs. Based on the guidelines these include:

—   material inputs from outside the enterprise;

—   fuel, excluding taxes;

—   electricity;

—   depreciation;

— reserve funds for maintenance;

— other expenditure for material consumption;

— sales costs related to material consumption (e.g. boxes, shelves); and

— The value of intermediate inputs provided by customers for processing in the enterprise.

The second approach is income-based; net industrial output is the sum of the income components generated within the production process:

— profit from sale of products;

— taxes related to sale revenue;

— wages and salaries;

— reserve funds for employees' benefits;

— interest; and

— other.

ii) The US census measures gross value added without deducting the cost of services purchased from outside the manufacturing sector. The production-based approach for China includes such services in net value added, because the "Production Cost Table" cited by SSB in its guidelines had an item called "other expenditure 1: for material consumption, 2: for non-material consumption," and the guidelines required inclusion of only the former in intermediate input. The income-based approach also includes these services in net value added because the same guidelines required inclusion of "other expenditure for non-material consumption" in net value added. Thus once Chinese value added has been put on a gross rather than a net basis, it becomes consistent with the US census concept of value added.

iii) Chinese enterprises provide a variety of welfare and other services to their employees. These include agricultural activities, construction, transportation operations, health services, child care, educational services, recreational services, meals and housing services. The guidelines, however, make it clear that gross value of output or net value added do not include these services. Those for the production-based method (SSB, 1987*a*) required exclusion of non-industrial productive activities (agriculture, construction, transportation, housing, public utilities and services) from gross value of output, and those governing the income-based procedure excluded wages and salaries of people engaged in non-industrial production (SSB, 1987*a*).

Not including the value of these services in the measurement of output understates gross output and gross value added for the specific industry or branch related to the employment registered in the census or other statistical sources, because this employment refers to total persons engaged in that industry or branch. Whether the value of these services has been reallocated to the service sector remains unknown, but the effect on an SNA basis of neglecting it in Chinese manufacturing statistics does not affect the real output comparison for the manufacturing sector itself.

iv) More serious problems arise in comparisons of labour productivity. Because Chinese census employment figures for manufacturing include employees who produce services or non-industrial output, while gross output and gross value added figures exclude the value of these services, the use of unadjusted employment figures gives a strong downward bias to Chinese labour productivity figures. The estimates have tried to adjust for this bias. Vol. 8 of the industrial census provides information on numbers of persons providing services within manufacturing. On average, service activities account for 9.8 per cent of total manufacturing employment. Table 3.A.20 contains calculations of employment excluding services, and adjusted labour input figures appear in all other relevant tables. Even after this adjustment, however, labour productivity figures may still have a downward bias. The 9.8 per cent estimate of service employment in manufacturing seems rather modest, and the ratio varies among industries. The adjustment may be insufficient for large and medium scale enterprises, although township and village enterprises probably would not have so many people engaged outside their main productive activities.

v) The gross value of output for commodities listed in the Chinese census includes indirect taxes (SSB, 1993a), while the gross value of output in the US census is at factor cost. The inclusion of indirect taxes in China biases unit value ratios and PPPs upwards. At sample industry level one can readjust PPPs, if one has information on indirect taxes. The Chinese census does not report indirect taxes as a proportion of gross value of output at market prices, but it supplies information on indirect taxes in a table on total sales revenues (Vol. 3). Application of the ratio between indirect taxes and sales revenues to gross value of output at market prices served to derive estimates of indirect taxes at sample industry and branch levels.

Subsidies are not included in the gross value of output. In Chinese statistical practice, they are reported as negative government income, but not regarded as positive income to enterprises. Therefore, there was no need to readjust PPPs for subsidies.

vi) At industry level, the US census employment figures exclude people in head offices and auxiliary establishments. The Chinese data, on an enterprise basis, include head office and auxiliary employment (SSB, 1993a). The US employment figures needed adjustment to include head office and auxiliary employment at branch level. The general summary volume of the census had such information for 1987, yielding the proportions used to adjust the employment figures for 1985.

vii) The Chinese census data are collected on an enterprise basis, rather than by establishments as in the United States. Nevertheless, China arranges the data on production quantities, gross value of output, value added and employment so that they seem to refer to the typical products produced by specific industries, notwithstanding that data collected from enterprises usually refer to a wide range of productive activities.

viii) The US census shows gross value of shipments — gross output plus inventories sold — other than the gross value of output. The Chinese data refer to gross output, sold and unsold. One might argue that centrally planned economies characteristically carry huge inventories, much of which will be junked rather than eventually sold. If true, this would create an upward bias in the measure of Chinese output. On the other hand, the difference between value of shipments and value of output consists of annual changes in inventories, irrespective of their overall level. Inventory changes constitute a very small proportion of gross output in the United States. Production of unsaleable items in China, leading to increases in inventories, might create some upward bias in the productivity comparisons for a given year. In the authors' judgement, however, this is not a major source of bias and they have not attempted to correct for it.

ix) The Chinese listing of products refers to 1985, the US listing to 1987. The procedure used to achieve comparability began with computation of the industry PPPs, using Chinese 1985 unit values and US 1987 unit values. Subsequently the PPPs were adjusted to a 1985 basis using US price deflators for each sample industry for the period 1985-87. The sample-industry price deflators were calculated as follows. The *US Industrial Outlook 1989* (US Dept. of Commerce, 1989 *b*) provides gross value of output by industry in constant 1982 dollars for both 1985 and 1987. The volume ratio of 1985 to 1987, applied to 1987 output in 1987 dollars from the *1987 Census of Manufacturing* (US Dept. of Commerce, 1990), resulted in 1985 output in 1987 dollars. Finally, dividing the figures for 1985 output in 1987 dollars by figures for 1985 output at 1985 current prices from the *Annual Survey of Manufactures* permitted derivation of an index for 1985-87 price changes (see Szirmai and Pilat, 1990, for a more detailed discussion of this procedure)

x) The extremely detailed Chinese product listings often are not mutually exclusive within industries, e.g. by quality of inputs, by size, by use etc. Items seldom add up to category totals and the product listings had to be screened very closely before they could be used.

xi) The Chinese census contains little detailed information on output values of specific products, which could be used to calculate unit values. Information on the gross value of industrial output, collected on an enterprise basis, refers to roughly defined categories of products. This study derived unit-value ratios by combining value added figures from volume three of the census, with quantity information from volume ten. Volume three provides some 600 output values for roughly defined categories of products. This scanty information limited the number of commodities or commodity groups for which unit values could be calculated. It was not always clear whether the categories having output values matched those with quantity information. As a result the unit values are extremely rough, making the findings tentative.

xii) In some industries such as dairy products, the value information on the Chinese side was so limited, that it permitted only a Paasche comparison, applying US prices to Chinese quantities. Proxy Laspeyres for these sample industries came from applying the average ratio of Laspeyres to Paasche PPPs .

xiii) The Chinese quantity information is far more detailed than the value information because value information is reported only for large product categories on an enterprise basis (see SSB, 1987a). On a quantity basis many more refined matches could have been made. Further research could explore two avenues. One could put the whole comparison on a Paasche basis, consistently applying US prices to Chinese quantities. The alternative would update or backdate to 1985 the long lists of administrative prices available for 1980 and 1990. (Updating the 1980 administrative prices could involve calculating implicit 1980-85 price indices from the census by comparing 1985 output in current prices with 1985 output at 1980 prices).

Reconciliation for Manufacturing between China's 1985 Census and the 1987 Input-Output Table

The comparison in the manufacturing sector uses the industrial censuses of the two countries, the most reliable data for labour productivity comparisons because both the labour input and the value added figures derive from single sources. One should, however, compare census data with other sources such as input-output tables and national accounts. Although this kind of reconciliation has been made at national level, one for the manufacturing sector between the 1985 census and the 1987 input-output table remains necessary. Table 3.A.22 presents a first step. It compares data for manufacturing from the 1985 census, the 1987 input-output table and the *Industrial Statistical Yearbook of China, 1993* (SSB, 1993a), re-arranged into 15 ICOP branches according to similar value added concepts. Adding depreciation adjusted the census data from net value added at market prices to gross value added at market prices. From the building blocks of the 1987 input-output table one can reconstruct both SNA and MPS concepts. Here we use the SNA concepts, with the 1987 data recategorised into 15 ICOP branches and subsequently backdated to 1985 using time series of current net value added per branch of manufacturing from the *Industrial Statistical Yearbook of China, 1993* (see Szirmai and Ren, 1995 for detail). The aggregates from the input-output table are very similar to the national accounts aggregates published in the *Statistical Yearbook of China*.

The main finding in this table is the relatively large discrepancy between manufacturing gross value added at market prices from the input-output table and that from the census, although the branch proportions of value added are rather similar. The difference arises because the input-output table covers more activities than the census, which is restricted to so-called "independent accounting units" and excludes the self-employed, other informal enterprises and, especially, township and village enterprises. The table finds almost no divergence between figures for net value added at market prices from the census and the industrial statistics yearbook — which

Table 3.A.22. **Reconciliation of Chinese Census, Input-Output and *Industrial Statistical Yearbook* Data for Manufacturing, 1985**
(Values in million yuan)

	Census					Input-Output Table		Yearbook	
	Gross value added at factor cost	Gross value added at market prices		Net value added at market prices		Gross value added at market prices		Net value added at market prices	
	Value	Value	% of total	Value	% of total	Value	% of total	Value	% of total
Food manufacturing	8 545	10 850	4.4	9 868	4.3	13 272	4.3	9 868	4.3
Beverages	3 217	5 352	2.2	4 999	2.2	7 708	2.5	4 990	2.2
Tobacco products	489	11 760	4.8	11 676	5.1	13 270	4.3	11 676	5.1
Textile mill products	18 738	26 849	10.8	25 050	11.0	33 152	10.8	25 050	11.0
Wearing apparel	4 342	5 139	2.1	4 900	2.2	7 293	2.4	4 900	2.2
Leather products and footwear	1 931	2 357	1.0	2 209	1.0	3 110	1.0	2 209	1.0
Wood products, furniture, fixtures	2 908	3 398	1.4	3 131	1.4	5 310	1.7	3 131	1.4
Paper products, printing, publishing	6 250	7 948	3.2	7 259	3.2	10 630	3.5	7 259	3.2
Chemical products (incl. oil)	25 141	37 538	15.2	33 925	14.9	45 352	14.8	33 925	14.9
Rubber and plastic products	6 486	9 032	3.6	8 463	3.7	11 518	3.8	8 463	3.7
Non-metallic mineral products	15 149	18 111	7.3	16 242	7.2	25 016	8.2	16 242	7.2
Basic and fabricated metal products	24 095	32 288	13.0	28 814	12.7	37 688	12.3	28 814	12.7
Machinery and transport equipment	41 506	48 754	19.7	44 168	19.4	53 219	17.4	44 168	19.4
Electrical machinery and equipment	16 137	20 135	8.1	18 847	8.3	24 143	7.9	18 847	8.3
Other manufacturing	6 702	8 021	3.2	7 546	3.3	15 366	5.0	7 547	3.3
Total manufacturing (incl. oil)	**181 814**	**247 532**	**100.0**	**227 096**	**100.0**	**306 047**	**100.0**	**227 089**	**100.0**

Sources: PRC, *Industrial Census, 1985* (OLG, 1987-88); Net value added from Vol. 3, p. 90 ff.; Gross value added (GVA) at market prices equals net value added plus depreciation from Vol. 3, p. 564 ff.; GVA at factor cost is derived from GVA at market prices using proportions of indirect taxes to sales from Vol. 3, p. 596 ff. *Input-Output Table 1987* (SSB, 1991), backdated to 1985 using indices of production from *Industrial Statistics Yearbook of China* (SSB, 1993a), which is also the source for the last two columns.

confirms that the yearbook's data for 1980, 1984 and 1985 were from the census. Finally, there is a large gap between gross value added at factor cost and at market prices from the census. The factor cost series has been constructed by deducting indirect taxes; if the numbers are in fact too low, the productivity comparisons will be biased downward.

Results at Branch Level.

PPPs first were calculated for 23 sample industries, then aggregated into thirteen branch PPPs (Table 3.5 in the text) according to the procedure already outlined. The branch PPPs equalled the sample industry PPPs in eight of the thirteen as there was only one sample industry in the branch. The PPP for "other manufacturing" comes from the quantity-weighted average of all unit-value ratios from all sample industries. The PPP for total manufacturing is the weighted average of branch PPPs, with value added weights. The wearing apparel branch had no matches because of insufficient Chinese quantity information and its PPPs depend on the weighted average of those for textile mill products as well as leather products and footwear.

Electricity, Gas and Water Supply

This sector presented only rather simple measurement problems. The *Industrial Census of China, 1985* (OLG, 1987-88) provided the Chinese information. The figure for natural gas was excluded from the original data. Data for the United States came from Pilat's comparison between Japan and the United States in 1985 (Pilat, 1994). His original data source was various issues of the *Statistical Abstract of the United States.* The value of water supply output for the United States was based on input-output table information (Pilat, 1994). (Table 3.A.23.)

Construction

Given the heterogeneous nature of construction output, Pilat considered unfeasible a direct industry-of-origin comparison (Pilat, 1994). Following his approach, this ICOP comparison used the PPP derived from the expenditure-based (ICP) study, after reweighting and aggregating, to convert real output into the currency of the other country. The construction sector offers the only exception where the expenditure-comparison PPPs could be used in the production-based study without ambiguity because:

— the expenditure-based PPPs relate to specified buildings and are therefore more comparable between the two countries;

— expenditure on construction and output of the construction sector do not differ very much;

— no trade and transport margins occur in construction;

— construction output is for final use and not an intermediate input; and

Table 3.A.23. Basic Data for Public Utilities, China and the United States, 1985

	Quantities produced		Quantity relative	Value of output		Unit value		PPPs	
	China	United States	China/ United States	China (million yuan)	United States ($ million)	China (yuan)	US ($)	At US quantity weights	At Chinese quantity weights
Electricity (million kwh) (a)	406 118.51	2 234 000	0.17	29 197.55	149 666	0.0719	0.0644	1.1164	1.1164
Gas (billion BTU)	1 141 921.7	12 616 000	0.09	426.02	63 293	0.0004	0.0050	0.0744	0.0744
Water (million m³) (b)	13 118.56	52 498	0.25	1 922.87	7 568	0.1466	0.1442	1.0168	1.0168
Total utilities				31 546.44	22 527			0.8139	0.9340
Geometric mean								0.8719	

Notes: a) The value of electricity for China includes 1 736.62 million yuan of electricity supply from sources other than power stations. (b) The figure for water refers to the production of water.

Sources: Data for the United States from Pilat (1994). Data for China from *Industrial Census of China, 1985*, (OLG, 1987-88), Vol. 3 (natural gas excluded) and Vol. 10.

— most construction activity is domestic and hence international trade is almost non-existent in this sector.

The expenditure-based PPP for 1986 had to be backdated to 1985, using as deflators the housing rent index in the urban residents' consumer price index for China and the housing price index in the consumer price index for the United States. (Table 3.A.24.)

Transport and Communications

The approach in this sector resembles that taken for public utilities. Quantity indicators exist for most components of output (Mulder, 1994*a*), such as passenger- and ton-kilometres for transport, numbers of access lines and telephone calls for telecommunications and pieces of mail delivered for postal services. For transport and communications, structural differences between the two countries — such as the difference between private and public transport, different means of transportation used, the quality of transport services and the importance of terminal services — need attention in the PPP estimates (Mulder, 1994*a*; Smith, Hitchens and Davies, 1982). In China, for example, railways predominate in both passenger and freight transport. Very different stages of development between China and the United States explain differences in their use of air transport. Generally, the country at the more advanced stage of economic development would show higher productivity in the transport sector. Developing countries would show higher productivity levels, especially in passenger transport, if productivity were measured only in terms of passenger-kilometres as output, because trains and buses are much more crowded than their counterparts in advanced countries.

Adjustments for factors influencing the quality of service can help to deal with this problem. Of the several aspects of quality involved in the international comparison for this sector, overcrowding is the most important. Others include speed of transport, delays, respect of announced schedules, numbers of accidents and frequency of service. Hampered by a lack of data, this study made adjustments in the passenger transport sector only for overcrowding, and these were tentative and arbitrary; it reduced the total passenger-kilometres carried by rail by 20 per cent and cut bus passenger carriage by 30 per cent. Lack of information prevented any adjustment for the quality of terminal services, which should have special consideration. Aside from the movement of persons and goods, loading and unloading services constitute an important part of the output of the transport industry.

Table 3.A.25 contains the basic data derived from the output matches for transport and tele-communications. Data for 1987 were from the *Input-Output Tables of China, 1987* (SSB, 1991); other data used to shift from 1987 to 1985 and to reallocate figures among the categories were from the *Statistical Yearbook of China, 1986, 1994* (SSB, 1986, 1994). Data for the United States in 1985 came from Pilat (1994), who had originally used various issues of the *National Transportational Statistics-Annual Report* (US Dept. of Transportation) and the *Statistical Abstract of the United States, 1990*

Table 3.A.24. Calculation of PPPs for Construction, 1985

	ICP code	ICP Proxy PPP China weights	US weights	Geometric Mean	Expenditure China (yuan per person)	United States ($ per person)	Price index China	United States
Residential construction	10.000	1.2445	1.2445	1.2445	12.68	1 080.49		
Non-residential construction	11.000	0.8260	0.8579	0.8418	201.65	547.67		
Other construction	12.000	0.7950	0.7950	0.7950	12.17	200.55		
Construction in 1986		0.8401	1.0794	0.9522			1.0210	
Construction in 1985		0.8472	1.0866	0.9604				1.0297

Notes: The expenditure-based PPPs refer to 1986; reweighted PPPs were backdated to 1985 by the relevant price indices. The US price index is the housing component in the Consumer Price Index. The Chinese index is the housing rent component of the Urban Residents' Consumer Price Index.

Sources: Ren and Chen (1994); *Statistical Abstract of the United States, 1992* (US Dept. of Commerce, 1992); *Statistical Yearbook of China, 1994* (SSB, 1994).

(US Dept. of Commerce); the 1987 US data, from Mulder (1994*a*), originated in the *Statistical Abstract of the United States, 1991* (US Dept. of Commerce) and *National Transportation Statistics, 1994* (US Dept. of Transportation).

Wholesale and Retail Trade

This sector cannot support a comparison based on direct product matches because it produces no quantifiable output, and no proxy PPPs can be derived directly from the expenditure-side study as wholesale and retail trading is an intermediate sector. Mulder and Maddison (1993) and Mulder (1994*a*, 1994*b*) applied a *single-deflation procedure* to arrive at value added in comparable "prices" in binary comparisons of Mexico, France and Brazil with the United States. This approach converts value added in a sub-sector with PPPs of the goods traded, taken from the relevant expenditure categories of expenditure side studies. These studies also tried the *double-deflation technique*, using first the PPPs from ICP studies to convert sales for both countries under comparison, and then PPPs from ICOP studies to convert purchases of goods destined for resale from other industries. Other inputs were converted by the relevant ICOP PPPs and deducted to reach gross value added in a comparative sense. Pilat (1994) used the *Smith and Hitchens approach* to derive PPPs by converting sales of different wholesale and retail categories with PPPs for the corresponding ICP expenditure categories. After summing the sales in matched categories at both national prices and those of the other country after conversion, he derived reweighted average PPPs for both segments of the wholesale and retail trade sector and used them to convert GDP. The treatment here settled on the single-deflation procedure, using data from the *Statistical Yearbook of China, 1986* (SSB, 1986) and the *Statistical Abstract of the United States, 1989,* (US Dept. of Commerce, 1989), with PPPs from the expenditure-based study of Ren and Chen (Ren and Chen, 1994, 1995). It applied the PPPs for specific commodity categories to calculate PPPs for groups of goods, weighted by ratios of expenditure in the detailed categories and then backdated from 1986 to 1985 by the two countries' price indices. Table 3.A.26 shows the results.

Finance, Insurance and Real Estate

Finance

The ICOP approach requires proper definition and measurement of both the gross value of output and the physical output of financial institutions. Operating revenues of financial institutions serve for the former, whereas several approaches have been used to estimate banking output (see Mulder, 1995*b* for a detailed discussion). These studies fall into two categories. Efforts in the first group measure economic activities in banking services by "output in value", but they take different approaches — the M2 to GDP ratio (Goldsmith, 1983 and Pilat, 1994), the asset approach (Berger and Humphrey in Griliches, ed., 1992; Penazola Webb, 1985; Welch, 1993), the liquidity

Table 3.A.25. Basic Data for Transport and Communications, China and the United States, 1985

Output item	Quantity		China/US quantity relative	Gross value output (million)		Unit values			Gross value added (million)	
	China	US		Yuan	$	Yuan	$	Ratio (yuan/$)	Yuan	$
Passenger transport	(million passenger-km.)									
Rail	193 291	18 237	10.599	4 836.81	1 292	0.0250	0.0708	0.3532	3 663.16	997.28
Bus	120 742	69 295	1.742	3 467.49	8 376	0.0287	0.1209	0.2376	1 732.24	6 723.89
Air (Domestic)	7 061	366 589	0.019	1 161.73	33 924	0.1645	0.0925	1.7779	675.93	19 277.85
Air (International)	4 611	117 838	0.039	642.2	7 180	0.1393	0.0609	2.2858	373.65	4 069.57
Freight transport	(million ton-km.)									
Rail	812 566	1 411 369	0.576	16.030	26.660	0.0197	0.0189	1.0444	11 918.22	20 578.48
Truck	190 320	981 700	0.194	20 131.77	87 840	0.1058	0.0895	1.1822	10 942.07	39 859.25
Air (Domestic)	164	271	0.606	270.76	2 514	1.6510	9.2849	0.1778	184.06	1 424.91
Air (International)	251	6 263	0.040	149.68	1 525	0.5963	0.2435	2.4491	101.75	864.36
Ship (Coastal)	240 030	374 506	0.641	1 044.30	2 451	0.0044	0.0065	0.6648	3 532.65	903.28
Ship (Ocean)	65.63	681	0.096	1 261	10 989	19.2184	16.1366	1.1910	839.44	4 049.82
Pipeline (million tons)	60 300	907 645	0.066	1 430	8 300	0.0237	0.0091	2.5933	881.42	89.38
Total transport									34 844.59	98 788.07
PPPs for transport:										
Chinese weights								0.7524		
US weights								1.2357		
Geometric mean								0.9643		
Communications	(million units)									
Mail handled	5 740.99	140 098	0.041	611.4	27 736	0.1065	0.1980	0.5380	462.39	26 799.00
Total telephone calls	97 975	115 556.25	0.016	4 113,7	106 599			2.4574	3 110.92	102 998.00
Long distance calls	382.54	461 772.00	.001							
Telephone subscriptions	3.12	151.00	0.021							
Total communications									3 573.31	129 797.00
PPPs for communications										
Chinese weights								1.6812		
US weights								2.0611		
Geometric mean								1.8615		

Notes and Sources: See paragraph concerning this table on page 61.

approach (Gorman in Fuchs, ed., 1969) and the user cost approach (Berger and Humphrey in Griliches, ed., 1992). Research in the second category measures economic activities in the banking sector by "output in numbers", relating output in banking to the volume of services performed by each function of banking (Dean and Kunze, 1991; Frischtak, 1992; Gorman in Fuchs, ed., 1969; Mark, 1982; Mckinsey, 1992 and 1994; Speagle and Kohn, 1958); but they differ in choosing either one indicator, such as the number of cheques cashed, or a variety of them, like transaction services, deposit and saving account services, and credit services. Mulder (1995*b*) proposed looking at the economic activity of banking services from both the asset and liability sides of a bank's balance sheet. His approach combined the first and second types of studies and used both "values" and "numbers" to measure of output in banking. His approach required quite strong statistical support which, unfortunately, China's data cannot sustain.

This study used the approach adopted in Goldsmith (1983) and Pilat (1994), with a slight modification based on the rationale that China and the United States are in different stages of financial intermediation, and US banks provide more types of instruments than do Chinese banks. The comparison chose the GDPs of both countries as proxies for wealth. For China, M2 — which includes currency in circulation, demand deposits of firms and institutions, and passbook savings and term deposits of households after deducting currency in circulation (see *Almanac of China's Finance and Banking, 1992*) — was used to calculate the indicator for the degree of financial intermediation. For the United States the same indicator was calculated from the sum of demand deposits, travellers cheques, other "checkable" deposits, savings deposits, money market deposit accounts, time deposits, money market mutual funds, overnight repurchase agreements and Eurodollars (see *Statistical Abstract of the United States, 1987,* US Dept. of Commerce, 1987).

The PPPs for China's GDP, from the expenditure-based study, were used to translate GDP in original currencies into the other currencies. The ratios of the degree of financial intermediation computed for both countries were used to derive the quantities of financial services. These quantities provided ratios in the sectors between the two countries. Finally, application of these ratios allowed derivation of China's financial sector GDP in dollar terms and that for the United States in China's currency. PPPs in Chinese weights, US weights and the Fisher base came from these sectoral GDP figures (Table 3.A.27).

Insurance

Pilat based his comparison on the number of life insurance policies, the largest part of the insurance industry. China has no such data. This study developed the comparison from total premiums — not really a quantity indicator but similar conceptually to the M2 used for the financial sector. Premium data for the United States came from the *Statistical Abstract of the United States, 1987, 1992* (US Dept. of Commerce, 1987, 1992) and data for China from the *Statistical Yearbook of China, 1994* (SSB, 1994). PPPs for GDP of the economy from the expenditure-based study were used to convert the valuation of premiums. PPPs were calculated from the sectoral GDPs in the insurance sector on the same value base between two countries (Table 3.A.7).

Real Estate

Pilat used data on the gross residential capital stock taken from a study by Maddison, which applied the perpetual inventory method to calculate gross capital stocks (Maddison, 1993). Pilat used a PPP for residential investment from ICP to estimate the relative real value of the residential stock between the two countries. Maddison's study provided the US data used here. For China an effort should be made to estimate the capital stock by the perpetual inventory method not only for this comparison but also for other economic analysis, such as explanation of the productivity differential and productivity trends. The poor availability of information in China, especially the unsatisfactory data for 1957-78, prevented such an estimate.

The careful comparison of gross rent in the expenditure study yielded PPPs that could have been used for this sector. An alternative is a rough estimate of the residential capital stock provided by Keidel in his World Bank study on China's national accounts (1992). Keidel based his estimate on the depreciation figures in the *Input-Output Tables of China, 1987* (SSB, 1991) and an assumed depreciation rate of 5 per cent. A recent study on sectoral productivity trends in China based on Jorgenson's approach (Li *et al.*, 1993, in Chinese), derived depreciation rates for each sector based on different assumptions for the lifetimes of structures and equipment. It found Keidel's assumed depreciation rate approximately correct. This estimate of residential capital stock, therefore, and the PPP from the expenditure-based study for residential investment, were used to calculate the real value of the residential stock in China versus that of the United States in 1985. The resulting quantity relationship was applied to GDP in the real estate sector to compute the PPPs (Table 3.A.27).

Services and Government

This rubric covers education, health services, other services and government. In each case, this study used the PPPs from the expenditure-side analysis to estimate GDP in the sector and make the productivity comparisons. The PPPs were backdated

Table 3.A.26. Comparisons of Sales and PPPs in Wholesale and Retail Trade, China and the United States, 1985

(Sales recorded in billion)

	Annual sales		ICP	ICP Proxy PPPs		Annual sales	
	China (yuan)	United States ($)	Code	US weights	Chinese weights	United States (yuan)	China ($)
WHOLESALE TRADE							
Food and beverages	273.83	256.40	01.100-01.300	1.5739	1.0574	403.55	258.97
Drugs and toiletries		25.10	05.100	0.8483	0.2032		
Furniture and household furnishings	20.67	24.20	04.100-04.200	0.9197	0.7713	22.26	26.80
Motor vehicles and equipment	4.11	132.40	06.100-14.000	1.8273	2.0958	241.94	1.96
General machinery and equipment	22.09	165.80	15.000	5.4347	1.3984	901.08	15.79
Electrical machinery and equipment	12.19	88.75	04.300-16.000	3.4340	3.0190	304.77	4.04
Total matched sales	332.88	692.65				1 873.59	307.55
PPPs (Total wholesale trade)							
US weights							2.7050
Chinese weights							1.0823
Geometric mean							1.7110
RETAIL TRADE							
Food (a)	180.61	284.00	01.100	1.5281	1.0122	433.98	178.44
Eating and drinking	19.69	133.50	01.100-01.300	1.5739	1.0574	210.21	18.62
Clothing and footwear	69.54	74.30	02	0.4366	0.3766	32.44	184.64
Furniture and household furnishings (b)	16.89	37.50	04.100-04.200	0.9197	0.7713	28.89	18.36
Household appliances (c)	60.35	27.40	04.300-04.500	1.4762	0.6719	30.22	205.41
Fuel (d)	3.08	101.30	03.200	1.5796	0.7085	161.84	4.35
Drugs	10.06	46.20	05.100	0.8483	0.2032	39.19	49.51
Total matched sales	360.23	704.20				936.78	659.33
PPPs (Total retail trade)							
US weights							1.3303
Chinese weights							0.5464
Geometric mean							0.8526

Notes: Data for Wholesale Trade were estimated by deducting retail trade from the total for wholesale and retail and allocating into product categories by the ratios of the categories to the total in retail trade. The following notes apply only to the figures for China in the first column: (a) Excludes liquor. (b) The sum of towels, bedsheets, woollen blankets and building materials. (c) The sum of goods used daily, television sets, recorders, radios and cameras. (d) Excludes kerosene and coal.

Sources: The PPPs for China in 1986 are from the ICP Study in this volume. Data for Chinese sales from *Statistical Yearbook of China, 1986, 1994* (SSB, 1986, 1994). Data for the United States from Pilat (1994), US Dept. of Commerce (1992) and *Survey of Current Business* (US Dept. of Commerce, May 1993).

Table 3.A.27. **Comparisons of GDP and PPPs in Finance, Insurance and Real Estate: China and the United States, 1985**

	China	United States	China/United States
FINANCE			
Gross Domestic Product (million)			
Yuan	896 440	6 094 802	0.15
$	1 520 679	4 038 700	0.38
Degree of financial itermediation			
(M2 - Cash) / GDP	0.44	0.91	0.48
Quantity of financial services (million)			
Yuan	394 434	5 546 270	0.07
$	669 099	3 675 217	0.18
GDP in Finance (million)			
Yuan	33 270	467 827	0.07
$	29 275	160 800	0.18
PPP for financial services			
At Chinese weights			1.1365
At US weights			2.9094
Geometric mean			1.8184
INSURANCE			
Total premiums (billion)			
Yuan	2.71	565.78	0.0048
$	4.67	510.45	0.0091
GDP in Insurance (million)			
Yuan	885.75	184 973.71	0.0048
$	560.47	61 300.00	0.0091
PPPs in Insurance			
At Chinese weights			1.5804
At US weights			3.0175
Geometric mean			2.1838
REAL ESTATE			
Residential capital stock (million)			
Yuan	247 306	6 763 213	0.0366
$	198 719	5 434 482	0.0366
GDP in Real Estate (million)			
Yuan	11 298.04	308 973.18	0.0366
$	16 809.58	459 700.00	0.0366
PPPs in Real Estate			
At Chinese weights			0.6721
At US weights			0.6721
Geometric mean			0.6721

Sources: FINANCE: For China, GDP from *Statistical Yearbook of China, 1994* (SSB, 1994), banking data from *Almanac of China's Finance and Banking*, Beijing, 1992, GDP in Finance from Table 3.2 in text, and expenditure-based PPPs from the ICP study in this volume. Figures for the United States from Pilat (1994). INSURANCE: Data for China from *Statistical Yearbook of China, 1994* (SSB, 1994); premiums include US dollar income from international business. For the United States, premiums (health, life, property and automobile insurance) from *Statistical Abstract of the United States, 1987 and 1992* (US Dept of Commerce, 1987, 1992), GDP from Pilat (1994) and *Survey of Current Business* (US Dept. of Commerce, May 1993). REAL ESTATE: Figures for China from Keidel (1992), p. 4.2, backdated from 1987 using an assumed growth rate of 5 per cent and the price index for construction in Shan Don province, p. 10. Data for the US from Maddison (1993).

from 1986 to 1985 with relevant price indices from the *Statistical Yearbook of China, 1994* (SSB, 1994) and the *Statistical Abstract of the United States, 1992* (US Dept. of Commerce, 1992). The reasons varied for making the estimates from the ICP PPPs. In education, an attempt to follow Pilat by basing the output measurement on numbers of students (but not adjusting, as Pilat was able to do, for relative achievement levels, because the meagre data available for China would not support such an adjustment) produced an unbelievably low and thus useless PPP. For health services, the ICP study already had derived PPPs based on input measures. Lack of data and notorious difficulties of measurement governed the approaches taken for both other services (business, personal, recreational, legal and social services) and government. In other services, the detailed expenditure category PPPs were reweighted by per capita expenditures in each of them. One source of error in the expenditure-side PPPs for government was their estimation under an assumption of no international labour productivity differential. The ICOP productivity comparisons suggested that productivity in China was roughly a quarter of that in the United States.

Notes and References

1. This source contains no definition of large and medium sized enterprises, although a definition inconsistent by industry — based sometimes on asset size and sometimes on production capacity — does appear in SSB (1993*b*), pp. 463-79. The US census uses a consistent definition in terms of employment. According to the source used here, large and medium sized enterprises accounted in 1985 for 1.79 per cent of the total number of enterprises in the industrial sector, 54 per cent of net value added at current prices and 33.4 per cent of average employment (PRC, 1987/88, PRC, 1988). Net value added per person employed was 64 per cent higher in medium and large sized enterprise than in total manufacturing (7 044 yuan per person employed against 4 307 yuan per person employed).

2. Since the Chinese Industrial Census does not use any classification code system, the number of industries in the Census varies depending on the classifying procedures adopted by researchers. McGuckin *et. al* (1992) distinguish 28 industries. This study obtained 56 manufacturing industries by matching the Chinese Industrial Census to the ISIC.

Chapter 4

Assessing China's Growth Rates

The foregoing chapters have established the foundation for an examination of reported industrial and economic growth rates in China, their comparison with alternative estimates and the presentation of new calculations. The measurement of Chinese growth remains under debate as both a policy issue and a statistical question. The rate of growth, of course, has a key influence on making and evaluating economic policy; policy makers regard it as a direct indicator of economic performance and, in the long term, improvements in living standards of any country depend upon it. Recent literature on Chinese growth performance has suggested that official statistics tend to overestimate it. The fairly recent adoption of the SNA guidelines in China merely ensures comparability of *current*-price data if adherence to the SNA is rigorous. *Constant*-price data, however, should measure price changes derived from deflators based on the conventions and experiences of each country. Assessment of growth rates from constant-price figures thus remains necessary even as the Chinese statistical system moves towards the SNA concept of national accounts.

Recent studies (Perkins, 1988; World Bank, 1992b; Keidel, 1992) suggest three main reasons for overestimation of China's growth rates:

— *The lack of production indices based on samples of products.* Chinese statisticians base their indices on total coverage of output, supposedly at constant or "comparable" administrative prices (SSB, 1987a). Estimates of Chinese growth rates at constant prices compare figures on gross product at constant prices, rather than on gross output at current prices deflated by a price index. In practice, there is often little difference between constant-price and current-price production indices because enterprises sometimes misuse current prices when they have no constant prices, especially for new products in township and village enterprises. China's price indices suffer major shortcomings from irregularities introduced by weights which overemphasize items covered by list prices and underemphasize prices in transactions using negotiated and periodic market prices.

— *The lack of independently constructed price deflators which adequately reflect price increases.* Price indices customarily underestimate inflation. Most are implicit deflators derived from comparing indices of production at constant administrative prices and current prices.

— *The practice of not writing off unsalable inventories.*

Alternative Estimates of Chinese Growth

Alternative estimates are scarce. Most of them are studies dealing with industrial growth, undertaken by staff in SSB and published in Chinese. Liu (1989) pointed out several weaknesses in present procedures for calculating industrial gross value of output growth in constant prices:

— Double counting, which he estimated accounts for 47 per cent of the gross value of output;

— Indicators do not show properly the relative standings of different regions and industries;

— Because enterprises are classified into industries based on their main product, the gross value of output in some industries can be underestimated as enterprises spread their products across several industries.

Liu and Nie (1993) compared the prevailing comparable-prices procedure for calculating growth rates of gross value of output with a proposed single-deflation approach to estimate growth of industrial value added and net industrial output based on data from 9 246 large and medium-sized enterprises. They found growth rates of both industrial value added and net industrial output lower than those derived by the current approach.

The Industry Division at the SSB of Hunan Province (1989) did a very interesting study on the reliability of the procedure in use to measure the growth of gross value of output. They estimated an industrial production index for Hunan province for 1983-87, using a weighted average of the growth rates for each commodity, with weights based on the share of each commodity in the gross value of industrial output. They employed a Paasche index which used 1985 data to calculate the weights because these figures were better than those for 1982. They also calculated a set of weights based on the 1985 net value of industrial output which can be used to derive the growth rate. Their sample selected 438 commodities, representing nearly 400 of the 500 classification categories. The results showed growth rates based on the production-index approach systematically lower than those yielded by the comparable-prices approach (Table 4.1). They had 36 summary categories; ten showed discrepancies between the two measures of more than 20 per cent, eight of 15 per cent to 20 per cent and seven of 5 per cent to 15 per cent; eleven categories had differences of less than 5 per cent.

Table 4.1. **A Comparison of Growth Rates Based on Comparable Prices and the Production Index for Hunan Province**
(preceeding year = 100)

	1983	1984	1985	1986	1987
Production-Index Method	104	109	111	109	113
Comparable-Prices Method	107.8	113.6	116.4	113	116.9

Fu and Lie (1989) proposed replacing the comparable-prices approach by adjustment of price changes for individual commodities. Based on their calculations from data covering 345 enterprises in Liaoning province, they concluded that the new approach could improve the quality of measurement of growth rates and correct flaws in the current procedure, but they did not include their empirical estimates in their paper. Other studies also confirm that present methods for calculating growth rates produce upwardly biased estimates for township and village industry.

Wu (1993) tried to fill the gap in the GDP time series before 1978, using his regression equation estimated from data after 1978. Since he had put the whole series on a 1980 basis, his time series at 1980 constant prices suggested a long-term growth rate. His methodology remains based on official GDP figures, however, and does not overcome the deficiencies of the constant-price series based on 1952, 1957 and 1970 prices because the constant-price series for real output still contain the original price weights, even though they have been linked. Table 4.2 summarises his results for various periods.

Table 4.2. **Chinese GDP at 1980 Prices, 1952-90**
(growth rates in per cent per year)

Period	Gross Domestic Product (a)	GDP in industry (b)
1952-90	6.0	10.5
1952-87	6.0	10.6
1952-57	7.1	19.4
1957-70	3.8	9.3
1970-78	5.3	8.2
1978-87	9.3	10.1
1980-87	10.3	10.6
1980-90	9.0	10.0

Notes: (a) SNA concept. (b) Includes mining and construction.

Source: Wu (1993), table 3, pp.72. Wu's estimates were calculated from *Statistical Yearbook of China, 1991*, p.31.

Maddison (1995) used Wu's data for agriculture and industry at 1980 prices. For the service sector, he assumed that half of services move parallel to the joint product of agriculture and industry and half move parallel to population. For aggregate GDP this results in lower growth rates than Wu's procedures (a 5.3 per cent compound growth rate from 1952 to 1990, against Wu's 6 per cent).

A Re-assessment of Growth in Industrial Production

Indices of industrial production tend to overestimate growth for the same kinds of reasons as indices of total GDP. In China's statistical practice indices based on "comparable prices" treat three categories of products: (a) the mainly industrial products which fall under ministerial departments; (b) products which fall under local government; and (c) products for which information is supplied by firms to higher government agents. During the 1980s, ex-factory prices have emanated from each of the entities thus involved — i.e. central government, local government and enterprises themselves — for the products within their jurisdictions.

Soviet statisticians used a similar method to construct the Soviet industrial output index in the 1930s (see Gerschenkron, 1962). Western literature has discussed this issue extensively since the 1950s. Jasny (1951*a,b* and 1952) tried to construct Soviet price indices by which he deflated computed values of industrial output at current prices. Hodgman (1954) produced an index of Soviet industrial output, weighted by payroll data in the individual branches and sub-branches of Soviet industry in 1934.

This study has taken the "deflator" approach. It deflated industrial output at current prices by price indices at the individual industry level. It derived new growth rates by deflating the gross value of output and net value added at current prices by the industrial producer price index, industry by industry. The results suggest lower growth rates than the official ones for industry (broadly defined to include mining, logging, utilities and manufacturing) and manufacturing proper from 1980 to 1992. This exercise has shown that simply a change of methodology can improve the reliability of growth estimates to some extent. Table 4.3 compares the growth rates from Wu's estimates, the official sources and the estimates of the current study.

The new estimates place the growth rate of gross value of output in total manufacturing from 1980 to 1992 at 9.6 per cent per annum and that for net value added at 7.6 per cent per annum. The growth rates for total industry (including mining, manufacturing, logging and utilities) were about the same as for manufacturing. The highest growth rates of net value added occurred in beverages (12.4 per cent), tobacco processing (11 per cent), wearing apparel (10.3 per cent) and electrical machinery and equipment (10.2 per cent). The lowest arose in basic and fabricated metals (5.5 per cent), textiles (4.2 per cent), oil refining (3 per cent) and wood products (1.6 per cent) (see Annex Table 4.A.3). With net value added consistently growing more slowly than gross value added in both manufacuring and industry as a whole, the share of net value added in the gross value of output declined sharply over these twelve years, from 34 to 27 per cent in industry and from 31 per cent to 25 per cent in manufacturing. Possible explanations for this trend include increasing specialisation and division of labour; increasing inefficiency in the use of intermediate inputs; and changes in pricing conventions and statistical concepts.

Table 4.3. **Compound Growth Rates in Industry and Manufacturing, 1952-92**

Period	Source and coverage	Per cent per annum	
1952-87	Official Source (gvo in industry)		11.0
	Wu (GDP in industry)	10.6	
1952-57	Official Source (gvo in industry)		18.0
	Wu (GDP in industry)	19.4	
1957-70	Official Source (gvo in industry)		10.0
	Wu (GDP in industry)	9.3	
1970-78	Official Source (gvo in industry)		9.3
	Wu (GDP in industry)	8.2	
1978-87	Official Source (gvo in industry)		10.4
	Wu (GDP in industry)	10.1	
1980-87	Official Source (gvo in industry)		11.0
	Wu (GDP in industry)	10.6	
	This Study (gvo in industry)		10.0
	(nva in industry)		8.5
	(gvo in manufacturing)		10.4
	(nva in manufacturing)		8.9
1980-90	Wu (GDP in industry)	10.0	
	This Study (gvo in industry)		8.5
	(nva in industry)		6.2
	(gvo in manufacturing)		8.5
	(nva in manaufacturing)		6.5
1980-92	This Study (gvo in industry)		9.5
	(nva in industry)		7.4
	(gvo in manufacturing)		9.6
	(nva in manufacturing)		7.6

Notes: Gvo = gross value of output; nva = net value added. The official figures exclude construction, which is included in Wu's estimates.

Sources: Official data from Annex Table 4.A.4. Wu's estimates from Table 4.2. Estimates of this study from Annex Table 4.A.3.

The official figures and Wu's estimates showed very high growth rates between 1952 and 1957, and Wu's figure was higher. Growth over the forty years covered by Table 4.3 was lowest between 1957 and 1978, picking up in the 1980s. Considering that Wu's estimates are based on official published data, it is not surprising that he found growth rates for all sub-periods very similar to the official figures, although they tended generally in the same direction as this study; for all sub-periods except 1952-57, his growth rates are somewhat lower.

This study has estimated a growth rate for gross value added in industry for the 1980-87 period a full percentage point lower than that from the official figures. For all sectors for which comparisons are possible (food, textiles, wearing apparel, leather, paper, petroleum, chemicals, building materials and machinery), the new growth rates are lower than those reported in the official figures, with the single exception of wearing apparel. In most sectors the growth rates of net value added fall well below those of gross output; net value added figures generally give a more modest picture of growth than gross output figures. In summary, both sources show rapid industrial growth in the 1980s, but the estimates of growth by this study tend to be substantially lower than those (including Wu's) calculated from older official sources. These rough comparisons offer support for the conclusion that independently calculated deflators lead to downward adjustments of growth rates for the important industrial sector of the economy.

A Re-assessment of China's Economic Growth

The focus now shifts from industry to an attempt at a new assessment of the growth of China's economy as a whole — GDP. The basic ideas and procedure, however, remain similar to those used for the industrial sector. Three deflators were chosen for the principal components of GDP — one each for the primary, secondary and tertiary sectors — to estimate time series for the components and GDP itself in constant prices. Table 4.4 presents the new series and compares the derived growth rates with the corresponding official figures.

Table 4.4. **GDP and its Components in 1985 Prices, 1985-94**

Year	Primary industry	Secondary industry	Tertiary industry	GDP	Growth rate based on this study	Official growth rate	Difference	Inflation
	(billion yuan)				(preceding year = 100)			
1985	254.16	386.66	255.62	896.44				
1986	259.77	432.82	276.32	968.91	108.1	108.8	0.7	106.0
1987	268.89	468.89	308.68	1 046.46	108.0	111.6	3.6	107.3
1988	261.36	511.43	341.67	1 114.46	106.5	111.3	4.8	118.5
1989	250.83	476.31	330.27	1 057.41	94.9	104.1	9.2	117.8
1990	305.38	485.37	293.04	1 083.99	102.5	103.8	1.3	102.1
1991	328.69	538.91	336.14	1 203.74	111.0	109.3	-1.7	102.9
1992	348.63	648.53	374.73	1 371.88	114.0	114.2	0.2	105.4
1993	364.79	734.40	359.35	1 458.54	106.3	113.5	7.2	113.2
1994	357.54	795.32	365.02	1 517.89	104.1	111.8	7.7	121.7
Compound Growth Rate, 1986-94					106.0	109.8		

Note: Index for Inflation is the overall consumer retail price index.

Sources: Annex Tables 4.A.5 and 4.A.6.

As was the case for the industrial sector, these figures also suggest that use of the deflator technique produces lower estimated growth rates for China than those obtained by current methods. The difference in the compound rate for the nine years of rapid growth covered by Table 4.4 amounts to almost four percentage points. Except for one year (1991), the estimated annual growth rates are lower than the official figures. The accompanying inflation figures suggest that the size of the difference between the estimates and the official data may be correlated with the rate of inflation.

Concluding Remarks

This chapter has tried to assess the degree of upward bias in estimates of growth for the industry sector and the economy as a whole. Caution is imperative, however, for anyone who wants to use the quantitative re-assessment presented here to discuss China's economic performance, for two reasons:

— the deflators themselves are subject to the published sources. Hence there is no assurance of consistency in the prices used to construct indices or those embedded in the gross value of output for individual industries or sectors;

— the GDP and its three components are valued on a "net" basis — with intermediate inputs excluded — while the price indices are constructed on a "gross" basis which includes these inputs. A better approach would be that associated with Geary (1944) and Fabricant (1940), namely deflated commodity outputs less deflated commodity inputs by industry. A lack of data prevented use of this method in the present study.

At the end of the day, resolution of the debate on Chinese growth rates will depend on the improvement of the procedures adopted by SSB and the data sources that it uses in its routine work to measure China's growth.

Methodological Discussion and Statistical Documentation

Re-assessment of Chinese Industrial Growth

The output data in current prices derive from the 1993 *Industrial Statistics Yearbook* (SSB, 1993) (see Table 4.A.1). Since 1987 Chinese national income statistics have been calculated on an SNA basis, which is reflected in the 1987 input-output table and assumed to hold as well for the data in the 1993 *Yearbook*. In any event, the differences between material product concepts and SNA are small for manufacturing, where most of the output is physical.

The 1994 *Statistical Yearbook of China* (SSB, 1994) presents producer price indices for fourteen industries (Table 4.A 2) in terms of changes relative to the previous year. The indices have been linked to derive price indices for the period 1980-92 in the second part of the table. The derived indices with 1980 as base year have been applied to the current-price gross output and net value added figures in Table 4.A.1 to calculate the constant-price figures in Table 4.A.3, recategorised into the 15 branches of manufacturing commonly distinguished in other ICOP studies.

Table 4.A.4 presents growth rates based on time series for gross value of output (material-product concept, prior to introduction of the SNA concept) at constant prices for 15 branches of industry from 1952 to 1987, taken from the *Industrial Statistical Yearbook of China, 1988* (SSB, 1988a). The original time series were valued at different constant prices (1952, 1957, 1970 and 1980) and have all been converted to the 1980 base. "Industry" here is a wider concept than manufacturing; it includes mining, utilities and logging. In fact, mining activities appear variously in the metallurgical industry, the coal industry and the petroleum industry, and logging is classified within forestry.

Table 4.A.1. Gross Value of Output (GVO) and Net Value Added (NVA) by Industry in China, 1980, 1984-92

(hundreds of millions of yuan, in current prices)

Category of industry and data series		1980	1984	1985	1986	1987	1988	1989	1990	1991	1992
Total	GVO	4 702.54	6 818.36	8 434.72	9 436.34	11 318.56	14 586.45	17 473.89	18 689.22	22 088.68	27 724.21
	NVA	1 598.26	2 235.13	2 736.63	2 978.70	3 487.71	4 301.41	4 903.41	5 093.25	5 915.10	7 446.95
A1 State-owned enterprises	GVO	3 798.88	5 183.86	6 167.09	6 754.12	7 996.76	9 946.70	11 872.96	12 570.45	14 371.73	17 091.10
	NVA	1 302.63	1 728.85	2 039.02	2 178.13	2 530.03	3 062.98	3 460.23	3 568.70	4 019.13	4 843.98
A2 Collective enterprises	GVO	870.59	1 559.19	2 149.24	2 536.45	3 143.50	4 219.58	4 945.33	5 246.50	6 177.89	8 106.42
	NVA	285.18	485.43	666.19	762.87	893.97	1 135.17	1 288.10	1 323.38	1 551.21	2 009.74
A3 Other ownership	GVO	33.07	75.31	118.39	140.77	241.30	420.17	655.60	872.28	1 539.06	2 526.69
	NVA	10.45	20.08	31.42	37.70	63.71	103.28	155.08	201.17	344.76	593.23
B1 Light industry	GVO	2 153.09	3 097.83	3 814.87	5 316.86	5 246.91	6 881.92	8 149.31	8 776.76	10 229.85	12 217.69
	NVA	642.13	861.40	1 060.02	1 208.82	1 424.40	1 822.67	2 068.09	2 212.50	2 555.52	3 086.06
B1.1 Using agricultural inputs	GVO	1 625.38	2 249.59	2 701.95	2 990.81	3 647.90	4 717.01	5 626.37	6 119.47	7 000.07	8 278.98
	NVA	441.42	575.45	703.52	793.90	954.66	1 227.02	1 412.08	1 515.47	1 703.16	2 031.32
B1.2 Using non-agricultural inputs	GVO	527.71	848.25	1 112.92	1 326.04	1 599.01	2 164.91	2 522.94	2 657.28	3 229.78	3 938.71
	NVA	200.41	285.95	356.51	414.91	469.74	595.66	656.01	697.03	852.36	1 036.74
B2 Heavy industry	GVO	2 549.45	3 720.72	4 619.86	5 119.48	6 134.65	7 704.53	9 324.58	9 912.47	11 858.83	15 506.52
	NVA	956.13	1 373.72	1 676.61	1 769.88	2 063.31	2 478.76	2 835.32	2 880.75	3 359.57	4 378.89
B2.1 Mining	GVO	346.58	486.20	580.76	634.38	757.33	873.94	1 073.63	1 200.29	1 386.98	1 628.04
	NVA	175.81	251.61	289.53	304.88	376.40	404.83	446.80	495.51	555.79	661.82
B2.2 Materials	GVO	1 049.00	1 445.49	1 741.63	2 023.75	2 401.24	2 972.08	3 724.01	4 122.15	4 947.54	6 364.93
	NVA	390.28	528.02	619.00	683.87	784.15	937.92	1 083.43	1 099.48	1 288.82	1 651.84
B2.3 Processing	GVO	1 153.87	1 788.83	2 297.49	2 460.90	2 976.07	3 858.51	4 526.94	4 590.03	5 524.32	7 513.55
	NVA	390.05	594.09	768.08	781.13	902.15	1 136.01	1 305.09	1 285.57	1 514.97	2 065.24
C1 Large enterprises	GVO	1 604.14	2 166.62	2 545.61	2 868.41	3 528.05	4 484.65	5 769.30	4 509.21	7 959.64	10 081.40
	NVA	649.88	846.37	993.19	1 047.60	1 283.99	1 543.08	1 832.08	1 999.98	2 364.40	3 335.85
C2 Medium enterprises	GVO	1 022.67	1 350.53	1 637.07	1 831.37	2 222.89	2 872.71	3 454.29	3 693.93	4 409.49	5 836.14
	NVA	341.48	425.64	516.29	571.81	657.16	826.88	930.31	926.38	1 125.47	1 503.03
C3 Small enterprises	GVO	2 075.73	3 301.21	4 252.04	4 736.56	5 630.61	7 229.09	8 250.31	8 486.08	9 722.56	11 806.67
	NVA	606.90	945.12	1 227.15	1 359.28	1 546.56	1 931.47	2 141.03	2 130.88	2 452.23	2 826.60

Table 4.A.1. (continued)

Category of industry and data series		1980	1984	1985	1986	1987	1988	1989	1990	1991	1992
Mining (author's total)	GVO	326.52									
Coal mining	GVO	135.42	183.70	222.75	235.55	253.33	309.48	408.09	457.53	518.86	612.34
	NVA	62.50	81.54	91.52	97.53	101.79	129.12	160.24	158.09	177.42	286.00
Petroleum and gas	GVO	123.19	178.73	215.13	231.78	292.17	302.31	362.37	427.20	514.95	611.22
	NVA	69.14	108.15	125.58	127.35	174.28	151.92	148.82	203.53	230.37	360.81
Black metal mining	GVO	8.99	13.11	17.36	19.40	22.36	26.15	30.40	36.99	47.76	59.37
	NVA	3.87	6.17	7.70	8.43	8.93	10.09	11.15	12.70	16.25	23.65
Coloured metal mining	GVO	21.45	28.84	37.03	44.15	56.03	70.90	93.78	103.11	113.45	125.63
	NVA	8.94	11.41	15.51	17.95	22.20	26.68	35.00	37.36	40.18	50.02
Building materials and other non-metal mining	GVO	19.58	29.62	33.35	41.18	47.66	63.02	79.82	89.88	99.43	125.26
	NVA	10.59	15.60	17.22	18.50	20.10	25.82	31.21	33.12	39.96	48.07
Salt mining	GVO	17.87	18.85	18.54	23.04	23.65	31.30	42.12	38.73	42.68	50.96
	NVA	14.26	14.27	13.48	16.89	15.90	20.17	25.87	21.32	24.98	31.89
Other mining	GVO	0.02	0.03	0.04	0.14	0.07	0.08	0.10	0.16	0.20	0.47
	NVA	0.01	0.02	0.02	0.08	0.03	0.04	0.04	0.07	0.07	0.11
Logging: timber and bamboo	GVO	38.62	53.29	56.53	64.81	87.30	104.85	104.12	92.07	100.92	105.50
	NVA	20.89	29.07	32.41	35.65	49.63	62.16	61.99	52.92	57.57	62.10
Total utilities	GVO	203.44									
Producing and supplying water	VPB	10.73	16.54	19.23	22.08	25.85	31.76	37.03	45.32	64.98	80.77
	NVA	5.25	7.57	8.42	9.42	10.14	11.99	12.28	14.19	25.14	40.03
Electricity, steam and hot water	GVO	192.71	256.66	293.21	309.87	362.27	431.19	557.18	676.63	828.37	1 021.30
Production and supply	NVA	111.61	137.13	153.79	142.89	157.02	173.65	199.51	242.83	284.12	481.46

113

Table 4.A.1. (continued)

Category of industry and data series		1980	1984	1985	1986	1987	1988	1989	1990	1991	1992
Manufacturing (author's total)	GVO	4 133.96									
ICOP Branches of manufacturing											
1/2 Food and beverages	NVA	80.07	121.44	145.30	165.20	200.11	265.89	295.11	316.11	401.05	445.50
1 Food	GVO	393.63	553.15	632.91	704.36	806.36	1 038.50	1 203.02	1 265.84	1 473.35	1 671.91
	NVA	55.90	80.44	95.40	112.21	131.33	168.98	191.07	200.63	248.65	260.9
2 Beverages	GVO	67.27	120.53	149.91	167.92	228.60	306.60	348.60	384.97	462.45	568.40
	NVA	24.17	41.00	49.90	52.99	68.78	98.91	104.04	115.48	152.40	184.60
3 Tobacco processing	GVO	86.03	164.91	202.26	224.53	277.12	367.98	450.89	511.99	547.45	646.52
	NVA	53.31	103.04	116.76	140.14	170.74	222.24	260.79	297.50	316.27	351.96
Forage [included in (1)]	GVO	2.14	13.27	24.87	36.83	51.09	88.59	114.73	123.52	153.37	199.65
	NVA	0.28	1.76	3.28	4.90	6.59	10.98	12.94	14.08	19.48	21.62
4 Textiles	GVO	699.11	888.24	1 056.44	1 163.30	1 373.49	1 728.16	2 109.57	2 291.08	2 533.27	2 899.16
	NVA	199.77	202.42	250.50	284.09	321.83	407.33	477.59	492.61	502.78	548.03
5 Clothing	GVO	107.05	141.71	171.78	186.88	227.51	285.98	352.68	414.64	522.95	681.58
	NVA	25.77	37.83	49.00	52.74	61.30	73.61	90.67	100.86	122.43	147.16
6 Leather, fur and their manufactures	GVO	50.10	61.28	84.09	100.14	119.84	150.20	175.32	199.11	253.35	325.10
	NVA	13.38	15.91	22.09	26.04	30.21	34.07	38.59	45.16	55.55	62.64
7 Timber processing and bamboo, cane and straw manufactures	GVO	30.60	49.28	56.74	64.06	80.22	100.19	106.78	103.23	122.27	157.26
	NVA	9.52	14.58	16.27	18.28	22.21	26.37	27.67	24.03	28.11	36.19
8 Paper and paper products	GVO	87.92	122.77	153.86	177.19	228.89	309.91	372.12	388.71	423.44	492.94
	NVA	27.54	35.01	45.09	50.66	62.77	83.82	92.22	93.24	98.71	113.74
8 Printing	GVO	47.15	66.74	84.04	93.47	111.93	138.56	158.23	173.39	216.41	262.36
	NVA	14.68	21.89	27.50	30.34	34.68	40.69	46.45	49.57	59.30	73.19
15 Culture; education and sports products	GVO	21.82	30.14	37.65	43.79	58.49	66.87	76.08	90.11	117.12	147.62
	NVA	8.57	11.18	13.64	15.51	19.47	21.08	22.92	25.62	33.14	37.73
15 Arts and crafts products	GVO	36.15	43.56	79.54	80.44	103.79	138.32	170.51	190.93	219.39	283.44
	NVA	14.25	16.19	23.01	27.98	35.44	44.06	53.52	57.35	65.53	74.29

Table 4.A.1. (concluded)

Category of industry and data series		1980	1984	1985	1986	1987	1988	1989	1990	1991	1992
9 Petroleum processing	GVO	169.24	229.78	255.98	297.87	338.71	392.33	457.33	501.87	714.85	900.25
	NVA	68.41	95.24	105.47	121.25	129.94	140.47	133.36	129.81	168.76	224.66
9 Coke, coals gas and coal products	GVO	14.86	19.98	25.44	27.53	32.89	42.00	56.45	71.35	84.37	92.91
charbon	NVA	2.57	3.51	4.91	5.60	6.09	6.58	7.66	9.96	12.21	14.46
9 chemicals	GVO	355.01	526.08	564.85	638.89	819.28	1 091.91	1 375.30	1 492.01	1 625.07	1 911.16
	NVA	108.28	159.80	165.40	179.95	231.59	312.01	369.66	395.35	418.27	514.85
9 Medical products	GVO	69.78	113.73	127.28	154.39	207.63	289.11	323.09	356.14	435.55	569.03
	NVA	22.18	33.47	36.52	52.53	57.88	80.17	83.10	93.80	131.26	160.26
9 Chemical fibres	GVO	33.75	60.11	79.30	99.28	129.01	172.06	233.82	272.42	325.39	371.45
	NVA	12.4	19.11	26.95	32.46	40.11	51.19	60.96	76.71	94.59	116.69
10 Rubber products	GVO	88.21	117.14	138.13	148.28	166.05	207.15	264.33	284.90	317.28	381.28
	NVA	32.52	40.30	46.56	47.52	49.21	56.07	70.36	76.68	87.85	106.33
10 Plastic products	GVO	66.34	113.60	141.19	161.95	207.90	324.49	347.42	349.82	439.23	566.00
	NVA	18.95	30.53	38.07	41.46	51.71	73.36	80.10	83.03	98.20	123.84
11 Building materials and other non-metallic mineral products	GVO	201.02	325.42	422.70	516.89	593.22	752.91	891.89	890.57	1 055.40	1 422.40
	NVA	80.54	124.89	162.42	197.27	212.93	260.10	284.18	274.27	338.93	491.48
12 Ferrous metal smelting and pressing	GVO	315.31	419.75	542.56	660.53	766.15	931.06	1 140.02	1 298.78	1 538.50	2 080.78
	NVA	96.59	137.51	167.78	193.30	227.05	273.50	325.37	314.31	374.65	583.91
12 Non-ferrous metal smelting and pressing	GVO	124.09	160.84	196.63	232.74	276.00	352.40	471.53	509.46	573.55	709.11
	NVA	29.27	35.19	44.81	51.53	61.38	80.24	103.54	98.07	107.29	142.45
12 Metal products	GVO	124.77	177.30	233.63	274.08	338.03	411.54	494.23	522.57	615.23	800.43
	NVA	43.03	58.27	75.55	86.42	100.15	117.99	136.50	140.90	159.34	187.51
13 Machinery	GVO	467.35	709.38	935.27	1 015.97	1 233.03	1 554.31	1 726.63	1 674.05	1 995.40	2 671.52
	NVA	169.44	241.77	320.23	339.03	388.72	472.79	519.79	483.85	565.00	741.42
13 Transportation equipment	GVO	52.82	274.87	380.11	346.73	425.96	574.45	670.09	713.87	975.75	1 544.01
	NVA	172.31	83.71	121.45	100.88	119.06	156.84	174.15	187.39	244.92	381.67
14 Electrical machinery and equipment	GVO	152.32	250.87	355.28	406.78	480.90	665.76	849.76	797.09	917.12	1 236.17
	NVA	51.35	79.93	112.53	120.65	134.20	176.28	223.07	209.90	238.36	287.96
14 Electronic and communication equipment	GVO	76.05	169.42	243.91	241.58	339.01	497.45	551.24	584.19	764.69	928.39
	NVA	26.27	56.62	75.94	67.65	88.96	126.66	142.49	146.21	184.20	205.62
15 Instruments	GVO	40.00	58.54	69.56	71.05	81.53	101.05	113.13	110.12	136.71	182.61
	NVA	17.59	24.69	29.50	29.06	31.72	38.17	43.07	40.33	49.51	58.85
15 Other industry	GVO	11.7	19.41	28.29	55.88	45.46	58.60	72.43	73.48	89.30	112.81
	NVA	4.03	6.47	9.32	15.78	12.74	15.67	18.83	18.69	22.27	26.08

Source: SSB, *Industry Statistical Yearbook of China, 1993* (SSB, 1993), pp. 142-154.

115

Table 4.A.2. Producer Price Index for Industrial Products, by Sector, 1979-92

	1979	1980	1981	1982	1983	1984	1985	1986	1987	1988	1989	1990	1991	1992
					(preceding year = 100)									
Overall index	101.5	100.5	100.2	99.8	99.9	101.4	108.7	103.8	107.9	115.0	118.6	104.1	106.2	106.8
Metallurgical products (a)	101.6	106.2	101.8	101.0	101.3	103.8	114.3	107.4	107.0	115.4	121.0	110.3	114.2	114.2
Power industry	101.7	98.4	101.6	98.9	105.6	102.1	103.4	102.4	103.1	101.7	105.9	107.4	116.9	108.8
Coal industry	113.4	106.4	102.6	101.9	101.5	102.6	117.6	96.8	102.8	110.6	112.2	106.2	113.1	116.1
Petroleum products (b)	100.6	102.1	99.3	100.5	106.3	112.0	107.2	104.6	104.0	106.8	108.4	107.1	118.8	115.3
Chemicals	99.6	98.2	97.2	99.6	101.0	102.4	102.9	102.9	112.2	120.4	119.4	101.6	102.4	102.7
Machine building	99.9	97.5	98.6	99.3	99.3	101.1	111.8	102.8	104.9	111.8	121.2	102.8	102.8	106.6
Building materials	103.5	102.5	101.6	102.2	102.7	102.0	115.4	113.7	105.6	113.4	123.6	99.6	106.1	111.1
Wood products (c)	102.5	104.5	111.3	105.8	100.3	103.2	114.9	107.1	144.9	119.6	115.7	94.6	100.4	105.9
Food products	103.6	101.2	102.3	103.1	100.8	101.7	105.5	102.5	109.4	116.3	114.3	101.0	103.3	106.2
Textiles	97.9	101.6	99.1	96.5	94.8	96.6	104.3	102.6	108.3	122.3	122.4	107.2	104.1	99.3
Clothing (sewing industry)	101.1	100.8	99.9	96.1	95.7	100.4	105.1	100.0	109.6	116.2	118.9	109.1	109.0	100.8
Leather products		102.4	101.7	99.5	1'00.9	100.6	112.1	101.7	102.9	114.4	118.3	106.3	109.0	112.8
Paper products	108.3	100.5	100.6	100.3	101.1	99.7	113.7	105.7	112.1	120.7	123.0	102.3	102.9	102.7
Cultural products, etc.		101.6	99.0	100.0	99.9	100.4	103.2	99.6	120.0	112.1	111.0	107.3	105.8	102.3
					(1980 = 100)									
Overall index	99.5	100.0	100.2	100.0	99.9	101.3	110.1	114.3	123.3	141.8	168.2	175.1	186.0	198.6
Metallurgical products (a)	94.2	100.0	101.8	102.8	104.2	108.1	123.6	132.7	142.0	163.9	198.3	218.7	249.8	285.2
Power industry	101.6	100.0	101.6	100.5	106.1	108.3	112.0	114.7	118.3	120.3	127.4	136.8	159.9	174.0
Coal industry	94.0	100.0	102.6	104.5	106.1	108.9	128.0	123.9	127.4	140.9	158.1	167.9	189.9	220.5
Petroleum products (b)	97.9	100.0	99.3	99.8	106.1	118.8	127.4	133.2	138.6	148.0	160.4	171.8	204.1	235.3
Chemicals	101.8	100.0	97.2	96.8	97.8	100.1	103.0	106.0	229.0	143.2	171.0	173.7	177.9	182.7
Machine building	102.6	100.0	98.6	97.9	97.2	98.3	109.9	113.0	228.52	132.5	160.6	165.1	169.7	180.9
Building materials	97.6	100.0	101.6	103.8	106.6	108.8	125.5	142.7	250.7	170.9	211.2	210.4	223.2	248.0
Wood products (c)	95.7	100.0	111.3	117.8	118.1	121.9	140.0	150.0	217.3	259.9	300.7	284.5	285.6	302.5
Food products	98.8	100.0	102.3	105.5	106.3	108.1	114.1	116.9	127.9	148.8	170.0	171.7	177.4	188.4
Textiles	98.4	100.0	99.1	95.6	90.7	87.6	91.3	93.7	101.5	124.1	151.9	162.9	169.6	`168.4
Clothing (sewing industry)	99.2	100.0	99.9	96.0	91.9	92.2	96.9	96.9	106.3	123.5	146.8	160.2	174.6	176.0
Leather products	97.7	100.0	101.7	101.2	102.1	102.7	115.1	117.1	120.5	137.8	163.1	173.3	188.9	213.1
Paper products	99.5	100.0	100.6	100.9	102.0	101.7	115.6	122.2	137.0	165.4	203.4	208.1	214.1	219.9
Cultural products, etc.	98.4	100.0	99.0	99.0	98.9	99.3	102.5	102.1	122.5	137.3	152.4	163.5	173.0	177.0

Notes: (a) Includes metal mining. (b) Includes petroleum refining. (c) Includes logging.

Source: *Statistical Yearbook of China, 1994* (SSB, 1994), p. 246. Figures in bottom half of table are calculated from those in top half.

Table 4.A.3. **Gross Value of Output and Net Value Added at 1980 Prices by Branch of Manufacturing, China, 1980-92**
(hundreds of millions of 1980 yuan; compound growth in per cent per year)

Industry branch and data series		1980	1984	1985	1986	1987	1988	1989	1990	1991	1992	Compound growth
Total	GVO	4 702.5	6 731.0	7 660.2	8 256.1	9 177.9	10 284.9	10 388.6	10 673.5	11 878.5	13 959.8	9.5
	NVA	1 598.3	2 208.5	2 485.3	2 606.1	2 828.1	3 032.9	2 915.2	2 980.5	3 180.9	3 749.7	7.4
	Ratio	0.34	0.33	0.32	0.32	0.31	0.29	0.28	0.27	0.27	0.27	
1-2 Food and beverages	GVO	463.04	635.34	708.07	777.54	849.06	963.75	980.01	1 033.18	1 177.65	1 295.09	8.9
	NVA	80.35	113.94	130.25	145.48	161.60	186.12	181.17	192.27	237.05	247.94	9.8
	Ratio	0.17	0.18	0.18	0.19	0.19	0.19	0.18	0.19	0.20	0.19	
1 Food products	GVO	395.77	523.9	576.7	633.9	670.3	757.7	775.0	809.0	917.0	993.4	8.0
	NVA	56.18	78.0	86.5	100.2	107.8	119.6	120.0	125.0	151.1	150.0	8.5
	Ratio	0.14	0.15	0.15	0.16	0.16	0.16	0.15	0.15	0.16	0.15	
2 Beverages (a)	GVO	67.27	111.5	131.4	143.6	178.7	206.1	205.0	224.2	260.7	301.7	13.3
	NVA	24.17	37.9	43.7	45.3	53.8	66.5	61.2	67.2	85.9	98.0	12.4
	Ratio	0.36	0.34	0.33	0.32	0.30	0.32	0.30	0.30	0.33	0.32	
3 Tobacco products(a)	GVO	86.03	152.5	177.3	192.0	216.6	247.4	265.2	298.1	308.6	343.2	12.2
	NVA	53.31	95.3	102.4	119.9	133.5	149.4	153.4	173.2	178.3	186.8	11.0
	Ratio	0.62	0.62	0.58	0.62	0.62	0.60	0.58	0.58	0.58	0.54	
4 Textiles	GVO	699.1	1 014.2	1 156.6	1 241.3	1 353.3	1 392.2	1 388.5	1 406.7	1 494.1	1 722.0	7.8
	NVA	199.8	231.1	274.2	303.1	317.1	328.2	314.3	302.5	296.5	325.5	4.2
	Ratio	0.29	0.23	0.24	0.24	0.23	0.24	0.23	0.22	0.20	0.19	
5 Clothing	GVO	107.1	153.6	172.2	192.8	214.1	231.6	240.2	258.9	299.5	387.3	11.3
	NVA	25.8	41.0	50.5	54.4	57.7	59.6	61.8	63.0	70.1	83.6	10.3
	Ratio	0.24	0.27	0.29	0.28	0.27	0.26	0.26	0.24	0.23	0.22	
6 Leather and fur products	GVO	50.1	59.7	73.0	85.5	99.5	109.0	107.5	114.9	134.1	152.5	9.7
	NVA	13.4	15.5	19.2	22.2	25.1	24.7	23.7	26.1	29.4	29.4	6.8
	Ratio	0.27	0.26	0.26	0.26	0.25	0.23	0.22	0.23	0.22	0.19	

117

Table 4.A.3. (continued)

Industry branch and data series		1980	1984	1985	1986	1987	1988	1989	1990	1991	1992	Compound growth
7 Wood products and furniture(b)	GVO	53.5	70.5	74.3	76.7	65.6	66.2	62.8	64.9	74.4	89.7	4.4
	NVA	17.3	21.7	22.4	22.7	18.6	18.4	16.7	16.1	18.3	21.1	1.6
	Ratio	0.32	0.31	0.30	0.30	0.28	0.27	0.27	0.25	0.25	0.23	
8 Paper, paper products and printing(c)	GVO	135.1	186.3	205.7	221.4	248.7	271.2	260.7	270.1	298.8	343.4	8.1
	NVA	42.2	55.9	62.8	66.3	71.1	75.3	68.2	68.6	73.8	85.0	6.0
	Ratio	0.31	0.30	0.31	0.30	0.29	0.28	0.26	0.25	0.25	0.25	
9 Chemical products: Total	GVO	642.64	909.25	969.70	1 086.14	1 239.95	1 377.93	1 450.23	1 554.22	1 742.86	1 982.78	9.8
	NVA	213.84	295.23	308.80	345.12	375.25	408.95	388.33	407.05	450.72	534.98	7.9
	Ratio	0.33	0.32	0.32	0.32	0.30	0.30	0.27	0.26	0.26	0.27	
9 Oil refining and coal and coke products(d)	GVO	184.1	210.2	220.9	244.2	268.2	293.5	320.3	333.7	391.6	422.0	7.2
	NVA	70.98	83.1	86.7	95.2	98.2	99.4	87.9	81.4	88.7	101.6	3.0
	Ratio	0.39	0.40	0.39	0.39	0.37	0.34	0.27	0.24	0.23	0.24	
9 Chemicals(e)	GVO	458.5	699.0	748.4	841.9	971.8	1 084.4	1 129.9	1 220.6	1 351.3	1 580.7	10.7
	NVA	142.9	212.1	222.1	249.9	277.1	309.6	300.4	325.7	362.1	433.3	9.7
	Ratio	0.31	0.30	0.30	0.30	0.29	0.29	0.27	0.27	0.27	0.28	
10 Rubber and plastic products(f)	GVO	154.6	227.8	253.7	271.4	303.2	374.9	363.7	362.5	406.8	477.0	9.8
	NVA	51.5	69.9	76.9	77.9	81.8	91.3	89.5	91.2	100.1	115.9	7.0
	Ratio	0.33	0.31	0.30	0.29	0.27	0.24	0.25	0.25	0.25	0.24	
11 Building materials; other non-metallic mineral products	GVO	201.0	299.2	336.8	362.2	393.6	440.5	422.2	423.3	472.8	573.5	9.1
	NVA	80.5	114.8	129.4	138.2	141.3	152.2	134.5	130.4	151.8	198.2	7.8
	Ratio	0.40	0.38	0.38	0.38	0.36	0.35	0.32	0.31	0.32	0.35	
12 Basic and fabricated metal products(g)(h)	GVO	564.2	701.0	787.2	879.6	971.9	1 034.3	1 062.0	1 065.7	1 091.9	1 258.7	6.9
	NVA	168.9	213.6	233.2	249.6	273.6	287.9	285.1	253.0	256.7	320.4	5.5
	Ratio	0.30	0.30	0.30	0.28	0.28	0.28	0.27	0.24	0.24	0.25	

Table 4.A.3. (concluded)

Industry branch and data series		1980	1984	1985	1986	1987	1988	1989	1990	1991	1992	Compound growth
13 Machinery and transport equipment(I)	GVO	639.7	1 001.3	1 197.0	1 206.3	1 399.9	1 606.7	1 492.6	1 446.6	1 750.9	2 330.4	11.4
	NVA	222.3	331.1	401.9	389.4	428.5	475.2	432.2	406.6	477.3	620.9	8.9
	Ratio	0.35	0.33	0.34	0.32	0.31	0.30	0.29	0.28	0.27	0.27	
14 Electrical machinery and equipment(j)	GVO	228.4	414.9	544.2	567.3	664.8	820.2	832.9	788.9	904.4	1 089.9	13.9
	NVA	77.6	134.8	171.2	164.7	181.0	213.6	217.3	203.4	227.2	248.5	10.2
	Ratio	0.34	0.32	0.31	0.29	0.27	0.26	0.26	0.26	0.25	0.23	
15 Other industries(k)(l)	GVO	109.7	151.2	203.2	232.8	235.5	262.0	272.1	276.7	316.0	392.3	11.2
	NVA	44.44	58.3	71.0	81.8	80.9	85.4	87.0	84.4	95.6	106.1	7.5
	Ratio	0.41	0.39	0.35	0.35	0.34	0.33	0.32	0.31	0.30	0.27	
Total for manufacturing	GVO	4 134.0	5 976.9	6 864.0	7 392.9	8 255.8	9 199.9	9 200.6	9 364.6	10 473.0	12 437.8	9.6
	NVA	1 291.2	1 792.4	2 054.0	2 180.9	2 347.0	2 556.2	2 453.1	2 417.7	2 662.9	3 124.2	7.6
	Ratio	0.31	0.30	0.30	0.29	0.28	0.28	0.27	0.26	0.25	0.25	

Notes: GVO = Gross Value of Output; NVO = Net Value Added; Ratio = NVA/GVO. (a) Deflated with price deflator for wood products, assumed to include logging. (c) Deflated with price deflator for paper products. (b) Deflated with price deflator for food products. (d) Deflated with price deflator for the oil industry, assumed to include both crude oil production and refining. (e) Includes pharmaceuticals and chemical fibres, excludes oil refining. (f) In the absence of a separate index for rubber and plastics, this series was deflated with the overall price index for industry. (g) Includes ferrous and non-ferrous metals and fabricated metal products. (h) Deflated with the price index for the metallurgical industry, which probably refers to mining. The index shows very rapid price increases and this series may understate growth. (i) Deflated with the price index for machinery. (j) Includes electronic and communications equipment. In the absence of a separate price deflator, the overall price index for industry was used to deflate these figures. (k) Includes cultural products, arts and crafts, instruments and "other". (l) Deflated using the price deflator for cultural products for those products, that for arts and crafts for that sub-branch, and the overall price index for instruments and "other".

Source: GVO and NVA from Table 4-A-1; deflators from Table 4-A-2.

Table 4.A.4. Gross Value of Output by Industrial Branch (a), 1952-87, in 1980 Prices

(1980 = 100)

Year	Total	Metals	Power	Coal	Petroleum	Chemicals	Machinery	Building materials	Forestry	Food	Textiles	Apparel	Leather	Paper	Culture, Education, Crafts	Other
	(b)											(c)	(c)	(c)	(c)	(c)
1952	5.3	3.8	2.5	10.7	0.7	1.1	1.8	4.7	28.9	17.1	12.8	8.2	10.8	11.4	3.6	3.8
1953	6.9	5.2	2.9	11.8	0.8	1.5	2.9	6.5	39.5	21.4	15.7	11.5	12.9	13.1	5.6	
1954	8.0	6.3	3.5	14.3	1.1	1.9	3.4	7.2	46.6	24.5	17.2	11.9	13.1	14.9	6.5	
1955	8.5	7.9	4.0	16.8	1.7	2.1	3.8	7.3	42.1	26.9	16.6	11.9	12.9	16.7	7.3	
1956	10.9	11.1	5.3	19.6	2.4	3.1	5.9	10.3	51.9	29.1	20.0	16.6	16.5	21.5	9.3	
1957	12.1	13.6	6.2	23.6	2.7	4.3	6.8	11.7	55.0	31.8	19.4	16.5	20.0	27.2	9.1	12.9
1958	18.8	25.0	8.5	46.5	4.2	7.5	13.9	21.0	66.2	38.9	27.0	19.6	26.7	36.4	12.1	
1959	25.5	36.5	13.9	64.3	6.5	10.7	20.5	35.3	77.4	44.1	34.2	30.7	38.6	50.9	17.1	22.3
1960	28.4	46.6	20.1	72.4	8.1	12.8	28.1	40.0	81.9	39.6	27.4	18.7	41.1	53.9	20.8	
1961	17.5	25.9	16.5	49.8	6.3	9.2	13.5	15.9	49.1	32.5	18.4	18.0	26.9	31.8	14.1	
1962	14.6	19.4	15.9	37.9	7.5	8.4	9.8	9.3	42.8	29.1	16.5	17.2	20.2	30.7	12.2	22.1
1963	15.9	21.6	17.1	37.7	8.2	9.7	10.8	11.9	45.5	30.2	18.9	16.5	18.4	35.0	13.4	
1964	19.0	26.8	19.3	35.1	11.4	12.3	13.0	16.0	51.1	35.1	23.8	18.3	18.9	38.8	14.4	
1965	24.0	33.9	22.9	36.6	15.4	16.0	17.7	20.4	54.1	40.3	29.8	19.9	20.7	43.3	17.7	36.5
1966	29.0	41.1	28.2	41.8	21.2	22.6	23.9	27.8	55.6	36.7	32.4			44.1		
1967	25.0	30.2	26.0	30.6	18.5	19.8	17.8	22.1	47.4	36.0	29.6			40.6		
1968	23.7	24.3	25.0	33.1	21.2	17.3	15.5	18.5	38.0	36.0	27.7			35.3		
1969	31.9	37.7	34.0	41.3	23.6	26.6	24.7	26.3	46.1	37.6	35.5			45.9		
1970	41.6	51.8	39.6	58.0	36.0	35.7	36.9	32.0	49.2	45.4	43.8	40.3	41.8	50.9	35.9	73.9
1971	47.9	61.8	47.0	66.7	43.6	41.8	47.5	36.8	52.6	50.1	42.3	39.8	41.3	50.2	35.5	73.0
1972	51.0	65.1	51.6	69.0	49.6	46.1	50.1	42.8	59.5	55.7	42.6	40.3	41.8	53.7	36.0	74.0
1973	55.9	69.8	56.3	69.0	54.6	51.1	55.7	46.1	64.6	61.4	47.5	44.5	39.9	59.8	43.4	74.8
1974	58.0	61.1	56.9	66.5	62.2	49.5	58.4	45.8	66.0	63.1	47.0	47.0	42.0	56.3	47.3	69.4
1975	64.5	67.0	66.2	78.7	71.3	58.6	69.9	55.1	70.5	68.0	53.8	54.1	48.9	64.6	54.1	77.8
1976	65.3	61.7	68.7	79.2	79.8	57.9	70.5	60.5	75.8	68.4	53.6	58.3	52.8	64.7	56.1	84.4
1977	74.7	67.5	75.1	89.9	89.9	68.1	81.4	73.4	80.7	76.7	62.6	65.9	61.3	74.1	63.5	94.5
1978	84.8	85.7	85.7	102.2	92.5	84.4	90.7	84.8	89.3	83.0	71.9	67.4	66.6	83.9	74.1	98.9
1979	92.0	95.4	93.8	103.4	98.9	90.3	97.7	92.2	97.8	91.3	80.6	75.0	74.3	94.1	86.1	95.1
1980	100.0	100.0	100.0	100.0	100.0	100.0	100.0	100.0	100.0	100.0	100.0	100.0	100.0	100.0	100.0	100.0
1981	104.1	96.5	103.0	98.5	97.3	104.7	96.3	99.7	99.4	112.7	118.0	113.9	113.6	99.5	108.4	102.4
1982	112.2	102.6	109.5	104.1	99.3	116.6	109.2	113.7	106.4	123.4	119.5	109.8	107.9	106.5	115.1	112.2

Table 4.A.4. (concluded)

Year	Total	Metals	Power	Coal	Petroleum	Chemicals	Machinery	Building Materials	Forestry	Food	Textiles	Apparel	Leather	Paper	Culture, Education, Crafts	Other
	(b)											(c)	(c)	(c)	(c)	(c)
1983	124.0	110.7	116.4	111.6	106.9	131.2	128.4	125.4	110.0	129.7	131.8	118.8	110.5	117.1	119.3	126.5
1984	141.4	122.5	124.5	121.9	115.2	145.9	156.6	146.8	120.2	141.4	149.3	138.3	120.5	132.6	135.2	149.1
1985	166.8	140.4	144.2	130.5	128.5	164.0	199.3	179.1	126.2	155.4	175.5	154.2	148.2	154.9	189.7	184.0
1986	180.6	158.5	154.5	134.9	139.7	184.0	211.5	208.5	135.3	168.6	186.3	162.0	173.6	173.1	202.2	191.8
1987	207.3	173.8	170.6	140.7	149.9	215.4	257.4	234.8	149.3	187.5	208.6	187.9	202.2	198.8	246.5	213.0
Average Annual Growth Rates at 1980 Prices																
1952-87	11.0	11.6	12.9	7.6	16.7	16.3	15.1	11.8	4.8	7.1	8.3	9.3	8.7	8.5	12.8	12.2
1952-57	18.0	29.2	20.4	17.2	32.7	31.2	29.7	20.0	13.7	13.2	8.6	14.9	13.1	19.1	20.0	27.7
1957-70	10.0	10.8	15.3	7.2	21.9	17.7	13.9	8.0	-0.9	2.8	6.5	7.1	5.8	4.9	11.2	14.4
1970-78	9.3	6.5	10.1	7.3	12.5	11.4	11.9	13.0	7.7	7.8	6.4	6.7	6.0	6.5	9.5	3.7
1978-87	10.4	8.2	8.0	3.6	5.5	11.0	12.3	12.0	5.9	9.5	12.6	12.1	13.1	10.1	14.3	8.9
1980-87	11.0	8.2	7.9	5.0	6.0	11.6	14.5	13.0	5.9	9.4	11.1	9.4	10.6	10.3	13.8	11.4

Notes: (a) Gross Material Product. (b) Including mining, utilities and logging but excluding construction. (c) For wearing apparel, leather, paper, cultural products and "other", data from 1966 to 1971 needed for the growth rate calculations are missing, and for "other" they are missing also from 1952 to 1955 and for 1958, 1960, 1961, 1963 and 1964. The growth rates have been calculated by interpolation, using the movement for total industry after deduction of the branches for which data are available.

Source: *Statistical Yearbook of China, 1988* (SSB, 1989), pp. 54-55.

Re-assessment of China's Economic Growth

The 1995 *Statistical Yearbook* (SSB, 1995) contains time series for GDP and its components: primary (agriculture), secondary (mining, manufacturing, utilities and construction) and tertiary industry (services), at current prices from 1985 to 1994 (Table 4.A.5). It also provides indices derived by the comparable-price approach for GDP and its components. The exercise here applied the relevant price indices to the three components of GDP to obtain a new time series for GDP and its components at constant prices.

For primary industry the index for "overall farm and sideline products purchasing price" was chosen as the deflator. According to the SSB guideline, this index reflects the general level of purchasing prices for agricultural and sideline goods. The "industrial products producer price index", in an aggregated version, served as the deflator for secondary industry. This study's detailed assessment of growth rates in industry used the same index in disaggregated form. The index is on a "gross" base with sales values used as weights in aggregation of relative prices. For tertiary industry, the index for the "services" category was used, from the "overall residents consumer price indices". This index is available only from 1986 to 1994, which determined the time span covered. Table 4.A.6 shows all the price indices used in the deflation of the components of GDP.

Table A.4.5. **Basic Data for China's GDP and its Components, in Current Prices, 1985-94**
(billions of yuan)

Year	GDP	Primary industry	Secondary industry	Tertiary industry
1985	896.44	254.16	386.66	255.62
1986	1 020.22	276.39	449.27	294.56
1987	1 196.25	320.43	525.16	350.66
1988	1 492.83	383.10	658.72	451.01
1989	1 690.92	422.80	727.80	540.32
1990	1 853.07	501.70	771.74	579.63
1991	2 161.78	528.86	910.22	722.70
1992	2 663.54	580.00	1 169.95	913.59
1993	3 451.51	688.21	1 642.85	1 120.45
1994	4 500.58	943.80	2 125.90	1 430.88

Source: *Statistical Yearbook of China, 1995* (SSB, 1995), p.32.

Table 4.A.6. **Price Indices Used as Deflators of GDP Components, 1985-94**
(1985 = 100)

Year	Overall farm and sideline products purchasing price index	Industrial products producer price index	Services index
1985	100.0	100.0	100.0
1986	106.4	103.8	106.6
1987	119.2	112.0	113.6
1988	146.6	128.8	132.0
1989	168.6	152.8	163.6
1990	164.2	159.0	197.8
1991	160.9	168.9	215.0
1992	166.4	180.4	243.8
1993	188.7	223.7	311.8
1994	263.9	267.3	392.0

Note: Price indices were calculated from chain indices. Column four is a price index for services within the composite consumer price index.

Source: *Statistical Yearbook of China, 1994* (SSB, 1994, pp. 231, 246, 240) *and 1995* (SSB, 1995, pp. 233, 244, 249).

Chapter 5

A Time Series of China's GDP in Dollars

Introduction

Two conventional methods exist for extrapolating benchmark estimates to other years in international comparisons. Both approaches can serve to update or backdate estimates. The first is to obtain an estimate in constant dollars by using the growth rates computed from national currency GDP data in constant prices for China:

$$GDP_t^{t+n} = GDP_t^t \, x(1 + G_c)^n \qquad\qquad (5.1)$$

where:

GDP_t^{t+n} is Chinese GDP in year $t+n$ expressed in dollars of year t;

GDP_t^t is Chinese GDP in year t expressed in dollars of year t; and

G_c is the growth rate of Chinese GDP expressed in constant Chinese prices.

This estimate then is adjusted by the change in the US price index to arrive at an estimate in current dollars:

$$GDP_{t+n}^{t+n} = GDP_t^{t+n} \, x \, P_t^{t+n} \qquad\qquad (5.2)$$

where:

GDP_t^{t+n} is Chinese GDP in year $t+n$ in year t dollars;

GDP_{t+n}^{t+n} is Chinese GDP in year $t+n$ in year $t+n$ dollars; and

P_t^{t+n} is a dollar deflator

The second approach extrapolates the purchasing power parity by the relative rate of inflation between the country in question and the United States, as measured by implicit deflators, using equation 5.3:

$$PPP_{t+n} = PPP_t \, x \, \frac{P_t^{t+n(C)}}{P_t^{t+n(U)}} \qquad\qquad (5.3)$$

where:

PPP_t is the converter used for year t;

PPP_{t+n} is the converter used for year $t+n$;

$P_t^{t+n(C)}$ is a deflator for China; and

$P_t^{t+n(U)}$ is a deflator for the United States.

The extrapolated PPP is then used to convert national currency GDP data in current prices to reach an estimate of GDP in current dollars by equation 5.4:

$$GDP_{t+n(U)}^{t+n} = GDP_{t+n(C)}^{t+n} \, / \, PPP_{t+n} \qquad\qquad (5.4)$$

where:

$GDP_{t+n(C)}^{t+n}$ is Chinese GDP in year $t+n$ in current yuan;

$GDP_{t+n(U)}^{t+n}$ is Chinese GDP in year $t+n$ in current dollars; and

PPP_{t+n} is the converter.

In theory these two approaches should give identical results but in fact they usually do not, because the heterogeneity of the data prevents it. Generally, the second approach applies best to China because of the apparent tendency of the official figures to overstate the growth rate of Chinese GDP. The following computations try both approaches to explore how big a difference actually emerges between the two alternatives. The results presented here focus on updating the benchmark study, because problems with the data on economic aggregates and inflation rates before the 1980s make backdating the benchmark very difficult. The backdating of the estimates needs further work. When this study was in its final stage, the SSB published a revised time series for GDP for 1978-93 based on a tertiary-industry census. The revised time series could form the basis for later updates of the benchmark estimates.

Various Estimates of the Inflation Rate in China

The US GDP deflator serves adequately as a measure of inflation in the United States. A proper measurement of the inflation rate in China, a vital factor in the second approach, presents greater problems and affects the accuracy of the extrapolation of the benchmark estimates.

For present purposes, two alternative price indices can be used in updating the benchmark estimates of the PPPs based on the ICP and ICOP approaches. The "overall retail price indices" constitute an index which reflects the general retail price level, shows changes in the purchasing power of the currency and reveals the impact of inflation on expenditure in rural and urban areas (see SSB's guidance in SSB, 1987c). This price index represents the best choice of deflator for updating the PPP from the ICP approach in terms of coverage, the price information used in constructing the index and the function for which it was designed.

The "industrial products producer price index" can be used to adjust the benchmark PPPs from the ICOP study. Not a perfect choice, it reflects price changes in industry, only part of the entire economy treated by the ICOP study. Nevertheless, it is the only index from Chinese sources which uses producers' prices, in conformity with the prices underlying the ICOP PPPs.

Recent literature on the financial sector of China's economy has examined the downward-biased price index hypothesis (Chen and Hou, 1986, Feltenstein and Ha, 1991; Li, 1994; Yi, 1994). These studies concentrated on the accuracy of the retail price index as a measure of inflation in China. The authors generally acknowledge that this index understates actual inflation over the past decade. A free-market price index offers an alternative to the retail price index from official sources. Some of these studies tried to estimate their own price indices to measure inflation in China.

Two issues are involved here. One concerns measurement, of the difference between the downward-biased official price index and a correct one. It has the most relevance to updating the benchmark PPPs in the current study. The other bears on a theoretical concern with the difference between inflation which actually occurred in China and the potential inflation inherent in a high rate of growth of money supply and a downward movement in velocity. The newly estimated price indices in Chen and Hou (1986) and Feltenstein and Ha (1991) focus on this second issue. In order to compare the effects of different measurements of inflation on updating the PPP, these two estimated price indices were included as alternatives in the PPP extrapolations.

The Updated Benchmark Estimates

Table 5.1 assembles for convenience of comparison all of the updates of Chinese GDP and GDP per capita estimated by the various techniques, and with the various deflators, discussed above. Recall that all of these updates emanate from the benchmark estimates; thus they carry forward the possible margins of error in the benchmark studies (due to the various sources) under both the ICP and ICOP approaches. The updates therefore show a range into which Chinese GDP likely fell during these years. For 1989, the latest year for which all three parts of the table contain complete estimates, the range for GDP varies by about 47 per cent between $1 041.27 billion based on the deflator of Feltenstein and Ha and $1 562.36 billion derived from the ICP study using China's official growth rates. The range is narrower for the estimates central to this study — about 37 per cent in 1994 between the ICOP estimate of $2 188.39 billion based on extrapolated PPPs and the ICP's $3 007.68 billion based on the official growth

Table 5.1. **Estimated Levels of GDP and GDP Per Capita in China, 1985-94**

Market prices or factor cost of the years cited; GDP in $ billion; GDP per capita in $

	1985	1986	1987	1988	1989	1990	1991	1992	1993	1994
A. Fisher GDP benchmark GDP levels extrapolated by official SSB real growth indices, multiplied by US GDP Deflator										
GDP (ICP)		1 081.66	1 244.82	1 437.91	1 562.36	1 689.72	1 918.07	2 254.08	2 622.94	3 007.68
GDP (ICOP)	841.10	937.99	1 079.48	1 246.93	1 354.85	1 465.29	1 663.31	1 954.69	2 274.56	2 608.20
GDP Per Capita:										
(ICP)		1 013.94	1 148.32	1 305.26	1 396.65	1 488.50	1 666.76	1 934.89	2 225.78	2 523.57
(ICOP)	700.25	879.26	995.80	1 131.89	1 211.14	1 290.79	1 445.38	1 677.89	1 930.14	2 188.39
B. Official SSB nominal values converted to current dollars by using an update of the benchmark Fisher PPPs (yuan per dollar)[a]										
GDP (ICP)	982.88	1 081.66	1 218.90	1 332.21	1 337.02	1 495.26	1 760.56	2 117.86	2 485.55	2 731.45
GDP (ICOP)	841.10	945.25	1 059.26	1 192.96	1 189.19	1 304.38	1 488.09	1 766.63	1 892.77	2 118.31
GDP Per Capita:										
(ICP)	935.15	1 013.94	1 124.41	1 209.30	1 195.21	1 317.19	1 529.88	1 817.95	2 109.19	2 291.80
(ICOP)	800.25	886.07	977.15	1 082.90	1 063.06	1 149.05	1 293.12	1 516.46	1 606.16	1 777.35

(a) The benchmark Fisher PPPs (ICP 0.9432 and ICOP1.0658) from Tables 3.1 and 3.2 were updated by multiplying the official Chinese GDP yuan deflator and dividing by the US GDP dollar deflator.

Sources: Benchmark estimates and PPPs from Chapter 3; official growth rates from Chapter 4. In panel B of the table, the deflator for the United States is from OECD (1994) and IMF (1994); the deflator for China is from *Statistical Yearbook of China, 1994* (SSB, 1994).

rates. Because there seems to be a consensus, based on both the literature and the exploratory studies in this volume, that the official growth rates overestimate Chinese GDP, the updates using the growth approach (Panel A of Table 5.1) should be regarded as an upper bound on the likely real income.

Panel B of Table 5.1 shows the results of following the second approach, using the deflators of both countries to extrapolate the benchmark estimates of PPPs. Different deflators of course yield different outcomes. The deflator used in the time series shown in Panel B is the Chinese official price index.

Time series, like those presented here, of internationally comparable macro indicators based on purchasing power parity, support analyses which reveal perspectives different from those supplied by exchange rate conversions. A look at the openness of the Chinese economy provides a good example, as Table 5.2 illustrates. Using the exchange rate as the converter suggests that China has a very open economy. With the PPP as the converter, however, the measure of openness falls considerably and does not increase as rapidly over time. Although China's trade has grown very fast, its GDP has risen substantially as well; one would not expect that the openness of the economy would expand as dramatically as the exchange rate conversions suggest — almost a doubling of trade as a percentage of GDP in the decade covered by the table, with more than half of it occurring between 1993 and 1994 alone.

Table 5.2. **Measures of the Openness of the Chinese Economy**

Year	Trade as a per cent of GDP		
	Exchange rate converter	ICP PPP converter	ICOP PPP converter
1985	11.40	3.54	4.32
1986	12.50	3.41	4.06
1987	12.86	3.39	4.06
1988	12.81	3.86	4.48
1989	12.43	4.18	4.89
1990	14.90	3.86	4.60
1991	16.70	3.85	4.74
1992	17.14	3.91	4.87
1993	16.34	3.94	5.38
1994	22.67	4.33	5.81

Notes: Trade is measured as: (exports + imports)/2 (see Fukusaku and Solignac Lecomte, 1996). The benchmark PPPs are: ICP (1986) — 0.9432; ICOP (1985) — 1.0658. The trade figures in dollars were calculated from yuan-denominated figures and the exchange rate. The US GNP deflator and Chinese deflators (the CPI for the ICP estimates and the PPI for the ICOP estimates) were applied to the benchmark PPPs to obtain the PPP time series, which then were used to calculates time series for GDP in dollars on the ICP and ICOP bases, while the exchange rate was used to create a third dollar GDP series. The relevant trade values were then used to find percentages of each of the GDP numbers.

Sources: *Statistical Yearbook of China, 1994* (SSB, 1994). Trade data from p. 537. GDP in yuan from p. 32. Chinese CPI from p. 233 and PPI from p. 249. The US deflator and Chinese exchange rates are from IMF, *International Financial Statistics*, various issues.

Re-assessing Economic Growth Rates Based on the Dollar GDP Time Series

The construction of a Chinese GDP time series in US dollars makes possible a view of China's growth rate from an international perspective, by converting the current-dollar GDP figures in Table 5.1 to constant dollars and then deriving growth rates. Table 5.3 shows the results.

Table 5.3. **A Comparison of GDP Growth Rates in China**
(preceding year = 100, except as noted)

Year	Official growth rate	Growth rate derived by deflation	Growth rate from ICP based $ series	Growth rate from ICOP based $ series
1986	108.8	108.1	107.4	109.6
1987	111.6	108.0	109.3	108.7
1988	111.3	106.5	105.3	108.5
1989	104.1	101.0	96.2	95.5
1990	103.8	102.5	107.3	105.3
1991	109.3	111.0	113.4	109.8
1992	114.2	114.0	116.9	115.4
1993	113.5	106.3	114.5	104.5
1994	111.8	104.1	107.1	109.1
Compound growth rate in per cent per year	9.8	6.0	8.4	7.3

Sources: The official growth rate and the rate derived by deflation (columns two and three) are from Chapter 4. Columns four and five were calculated using series of GDP in current dollars (Table 5.1) from the ICP and ICOP approaches in Chapter 3.

The two time series in US dollar terms from the ICP and ICOP approaches suggest compound growth rates lower than the official growth rates, a result consistent with the literature and the findings of this study. The assessment of the economic meaning of growth rates derived from an international comparison of this sort, however, requires closer consideration.

Using foreign prices to explore the growth rates of a country has a long history in economics. A famous study dates back to Gerschenkron (1962), who attempted to measure the growth of output in Soviet heavy industry with a dollar index for 1927-37. At that time, Soviet statistical practice used a comparable price approach similar to that in Chinese statistical convention. Gerschenkron pointed out the advantages and disadvantages of his approach before he introduced the quantitative results. One advantage still relevant to the present study was that American prices better reflected opportunity cost. A key shortcoming lay in the very remote vantage point it chose from which to view Soviet industrial development. For the present study, this point should be stressed again. The underlying assumption is that the country whose weighting system is chosen to measure Chinese industrial output should be as similar as possible to China in its stage of economic development and have a comparable range of measurable output. The choice of US prices satisfies the second requirement but certainly does not meet the first one.

Balassa and Bhagwati discussed the same issue in another context (see their comments on Daly's paper, "Uses of International Price and Output Data" in Daly, 1972). Balassa supported the use of other countries' prices to measure economic growth in a country whose prices were distorted by protective measures. Based on his empirical work on some developing countries, the use of world market prices usually suggested lower growth rates than the official ones (Balassa, 1970; Balassa et al., 1970). Bhagwati, however, had reservations concerning the measurement of growth rates at foreign prices. His comments focussed on Balassa's example which proposed that the income of a small country should be valued at world market prices because the country can affect the prices of neither its exports nor its imports. Bhagwati's important general message is that "A range of estimates of income and growth rates at international prices, instead of a single estimate, must be provided, using a sensitivity analysis approach, to emphasize that the calculations require heroic conceptual and measurement assumptions."

The present estimates of China's GDP growth rates derived from an international comparison are more complicated because of their derivation with the Fisher index which uses both Chinese and US prices in the weighting system. These new estimates based on international comparison remain valid here because:

— China is in a transition process with prices certainly distorted to some extent and not reflecting opportunity cost very well.

— Flaws in the comparable-price approach used to measure Chinese GDP at constant prices have been recognised and analysed elsewhere (e.g. World Bank, 1992b).

China's Comparative Standing in an International Framework

The new estimates of this study permit a comparison of China's per capita GDP with those of some Asian developing countries and transitional countries. The choice of countries in this comparison depends solely on the availability of ICP benchmark estimates. ICP now provides international comparisons for many countries every five years using the Geary-Khamis multilateral comparison framework [see Geary (1958) and Khamis (1972, 1984)] or other methods. Because the results of the present study are on a bilateral comparison basis and in order to make the two sets of estimates comparable in concept, the Fisher index estimates from this study have been adjusted by a factor of 1.187, the average ratio of the Geary-Khamis to Fisher measures for the four lowest-income countries in the ICP2 comparison. For the countries compared with China in Table 5.4, the figures show 1985 per capita GDP in 1985 Geary-Khamis dollars from ICP5. As benchmark estimates, they are comparable with the adjusted figures for China from this study. The figures on 1990 per capita GDP in 1990 Geary Khamis dollars for these countries are updates by Maddison (1995), who based them on growth rates calculated for changes in GDP volume in local constant prices and the US GDP deflator for the US price change between the two years — a procedure equivalent to the first method used in this study. The updated benchmark figures using the two methods of this study show a relatively significant gap for China in 1990; whether this would be the case for other countries is not known. Hence, the 1990 estimates in 1990 Geary-Khamis dollars for China and other countries may also be comparable even if different updating methods are used.

Table 5.4. **Comparison of China's Per Capita GDP with Those of Three Developing and Three Transition Countries, 1985 and 1990**

(in current Geary-Khamis dollars)

Year	China		India	Pakistan	Thailand	Hungary	Poland	Yugoslavia
	ICP	ICOP	ICP	ICP	ICP	ICP	ICP	ICP
1985	1 110	950	749	1 342	2 641	5 140	4 039	4 810
1990	1 564	1 364	1 088	1 791	2 641	6 529	4 349	5 206

Sources: Figures for China from this study, Chapter 3. Figures for other countries for 1985 from UN *et al.* (1994), and for 1990 from Maddison (1995).

On the evidence of these figures, China certainly remains a low-income country with much lower average GDP than dynamic Asian developing countries like Thailand. The comparison with transitional countries, showing China's GDP as a fraction of theirs, may provide a hint of why China has adopted a quite different reform approach (in the vast recent literature, see, e.g. Lee and Reisen, 1994) and probably would recommend caution in drawing lessons for China from the transition countries' situations, because the initial conditions of the transition differ so greatly between China and the eastern European countries.

Concluding Remarks

The updated estimates based on the benchmark studies revealed a quite significant discrepancy for the early 1990s. This has serious import. Extrapolations of benchmark estimates must be made carefully and interpreted cautiously.

The findings of this study provide a different perspective on China's economic performance over time. The indicator for openness suggests much less dependence on international trade than do exchange rate conversions. The initial conditions for reform and real income levels differ considerably between China and eastern European countries. These new perspectives may call for some revisions of the conventional evaluation of the economic performance and the transition strategy of China.

In the "Summary of 1985 Results" of "Phase V of The International Comparison Project" (UN *et al.* 1994), countries that participated in the 1985 ICP comparison were divided into four groupings. The countries which had a real per capita GDP of less than $1 500 belong to the low-level group. Based on both the ICP and ICOP benchmark estimates in this study and the estimates derived from ICP multilateral comparisons shown in Table 5.4, China definitely still remained classified among the low-income developing countries in 1985. For 1990, the dividing line could not be less than $1 500, considering inflation in the United States between 1985 and 1990 and economic growth in all countries. Hence China occupied the same neighbourhood in 1990 as in 1985. For the years after 1990 the relative standing of China appears around the margin of this grouping, at least in terms of the ICOP estimates.

Chapter 6

Chinese Manufacturing Competitiveness

Since the early 1980s, China has undergone two restructuring processes: industrialisation and the transition from a centrally planned to a market economy. China's successful, trade-driven development strategy plays a very important role in these two dimensions of development [Fukasaku and Wall (1994); Anderson (1990); Garnaut and Liu (1992); Lardy (1992); Lee and Reisen, (1994)]. To better understand the role of trade in the Chinese economy, the production-side (ICOP) estimates of this study make it possible to explore the comparative advantage and competitiveness of Chinese manufacturing by looking at relative levels of prices derived from sectoral purchasing power parities, sectoral comparative productivity, and comparative unit labour costs for several benchmark years during 1980-90 (see Pilat and van Ark (1994) for discussion on this approach).

Relative Prices of Manufactured Products

Price differences between countries for similar products influence competitiveness. They certainly have more importance for China than comparative productivity levels because it has not yet achieved major relative productivity gains. The comparisons in Table 6.1 use the PPPs developed in Chapter Three, based on ex-factory prices. If the PPP of a manufacturing branch in China is below the exchange rate, the relative price level (the PPP divided by the exchange rate) in that branch will be lower than that for the country under comparison. The country with lower relative price levels — with an exchange rate, in other words, higher than the PPPs in manufacturing — can compete favourably against the other country in the world market.

During the 1980s, all major Chinese manufacturing branches experienced improved price competitiveness due largely to the depreciation of the yuan (see Fukasaku and Wall, 1994 for detailed discussion on the evolution of China's exchange rate regime), which more than offset the effects of persistent high inflation in China. Had the exchange rate remained at its 1985 level, for example, the relative price level for all manufacturing would have reached 109.31 (US = 100) in 1994; the actual

135

Table 6.1. **Chinese Manufacturing PPPs and Relative Price Levels by Major Branches of Manufacturing, 1985-94**

(US = 100 for relative price levels)

Year	Food, beverages and tobacco		Textiles, apparel and leather		Chemicals and allied products		Basic and fabricated metals		Machinery and equipment		Other manufactures		All manufacturing		Exchange rate
	PPP	Relative price level	PPP	Relative price level	PPP	Relative price level	PPP	Relative price level	PPP	Relative price level	PPP	Relative price level	PPP	Relative price level	
1985	1.32	44.96	1.37	46.52	1.50	51.15	0.99	33.77	1.78	60.53	1.17	39.91	1.45	49.38	2.9367
1986	1.33	38.50	1.39	40.31	1.56	45.21	1.09	31.14	1.81	52.29	1.14	33.14	1.56	45.22	3.4528
1987	1.44	38.65	1.49	40.06	1.77	47.54	1.15	30.99	1.87	50.23	1.35	36.24	1.64	44.12	3.7221
1988	1.58	42.36	1.77	47.57	1.93	51.79	1.21	35.52	2.01	54.11	1.46	39.33	1.82	48.95	3.7221
1989	1.74	46.34	2.12	56.21	2.27	60.29	1.46	38.74	2.35	62.39	1.56	41.54	2.06	54.67	3.7651
1990	1.71	35.83	2.20	46.09	2.32	48.61	1.66	34.75	2.34	48.88	1.62	33.96	2.07	43.20	4.7832
1991	1.77	33.26	2.27	42.60	2.39	44.95	1.97	36.95	2.37	44.43	1.68	31.59	2.18	40.96	5.3234
1992	1.86	33.73	2.24	40.68	2.41	43.77	2.27	41.18	2.53	45.82	1.70	30.74	2.31	41.90	5.5146
1993	2.06	35.81	2.33	40.41	2.61	45.23	3.54	61.48	3.02	52.49	1.84	31.99	2.82	49.00	5.7620
1994	2.55	29.63	3.20	37.18	2.80	32.49	3.46	40.13	3.28	38.08	1.98	22.97	3.21	37.19	8.6187

Sources: PPPs from Chapter 3 and exchange rates from SSB, *Statistical Yearbook of China*, various issues

recorded value was 37.19, well below the 1985 level. In the decade covered by the table, there were two episodes (1987-89 and 1991-93) when relative price levels rose when inflation exceeded exchange rate changes. It seems possible to forecast a similar pattern in the near future because further strong depreciation of the Chinese currency cannot be expected and inflation has yet to be brought under complete control.

Chinese Manufacturing Productivity Performance

Comparative Productivity Levels, 1985

Table 6.2 presents comparisons of real gross value added. On a census basis and using the geometric average of PPPs, Chinese industrial GDP was 12.5 per cent of that in the United States, twice as high as the figure one would find using the exchange rates. The use of PPPs corrects to a considerable extent for underestimation of Chinese GDP due to converting at the official exchange rate, because it evaluates both Chinese and US production at the same sets of prices.

Table 6.3 moves to comparisons of gross value added per person. For all manufacturing Chinese labour productivity was 4.8 per cent of the US level. The highest levels occurred in electrical machinery and equipment (11.4 per cent of the US level), leather products and footwear (10.8 per cent) and metal products (9.5 per cent). Low relative productivity is found in machinery and transport equipment (2.9 per cent), food manufacturing (2.8 per cent), paper products, printing and publishing (3.2 per cent), tobacco products (3.5 per cent) and wood products (3.6 per cent).

Low relative productivity in Chinese manufacturing does not arise from excessively high PPPs. On the contrary, the PPPs are very low. Application of the exchange rate to Chinese value added per person from the census would result in much lower figures. One possible explanation for low productivity is that the comparison includes small scale enterprises which have very low productivity in China. A second may lie in wasteful use of both intermediate and factor inputs. Chinese enterprises often hoard labour extensively.

An extremely labour-intensive small-scale sector exists in many low-income countries, with labour productivity far below that in medium-sized and large-scale manufacturing (see e.g. Szirmai, 1994, for Indonesia, and van Ark, 1991, for India). Figures in current yuan show that value added per person in medium-size and large Chinese manufacturing enterprises is 1.64 times as high as in the whole of manufacturing (see *Industrial Census 1985*, OLG, 1987-88). In the United States, labour productivity in the same manufacturing group (defined as excluding establishments with fewer than 20 employees) is only 1.023 times that in total manufacturing[1]. After a rough adjustment for these differentials, labour productivity among large and medium-sized Chinese manufacturers measures at about 7.7 per cent of the US level.

Table 6.2. Gross Value Added by Major Manufacturing Branch, China and the United States, 1985

	At Chinese prices (Yuan million, ratio as per cent)			At US prices (in $ million, ratio as per cent)			Geometric Mean of ratios
	China	United States	China/US Ratio	China	United States	China/US Ratio	
1 Food products	8 544.6	150 103.6	7.00	5 598.9	84 853.3	6.60	6.1
2 Beverages	3 217.1	17 508.2	18.40	3 544.8	19 292.7	18.40	18.4
3 Tobacco products	488.5	4 608.6	10.60	1 325.2	11 893.7	11.15	10.9
4 Textile mill products	18 737.7	30 852.2	60.73	13 015.6	20 693.3	62.90	61.8
5 Wearing apparel	4 341.9	37 990.6	11.43	3 133.3	27 728.4	11.30	11.4
6 Leather products and footwear	1 931.1	3 463.9	55.75	2 290.0	4 107.5	55.75	55.8
7 Wood products, furniture and fixtures	2 907.7	65 032.6	4.50	1 679.4	37 544.3	4.50	4.5
8 Paper products, printing and publishing	6 249.9	223 373.0	2.80	3 952.1	113 476.6	3.48	3.1
9 Chemical products	25 141.4	182 653.2	13.80	21 756.5	112 369.1	19.40	16.3
10 Rubber and plastic products	6 485.5	130 510.7	4.97	7 979.2	35 708.3	22.35	10.5
11 Non-metallic mineral products	15 148.9	33 019.9	45.88	29 180.4	28 877.7	101.05	68.1
12 Basic and fabricated metal products	24 095.4	70 904.3	33.98	16 170.9	107 400.0	15.06	22.6
13 Machinery and transport equipment	41 505.5	659 507.9	6.29	21 645.3	231 388.6	9.35	7.7
14 Electrical machinery and equipment	16 316.6	82 553.5	19.73	21 184.3	85 875.5	24.67	22.1
15 Other manufacturing	6 702.2	143 187.2	4.65	5 744.7	79 100.0	7,30	5.8
All manufacturing	181 814.1	1 835 269.6	9.9	158 200.5	1 000 142.0	15.8	12.5

Source: Census value added in national currencies from Tables 3.A.20 and 3.A.21; converted with PPPs from Table 3.5.

Table 6.3. **Gross Value Added per Person Employed, by Major Manufacturing Branch, China and the United States, 1985**

	At Chinese prices (in yuan; ratios in per cent)			At US prices (in $; ratios in per cent)			Geometric Mean of ratios
	China	United States	China/US ratio	China	United States	China/US ratio	
1 Food products	3 083	112 714	2.7	1 849	63 717	2.9	2.8
2 Beverages	3 544	88 825	4.0	3 635	97 878	3.7	3.8
3 Tobacco products	2 393	65 939	3.6	5 879	170 171	3.5	3.5
4 Textile mill products	3 025	45 056	6.7	1 906	30 220	6.3	6.5
5 Wearing apparel	2 297	34 798	6.6	1 568	25 398	6.2	6.4
6 Leather products and footwear	2 495	22 446	11.1	2 774	26 617	10.4	10.8
7 Wood products, furniture and fixtures	2 209	58 670	3.8	1 170	33 871	3.5	3.6
8 Paper products, printing and publishing	3 183	107 251	3.0	1 860	54 485	3.4	3.2
9 Chemical products	6 232	150 673	4.1	4 707	92 694	5.1	4.6
10 Rubber and plastic products	3 757	169 277	2.2	4 254	46 315	9.2	4.5
11 Non-metallic mineral products	2 459	59 994	4.1	4 422	52 468	8.4	5.9
12 Basic and fabricated metal products	4 747	30 943	15.3	2 780	46 870	5.9	9.5
13 Machinery and transport equipment	4 066	162 470	2.5	1 865	57 003	3.3	2.9
14 Electrical machinery and equipment	5 147	47 762	10.8	5 994	49 588	12.1	11.4
15 Other manufacturing	3 068	97 877	3.1	2 441	54 070	4.5	3.8
All manufacturing	**3 742**	**97 639**	**3.8**	**3 256**	**53 209**	**6.1**	**4.8**

Sources: Gross value added (census concept) from Table 6.2; employment from Tables 3.A.20 and 3.A.21.

Adjustment for small-scale manufacturing in China is fraught with uncertainties. The "Explanation of Industrial Statistical Indicators" (in SSB, 1993) provides definitions of size based on installed capacity, fixed capital stock or annual output, but the cut-off points are different for each manufacturing sector, even for a single indicator. Nevertheless, SSB (1993) data allow calculation of 94 as the average number of employees per enterprise in the small-scale sector, against 1 636 in medium-scale manufacturing and 4 794 in large-scale manufacturing. This would suggest a cut-off point of around 100 persons employed rather than the often used 20 or more. The data refer to enterprises rather than establishments, however, so a cut-off point of 20 per establishment would not be inconceivable. If a cut-off point of 100 or more persons employed is applied to both Chinese and US data, Chinese labour productivity in medium-sized and large-scale enterprises becomes about 7.2 per cent of the US level. For the time being, then, the Chinese estimate probably lies between 7.2 per cent and 7.7 per cent of the US level.

Labour productivity in Chinese manufacturing lies in the same range as the levels in other Asian low-income countries. For medium-sized and large-scale manufacturing in India van Ark (1991) estimated gross value added per person in 1985 at 7.7 per cent of the US level, a striking similarity in light of often highly favorable comparisons of Chinese economic performance with that of India. Labour productivity in Indonesian manufacturing in 1985, excluding establishments with fewer than 20 employees, was 10.5 per cent of the US level, substantially higher than in both China and India (Szirmai, 1994)[2].

Net Value Added Per Person Employed in Chinese Manufacturing

Table 6.4 presents a 1980-92 time series for Chinese net value added per person employed; it combines the figures on net value added at constant prices with those on labour input. Average labour productivity in manufacturing increased by 3.4 per cent and that in all industry (including mining, logging and utilities) by 3.3 per cent per year over the period. Performance varied substantially from branch to branch. The data suggest negative productivity growth in oil refining (-4.0 per cent per year), textiles (-1.5 per cent) and wood products (-0.8 per cent). High productivity growth occurred in machinery and equipment (5.6 per cent), wearing apparel (4.9 per cent) and chemical products excluding oil refineries (4.6 per cent).

Comparative Productivity Over Time

Table 6.5 extrapolates the 1985 benchmark figures using Chinese and US time series of real value added per person employed. Its most important finding is the absence of significant change in aggregate Chinese relative labour productivity in manufacturing between 1980 and 1992. It began at 4.9 per cent of the US level in 1980, rose slightly to a peak of 5.2 per cent in 1982, declined steadily to 4.2 per cent in 1990, then recovered to 4.9 per cent of the US level in 1992, the same as in 1980. At branch level the trends varied. There were relative productivity gains in food, beverages and tobacco, wearing

Table 6.4. "Productivity in Chinese Industry: Net Value Added per Person Employed, 1980-92."

(Constant 1980 yuan and index numbers, 1980=100; Growth=compound annual rate in per cent)

ICOP Branch Industry Category	1980	1981	1982	1983	1984	1985	1986	1987	1988	1989	1990	1991	1992	Growth
Total Industry	3 178.5	3 275.3	3 375.1	3 477.8	3 583.7	3 763.1	3 818.7	3 875.1	4 034.2	3 863.2	3 795.7	3 993.5	4 682.4	
	100.0	103.0	106.2	109.4	112.7	118.4	120.1	121.9	126.9	121.5	119.4	125.6	147.3	3.28
1/2.	2 976.3	2 982.9	2 989.5	2 996.1	3 002.7	3 087.4	3 221.7	3 361.8	3 760.8	3 703.7	3 877.5	4 641.8	4 821.7	
	100.0	100.2	100.4	100.7	100.9	103.7	108.2	113.0	126.4	124.4	130.3	156.0	162.0	4.10
1.	2 586.9	2 584.2	2 581.6	2 578.9	2 576.2	2 701.6	2 855.4	3 016.0	3 281.2	3 308.7	3 396.9	4 008.1	3 971.0	
	100.0	99.9	99.8	99.7	99.6	104.4	110.4	116.7	126.8	127.9	131.3	154.9	153.5	3.64
2	4 577.7	4 556.7	4 535.9	4 515.1	4 494.5	4 302.3	4 329.4	4 356.8	5 102.8	4 835.8	5 262.0	6 430.2	7 173.5	
	100.0	99.5	99.1	98.6	98.2	94.0	94.6	95.2	111.5	105.6	115.0	140.5	156.7	3.81
3	39	40	41	42	43	42	45	49	52	52	58	57	58	
	576.8	526.8	499.6	495.7	515.7	332.1	995.0	974.9	548.0	186.2	504.8	435.3	379.7	
	100.0	102.4	104.9	107.4	110.0	107.0	116.2	126.3	132.8	131.9	147.8	145.1	147.5	3.29
4	4 195.8	4 014.5	3 841.1	3 675.2	3 516.4	3 802.0	3 759.7	3 717.9	3 661.1	3 440.5	3 257.7	3 094.2	3 482.1	
	100.0	95.7	91.5	87.6	83.8	90.6	89.6	88.6	87.3	82.0	77.6	73.7	83.0	-1.54
5	1 907.1	1 974.0	2 043.2	2 114.9	2 189.1	2 438.1	2 542.7	2 651.5	2 751.0	2 846.7	2 765.0	2 887.3	3 388.0	
	100.0	103.5	107.1	110.9	114.8	127.9	133.3	139.0	144.3	149.3	145.0	151.4	177.7	4.91
6	2 229.3	2 175.6	2 123.2	2 072.0	2 022.1	2 224.1	2 390.5	2 569.3	2 508.4	2 430.8	2 550.8	2 666.1	2 609.6	
	100.0	97.6	95.2	92.9	90.7	99.8	107.2	115.3	112.5	109.0	114.4	119.6	117.1	1.32
7	1 550.9	1 542.2	1 533.6	1 524.9	1 516.4	1 486.3	1 338.4	1 205.3	1 206.6	1 105.3	1 051.9	1 191.6	1 408.7	
	100.0	99.4	98.9	98.3	97.8	95.8	86.3	77.7	77.8	71.3	67.8	76.8	90.8	-0.8
8	2 526.3	2 579.0	2 632.8	2 687.7	2 743.8	2 858.1	2 852.0	2 845.8	2 910.5	2 637.0	2 595.8	2 684.0	3 028.8	
	100.0	102.1	104.2	106.4	108.6	113.1	112.9	112.6	115.2	104.4	102.8	106.2	119.9	1.52
9a	19	19	19	19	19	18	18	17	15	13	11	11	12	
	860.1	697.3	535.9	375.8	216.9	971.6	071.9	214.9	960.9	196.2	741.6	121.2	107.0	
	100.0	99.2	98.4	97.6	96.8	95.5	91.0	86.7	80.4	66.4	59.1	56.0	61.0	-4.04
9b	4 191.2	4 418.8	4 658.9	4 912.0	5 178.8	5 186.3	5 451.2	5 729.6	5 995.0	5 655.1	5 845.9	6 171.3	7 172.4	
	100.0	105.4	111.2	117.2	123.6	123.7	130.1	136.7	143.0	134.9	139.5	147.2	171.1	4.58
9	5 678.2	5 877.8	6 084.3	6 298.2	6 519.6	6 514.8	6 724.6	6 941.2	7 067.3	6 495.5	6 498.0	6 763.5	7 774.2	
	100.0	103.5	107.2	110.9	114.8	114.7	118.4	122.2	124.5	114.4	114.4	119.1	136.9	2.65

Table 6.4 (concluded)

ICOP Branch Industry Category	1980	1981	1982	1983	1984	1985	1986	1987	1988	1989	1990	1991	1992	Growth
10	3 814.9	3 844.3	3 874.1	3 904.0	3 934.2	3 964.9	3 878.9	3 794.9	4 036.7	3 958.7	3 912.5	4 060.2	4 619.6	
	100.0	100.8	101.6	102.3	103.1	103.9	101.7	99.5	105.8	103.8	102.6	106.4	121.1	1.61
11	1 765.8	1 804.0	1 842.9	1 882.7	1 923.4	1 947.7	1 929.6	1 911.6	2 025.5	1 861.0	1 866.1	2 114.2	2 755.3	
	100.0	102.2	104.4	106.6	108.9	110.3	109.3	108.3	114.7	105.4	105.7	119.7	156.0	3.78
12	3 391.7	3 480.4	3 571.3	3 664.7	3 760.4	3 887.9	4 008.6	4 133.0	4 203.5	4 104.2	3 599.2	3 592.6	4 367.2	
	100.0	102.6	105.3	108.0	110.9	114.6	118.2	121.9	123.9	121.0	106.1	105.9	128.8	2.13
13	2 167.1	2 334.3	2 514.2	2 708.1	2 917.0	3 393.9	3 410.5	3 427.2	3 709.7	3 416.7	3 194.0	3 635.5	4 661.7	
	100.0	107.7	116.0	125.0	134.6	156.6	157.4	158.1	171.2	157.7	147.4	167.8	215.1	6.59
14	2 766.8	3 038.3	3 336.5	3 663.9	4 023.4	4 701.8	4 596.7	4 493.9	5 157.1	5 233.8	4 742.1	4 968.6	5 342.5	
	100.0	109.8	120.6	132.4	145.4	169.9	166.1	162.4	186.4	189.2	171.4	179.6	193.1	5.64
15	2 457.1	2 490.3	2 523.9	2 558.0	2 592.5	2 910.1	2 792.7	2 680.0	2 859.4	2 918.0	2 744.5	2 964.2	3 345.5	
	100.0	101.4	102.7	104.1	105.5	118.4	113.7	109.1	116.4	118.8	111.7	120.6	136.2	2.61
Total manufacturing	3 084.4	3 177.3	3 273.0	3 371.6	3 473.2	3 697.5	3 743.7	3 790.4	4 005.9	3 847.5	3 753.9	3 962.8	4 610.4	
	100.0	103.0	106.1	109.3	112.6	119.9	121.4	122.9	129.9	124.7	121.1	128.5	149.5	3.41

Notes: ½. Food and beverages; 1. Food manufacturing; 2. Beverages; 3. Tobacco products; 4. Textiles; 5. Clothing; 6. Leather, fur and their products; 7. Wood products and furniture; 8. Paper, paper products and printing; 9a. Oil refining, coal, coking and coal products; 9b. Chemicals, excluding, oil refining; 9. Chemicals, total; 10. Rubber and plastic products; 11. Building materials and other non-metallic minerals; 12. Basic and fabricated metals; 13. Machinery and transportation equipment; 14. Electrical machinery and equipment; 15. Other industry.

Sources: Net value added from SSB (1993a), pp.142-154; deflators from SSB (1993c), Table T7.24, p. 238; and employment from SSB (1993a).

142

Table 6.5. **Comparative Productivity by Manufacturing Branch, China and the United States, 1980-92**

(United States = 100)

	1980	1981	1982	1983	1984	1985	1986	1987	1988	1989	1990	1991	1992
Food and beverages	3.5	3.5	3.3	3.2	3.2	3.1	3.3	3.4	3.6	3.7	3.7	4.5	4.6
Tobacco	2.3	2.4	2.7	2.9	2.9	3.5	3.2	4.4	5.0	5.5	6.4	6.9	7.5
Textile mills	8.2	7.9	7.4	6.4	6.3	6.5	5.9	5.9	5.9	5.3	4.8	4.3	4.6
Wearing apparel	5.4	5.7	5.9	5.7	6.0	6.4	6.3	6.2	6.2	6.1	5.8	5.9	6.7
Leather and footwear	11.1	11.0	10.6	10.4	9.8	10.8	12.3	11.5	10.6	10.0	10.3	10.0	8.6
Wood products, furniture and fixtures	3,8	4.3	4.1	3.8	3.6	3.6	3.2	2.6	2.7	2.5	2.5	2.8	3.3
Paper, printing and publishing	3.0	3.0	3.0	30	3.1	3.2	3.1	3.0	3.1	2.8	2.8	2.9	3.2
Chemicals, petroleum and coal products	5.8	5.8	5.6	5.0	4.6	4.6	4.3	4.1	4.0	3.7	3.9	4.1	4.6
Rubber and plastics products	5.8	5.3	5.3	4.9	4.8	4.5	4.4	4.1	4.4	4.1	4.0	4.0	4.3
Non-metallic mineral products	6.2	6.5	6.6	6.2	6.2	5.9	5.6	5.8	6.0	5.3	5.2	6.1	7.4
Basic and fabricated metal products	8.9	8.9	10.0	10.1	9.7	9.5	9.8	9.2	9.5	9.6	8.2	7.8	9.1
Machinery and transport equipment	2.6	2.9	3.1	2.8	2.7	2.9	2.7	2.6	2.6	2.4	2.2	2.5	3.0
Electrical machinery and equipment	7.5	8.1	9.0	9.4	10.0	11.4	10.8	9.2	10.1	9.5	8.2	7.9	8.2
Other manufacturing	3.8	3.5	3.6	3.7	3.2	3.8	3.3	3.1	2.8	2.9	2.6	2.7	3.0
All manufacturing	**4.9**	**5.0**	**5.2**	**4.9**	**4.8**	**4.8**	**4.7**	**4.5**	**4.6**	**4.3**	**4.2**	**4.4**	**4.9**

Notes and Sources: A time series for Chinese net value added per person was derived by combining the series on net value added at constant prices from Table 4.A.3 with a series on labour input from *Industrial Statistics Yearbook of China, 1993* (SSB, 1993). Note the drawback that these series refer to net value added while the benchmark is in terms of gross value added. The US series derive from the *National Income and Product Accounts* and the *Survey of Current Business* (US Dept. of Commerce, 1986 *a* and *b*). For a discussion of the US time series, see van Ark and Pilat (1993); They are reproduced as Annex Tables A.6, A.7 and A.8 to Szirmai and Ren (1995).

apparel, machinery and transport equipment, electrical machinery and equipment and non-metallic minerals. Six of the fourteen branches showed decreases in relative productivity, with a quite dramatic decline in textile mill products from 8.2 per cent of the US level in 1980 to 4.6 per cent in 1992. Chemical products and leather products also showed marked declines in relative performance.

Table 6.6 emphasizes the substantial productivity growth that has taken place in most branches of Chinese manufacturing. It shows clearly that China's modest *relative* productivity performance, overall and by manufacturing branch, occurred almost entirely because productivity also increased rapidly in the United States. Only in the textile mill branch, and to a lesser extent in wood products, was the relative decline associated with an absolute decline in labour productivity.

Table 6.6. **Changes in Labour Productivity by Manufacturing Branches,**
China and the United States, 1980-92
(Index values in 1992; 1980 = 100)

	China	United States	China/US Ratio
Food and Beverages	162.0	121.8	133.0
Tobacco Products	147.5	46.0	320.4
Textile Mill Products	83.0	148.1	56.0
Wearing Apparel	177.7	141.6	125.4
Leather Products and Footwear	117.1	151.8	77.1
Wood Products, Furniture and Fixtures	90.8	103.3	87.9
Paper Products, Printing and Publishing	119.9	112.7	106.4
Chemicals, Petroleum and Coal Products	136.9	172.9	79.2
Rubber and Plastics Products	121.1	160.9	75.3
Non-Metallic Mineral Products	156.0	132.3	117.9
Basic and Fabricated Metal Products	128.8	126.6	101.7
Machinery and Transport Equipment	215.1	191.4	112.4
Electrical Machinery and Equipment	193.1	177.5	108.8
Other Manufacturing	136.2	172.9	78.7
All Manufacturing	**149.5**	**151.4**	**98.7**

Source: See source notes for Table 6.4.

Table 6.7 puts China's manufacturing productivity further into an international perspective by comparing it with the results of other ICOP studies for Asia. Set against the other Asian giant, India, China appears to have very low productivity — but keep in mind that the benchmark for China includes small-scale manufacturing, while those for India (and Indonesia) are based on data for medium-sized and large-scale manufacturing only. Recall that after excluding small-scale manufacturing in both China and the United States, Chinese labour productivity in 1985 was estimated at between 7.2 per cent and 7.7 per cent of the US level. This puts China close to India, where the figure in 1985 was 7.7 per cent of the US level. While India showed a marked improvement in relative productivity between 1980 and 1986, however, China had no significant change over the same period. Chinese manufacturing in the 1980s exhibited extremely rapid growth of production, but no decrease in the productivity gap *vis-à-vis* the world productivity leader, the United States. Indonesia shows a similar pattern, but at a somewhat higher level of relative productivity. Given rapid productivity increases in Korea and Japan, the productivity gap between China and the leading Asian economies is growing. Further empirical research should check whether the picture emerging from the present data is reliable; direct comparisons between China and other countries at similar development stages may help. If the findings presented here have further support from other studies, explanations would be immediately required.

Table 6.7. **Real GDP per Person Engaged in Manufacturing: International Comparisons**
(US = 100)

Year	India (a)	Korea	Japan	Indonesia (a)	China
1970	7.0	13.8	58.9		
1971	6.3	15.8	57.8		
1972	6.1	14.5	59.9		
1973	6.0	15.4	61.6		
1974	6.0	14.3	63.4		
1975	5.8	17.6	64.1	7.7	4.5
1976	5.7	17.3	66.8	8.0	
1977	5.8	17.8	67.7	8.0	
1978	6.2	20.6	71.6	9.4	
1979	5.7	18.4	77.7	9.0	
1980	5.6	20.4	82.3	10.6	4.9
1981	6.1	22.7	84.3	11.5	5.0
1982	6.9	23.9	88.3	10.5	5.2
1983	7.1	25.3	83.7	9.9	4.9
1984	7.1	25.3	83.7	9.9	4.8
1985	7.7	24.5	85.0	10.5	4.8
1986	7.9	25.4	79.7	11.5	4.7
1987		26.4	81.8	10.0	4.5
1988		26.7	83.1	11.0	4.6
1989		28.9	87.1	10.5	4.3
1990			89.4	10.9	4.2
1991					4.4
1992					4.9

Note: The comparisons for India and Indonesia with the United States are for large and medium-sized establishments; those for Korea, Japan and China are for all manufacturing.

Sources: For India, van Ark (1991); for Japan, van Ark and Pilat (1993); for Korea, Pilat (1994); and for Indonesia, Szirmai (1994). The 1975 figure for China is from Szirmai and Ren (1995); the other figures for China are from Table 6.5.

Unit Labour Costs

The estimates of the major branch PPPs and productivity levels in manufacturing permit an exploration of Chinese manufacturing competitiveness from the perspective of unit labour costs. Table 6.8 compares such costs in dollars for China with those in US manufacturing. The methodology underlying these figures is described in the Annex to this chapter.

Table 6.8. **Chinese Unit Labour Costs by Major Branch of Manufacturing**
as a percentage of those in the United States, 1980-90

	1980	1984	1985	1987	1990
Food, beverages and tobacco	305.9	142.4	104.9	88.1	82.9
Textiles, apparel and leather products	99.1	70.2	55.7	48.7	63.0
Chemicals and allied products	72.0	54.9	48.4	45.2	54.6
Basic and fabricated metal products	64.9	32.3	27.3	30.5	36.4
Machinery and equipment	118.7	66.7	50.2	58.9	72.3
Other manufacturing	101.5	59.7	47.1	42.4	60.9
All manufacturing	**125.4**	**76.6**	**62.1**	**65.2**	**82.8**

Sources: See Annex.

Unit labour costs in Chinese manufacturing relative to those in the United States, fairly low in 1990, had fallen dramatically from 1980 until mid-decade when they began to rise. The gaps are relatively narrow for some major branches due to large productivity disparities. Trends in comparative unit labour costs depend not only on changes in productivity and labour costs (which are very low but recently rising rapidly in China), but also on exchange rate movements. In the face of recent increases in labour costs and because the room for further yuan depreciation seems limited, China's manufacturing appears to have only one way to maintain its cost competitiveness, namely to improve labour productivity.

Concluding Remarks

The comparison of labour productivity is useful but only part of the story. It has shown that no productivity catch-up process occurred between China and high-productivity leaders in the world and Asia, such as the United States, Japan and South Korea, notwithstanding that China has a very dynamic economy. Explanations for the huge gaps that remain would certainly provide new insights for policies to improve productivity levels. Such explanations would be helped by estimates of the stock of capital in the manufacturing sector by the perpetual inventory method, which has become routine in the official statistics of most OECD countries but is not yet applied to estimate the capital stock in China.

Jefferson (1992) suggested measurement error as a reason for the apparent absence of catch-up during this decade. Based on his own studies on the multi-factor productivity of Chinese industry, he found that "Within the state sector, during the first half of the 1980s, there has been a rise in the proportion of nonindustrial resources, both capital and labour, which has had the effect of overstating the rate of these two inputs and understating real factor productivity growth."

National income per person can rise as the result either of increases in the number of hours people work, the fraction of the population that is working, or of productivity. Since China had a typical dualistic economy and quite low real income in the early 1980s, the increase in per capita income may have come mainly from increases in the fraction of the population working — i.e. labour migration from agriculture to industry, including a shift of hidden unemployment in agriculture to employment in industry. If so, no inconsistency exists between the rapid increase in per capita income for the economy as a whole and the slow increase in labour productivity in manufacturing, the modern part of the economy.

Notes and References

1. This figure is calculated from the *US Census of Manufacturing, 1987, General Summary.* (US Dept. of Commerce, 1990). Table 1 from this source provides data on employment, including head office and auxiliary employment and gross value added. Table 4 provides a breakdown of employment (excluding auxiliary employment) and gross value added by employment size class. In calculating the productivity ratios we assume that all head office and auxiliary employment is in establishments with more than 20 persons employed.

2. This figure is an update of a benchmark comparison for 1991.

Methodological Notes and Source Documentation

Relative Prices of Manufactured Products

PPPs can show trends of relative price levels over time. In Chapter 3, they were calculated at sample industry, branch and manufacturing levels, and sectoral PPPs were derived for 15 branches. Here, these disaggregated PPPs were aggregated to 6 major branches by weighting with value added for each disaggregated branch. The next step extrapolated the PPPs for major branches in 1985 to other years using deflators from both countries' national accounts — the industrial products producer price index for China (see Table 4.A.2) and the US producer price index for the net output of major industry groups (see US Dept. of Labour, Bureau of Labour Statistics: *Producer Price Indexes,* Table 4, various issues).

Unit Labour Costs

The US Bureau of Labour Statistics regularly publishes trend estimates of manufacturing unit labour costs. For comparing unit labour costs between the two countries, the US labour costs per employee came from Pilat and van Ark (1994) and their data appendix. The same figures for China were estimated first for three years based on the 1985 industrial census (OLG, 1987-88) and then extrapolated for the rest of the 1980s. The labour costs refer to total compensation, including wages and salaries before tax, employer's social security contributions, contributions to pensions, insurance and health, and other expenses related to employment. One well-known characteristic of state-owned enterprises in China (especially large and medium-scale enterprises) is the large share of compensation to employees in kind through housing and other benefit programmes. If this factor were not taken into account, the study would overstate China's comparative advantage. The procedure used to estimate labour cost for China involved the following steps.

— Figures for wages and salaries for 1980, 1984 and 1985 for each industry in manufacturing were taken from the 1985 industrial census (OLG, 1987/88, Vol. 3). This is the only part of total compensation usually shown in the payroll.

— Ratios of bonuses to wages and salaries were estimated for state-owned enterprises from the 1985 industrial census, Vol. 8. These ratios were used to estimate the bonuses for all enterprises in manufacturing.

— The third step combined these ratios for 1985 with the ratios of bonuses to wages and salaries, on the underlying assumption of stability in the ratios during 1980-85.

Chapter 3's estimates of the average rent per person served as a base to derive the housing allowance as part of total compensation. The original housing allowance estimate for 1986 was applied to all manufacturing after backdating to 1985, 1984 and 1980. This procedure involved the assumption that the housing allowances have no variation among industries in manufacturing and changed only with inflation.

With the foregoing components, total compensation could be estimated for the 15 branches in manufacturing and further aggregated for the six major branches, based on the data from the 1985 industrial census. Because no data are available, compensation for the other years had to be extrapolated with the following procedure:

— It was assumed that the changes in 1985-86 and 1986-87 were the same as the change in 1984-85, in order to estimate a figure of total compensation for each major branch in 1987.

— A ratio between labour incomes in 1987 and those in 1990 for each sector was derived using data from the 1987 and 1990 input-output tables of China. These ratios were applied to total compensation for 1987 to calculate the total compensation for 1990.

Estimates of total compensation per employee for the benchmark years and labour productivity were used to estimate unit labour costs in Chinese currency, converted to unit labour costs in US dollars by the following formula:

$$ULC^{X(U)} = \frac{(LCH^{X(X)})/ER^{XU}}{(OH^{X(X)})/PPP^{XU}}$$

where ER^{XU} is the exchange rate between countries X and U, PPP^{XU} is the manufacturing PPP between them, $LCH^{X(X)}$ are the labour costs per person in country X in prices of X, and $OH^{X(X)}$ is value added per person in country X in its own prices.

Chapter 7

Conclusions

With PPPs rather than official exchange rates used as conversion factors, China has a much larger economy than people usually think. Measured on an internationally comparable scale, its aggregate GDP may be the second highest in the world, larger than those of Japan and Germany, and it has an enormous potential market.

China's per capita GDP in dollar terms is two or three times that suggested by the World Bank Atlas approach. The methods used in this study give a more realistic picture of Chinese markets. Given the relationship between consumption patterns and real income per capita, these new estimates should help investigation of consumer goods markets in China. At the same time, the PPPs and the relative price levels calculated from these PPPs have shown very low price levels in many industries in China. China's goods and services are very competitive in the world market and would have huge export potential if international trade barriers were removed. The new estimates of the openness of China's economy provide a fresh perspective on the trade-driven development strategy that China has adopted. These estimates deserve to be taken into account in evaluations of China's trade and economic performance over the past decade.

Although made for different benchmark years, the ICP and ICOP studies can be compared on a 1985 or 1986 base, which suggests relatively similar income levels. Because the updated estimates based on the benchmark studies revealed a quite significant discrepancy for the early 1990s, however, updating or backdating of estimates like these is risky and requires caution. It is better to have another benchmark estimate and cross-check the two against each other.

The study has demonstrated the necessity and feasibility of estimates based on the ICOP approach, especially as complements to ICP studies. The ICP and ICOP estimates of per capita GDP presented in this study, as well as those derived from ICP multilateral comparisons (Table 5.4), definitely still classify China as a low-income developing country. This category should be identified in purchasing power parity terms, with the per capita GDPs of all other countries in a comparison also measured by PPP-based converters. It would make no economic sense to claim exclusion of

China or any country from the low-income category because its per capita GDP based on a PPP-based converter is higher than some threshold derived by the Atlas approach or another exchange-rate method. The findings from this study have also suggested that the very different initial conditions under which China and eastern European countries started their transitions may explain to some extent why their strategies for transition have diverged.

The exploratory assessment of the growth rate provides evidence that official growth rates may overstate economic performance. Nevertheless, the economic development of China for more than a decade has been very impressive.

Several fields need further research:

— The benchmarks for both the ICP and ICOP estimates are far from perfect, which suggests the potential worth of another, later benchmark study using the most recent data. The ICOP approach may be the more feasible because the sample of prices in the ICP framework is time-consuming and expensive, and only official involvement could improve the reliability of the estimates by a large degree. The key factor for an ICOP study is a new industrial census which is under way for the benchmark year 1995. The SSB has recently undertaken a census of China's tertiary industry and published detailed data. A new input-output table has been compiled and issued. When a new industrial census is available to the public these new data will make possible an ICOP study with good chances of producing better estimates because the new data sources, especially the census of tertiary industry, should strengthen the comparison in the service sector, relatively weak in the present study.

— Another benchmark study for the early 1950s would aid assessment of long-term economic development of China since the early 1950s. It is hard to evaluate economic development over nearly four decades based on one benchmark study. A further study would throw light on economic development even if it is very rough. The price information provided in Chao (1963) and the detailed expenditure information estimated in Hollister (1958) could be the building blocks of reduced-information estimates in the ICP tradition.

— Tremendous gaps in labour productivity in manufacturing exist between China and the United States as well as other Asian countries. China's comparative productivity *vis-à-vis* these countries has not improved during the past decade of rapid growth, with no real productivity catch-up at all. Explanation of Chinese manufacturing labour productivity gaps can have considerable value for policy making.

— There is a strong case for augmenting the current study on the international competitiveness of Chinese manufacturing by estimating the total factor productivity gap, which demands estimates of China's capital stock.

— This study has examined the competitiveness of Chinese manufacturing from three perspectives: price levels, labour productivity and unit labour cost; the next step is to look at the linkage between measures of competitiveness and China's export performance over time. Similar ICOP studies have been done for Asian countries such as Japan, Korea, India and Indonesia. One can usefully examine their competitiveness in manufacturing, based on the approach adopted here, in an Asian context. In due time, based on such studies and similar ones for OECD countries (van Ark and Pilat have done this for the United States, Germany and Japan), a comparative study of competitiveness in manufacturing of OECD and Asian countries and their export performance would highlight important issues in international trade.

— This study has illustrated the many unusual methodological problems posed by comparisons between countries with large income gaps and very different institutional structures. Comparisons between countries with similar economic development levels would hold promise. The most interesting candidate for this kind of comparison is another Asian giant, India, which has much better organised data than China.

Finally, this study has at several points mentioned the major efforts under way by China's statistical authorities to improve the country's economic data and develop new systems and methodologies for collecting and reporting economic information in accordance with international statistical standards. These efforts can only be encouraged. The study of China's growth and development— and the evolution of policies to enhance them —depend upon the availability of the best and most accurate statistical information.

Bibliography

AHMAD, S. (1980), "Approaches to Purchasing Power Parity and Real Product Comparison Using Shortcuts and Reduced Information", *Staff Working Papers*, No. 418, World Bank, Washington, D.C.

AHMAD, S. (1983), "International Comparison of Chinese Prices", unpublished working paper, Comparative Analysis and Data Division, Economic Analysis and Projections Department, World Bank, Washington, D.C.

Almanac of China's Finance and Banking, (1992), Beijing.

ANDERSON, K. (1990), *Changing Comparative Advantages in China: Effects on Food, Feed and Fibre Markets*, OECD Development Centre, Paris.

ARK, B. VAN (1991), *Manufacturing Productivity in India: A Level Comparison in an International Perspective,* IDPAD, Occasional Papers and Reprints, 1991-5, New Delhi, The Hague.

ARK, B. VAN (1993*a*), *International Comparisons of Output and Productivity – Manufacturing Productivity Performance of Ten Countries from 1950 to 1990,* Monograph Series, No. 1, Groningen Growth and Development Centre, Groningen.

ARK, B. VAN (1993*b*), "The ICOP Approach: Its Implications and Applicability", *in* A. SZIRMAI, B. VAN ARK AND D. PILAT, (eds.), *Explaining Economic Growth – Essays in Honor of Angus Maddison*, North Holland, Amsterdam.

ARK, B. VAN AND D. PILAT (1993), "Productivity Levels in Germany, Japan, and the United States: Differences and Causes, *Brookings Papers on Economic Activity (Microeconomics),* Brookings Institution, Washington, D.C.

ACDA (citation abbreviation): US ARMS CONTROL AND DISARMAMENT AGENCY (1988), *World Military Expenditure and Arms Transfer*, ACDA Publication 131, Washington, D.C.

ASHBROOK, A.G., JR. (1972), "China: Economic Policy and Economic Results, 1949-71", in U.S. Congress, Joint Economic Committee, *The People's Republic of China: An Economic Assessment – A Compendium of Papers Submitted to the Joint Economic Committee, Congress of the United States*, US Government Printing Office, Washington, D.C.

BALASSA, B. (1970), "Growth Strategies in Semi-Industrial Countries", *Quarterly Journal of Economics*, February.

BALASSA, B. AND ASSOCIATES (1970), *The Structure of Protection in Developing Countries*, Johns Hopkins University Press, Baltimore.

155

BERGER, A.N. AND D.B. HUMPHREY (1992), "Measurement and Efficiency Issues in Commercial Banking", in GRILICHES (ed.), *Output Measurement in the Service Sectors*, National Bureau of Economic Research, University of Chicago Press, Chicago.

BHAGWATI, J.N. (1984), "Why Are Services Cheaper in the Poor Countries?" *Economic Journal*, Vol. 94.

BRABANT, J.M. (1985), "Exchange Rates in Eastern Europe: Type, Derivation, and Application", *Staff Working Papers*, No. 778, World Bank, Washington, D.C.

CAMPBELL, R.W. (1985), "The Conversion of National Income Data of the U.S.S.R. to Concepts of the System of National Accounts in Dollars and Estimation of Growth Rate", *Staff Working Papers*, No. 777, World Bank, Washington, D.C.

CHAO, K. (1963), *Yuan-Dollar Price Ratios in Communist China and the United States*, Occasional Papers, Center for Chinese Studies, University of Michigan, Ann Arbor, Michigan.

CHEN, N.R. AND C.M. HOU (1986), "China's Inflation, 1979-1983: Measurement and Analysis", *Economic Development and Cultural Change,* Vol. 34, No. 2

COLLIER, I.L. (1985), "The Estimation of Gross Domestic Product Growth Rate for the German Democratic Republic", *Staff Working Papers*, No. 773, World Bank, Washington, D.C.

EC COMMISSION *et al.* (1993), *System of National Accounts, 1993*, Luxembourg.

DALY, D.J. (ed.) (1972), *International Comparison of Prices and Output*, Columbia University Press, New York and London.

DEAN, E.R. AND K. KUNZE (1991), "Productivity Measurement in the Service Industries", paper presented at the Conference on Output Measurement in the Service Sector, Charleston.

DERNBERGER, R.F. (1980), "Quantitative Measures and the Analyses of China's Contemporary Economic Evolution: Problems and Prospects", *in* ECKSTEIN, A. (ed.), *Quantitative Measures of China's Economic Output,* The University of Michigan Press, Ann Arbor.

DIEWERT, W.E. (1986), "Microeconomic Approaches to the Theory of International Comparisons", Technical Working Paper No. 53, National Bureau of Economic Research, Cambridge, MA.

ECKSTEIN, A. (1961), *The National Income of Communist China*, The Free Press of Glencoe, Inc., New York.

ECKSTEIN, A. (1973), "Economic Growth and Change in China: A Twenty-Year Perspective", *The China Quarterly*, No. 54.

FABRICANT, S. (1940), *The Output of Manufacturing Industries, 1899-1937*, National Bureau of Economic Research, New York.

FALLENBUCHL, Z.M. (1985), "National Income Statistics for Poland, 1970-1980", *Staff Working Papers*, No. 776, World Bank, Washington, D.C.

FELTENSTEIN, A. AND J. HA (1991), "Measurement of Repressed Inflation in China", *Journal of Development Economics,* Vol. 36.

FISHER, J. (1922), *The Making of Index Numbers*, Houghton Mifflin, Boston.

FRISCHTAK, C. (1992), "Banking Automation and Productivity Change: The Brazilian Experience", *World Development*, Vol. 20, No. 12.

FUCHS, V.R. (ed.) (1969), *Production and Productivity in the Service Industries,* NBER Studies in Income and Wealth, Vol. 34, Columbia University Press, New York.

FU, X.C. AND G.Q. LIE (1989), " The Calculation of Industrial Growth Rate by the Industrial Gross Value of Output and the Changes of Prices of Products" (in Chinese: "Shi Yong Gong Ye Zong Chan Zhi He Chan Ping Jia Ge Bian Dong Ji Suan Gong Ye Zeng Zhang Lu"), *Journal of Statistical Studies.*

FUKASAKU, K. AND H.-B. SOLIGNAC LECOMTE (1996), *Economic Transition and Trade Policy Reform: Lessons From China*, processed paper, OECD Development Centre, Paris.

FUKASAKU, K. AND D. WALL, (1994), *China's Long March to an Open Economy,* Development Centre Studies, OECD, Paris.

GARNAUT, R. AND G. LIU, (eds.) (1992), *Economic Reform and Internationalization: China and the Pacific Region*, ALLEN & UNWIN, Singapore.

GEARY, R.C. (1944), "The Concept of Net Volume of Output with Special Reference to Irish Data", *Journal of the Royal Statistical Society,* Vol. 107.

GEARY, R.C. (1958), "A Note on Comparisons of Exchange Rates and Purchasing Power Between Countries", *Journal of the Royal Statistical Society,* Vol. 121.

GERSCHENKRON, A. (1962), *Economic Backwardness in Historical Perspective*, The Belknap Press of Harvard University Press, Cambridge, MA.

GILBERT, M. AND I.B. KRAVIS (1954), *An International Comparison of National Products and the Purchasing Power of Currencies*, OEEC, Paris.

GILBERT, M. AND ASSOCIATES (1958), *Comparative National Products and Price Levels*, OEEC, Paris.

GILBERT, M. AND W. BECKERMAN (1961), "International Comparisons of Real Product and Productivity by Final Expenditures and by Industry" *in* KENDRICK (ed.), *Output, Input, and Productivity Measurement*, Studies in Income and Wealth, Vol. 25, Princeton University Press, Princeton, NJ.

GOLDSMITH, R.W. (1983), *The Financial Development of India, Japan and the United States: A Trilateral Institutional, Statistical and Analytic Comparison*, Yale University Press, New Haven and London.

GORDON, M.J., F. LUO AND Z. WANG (1990), "On the International Comparison of China's GNP", mimeo. Faculty of Management, University of Toronto, Canada and Hongnan University of Finance and Economics, China.

GRILICHES, Z. (ed.) (1971), *Price Indexes and Quality Change*, Harvard University Press, Cambridge, MA.

HAN, K. (1982), "The Reminbi Exchange Rate and Profits and Losses in Foreign Trade", in Secretariat of the Chinese Association for International Trade (ed.), *Selected Articles on International Trade*, Trade Publishing House, Beijing.

HAVLIK, P. AND F. LEVCIK (1985), "The Gross Domestic Product of Czechoslovakia, 1970-1980", *Staff Working Papers*, No. 772, World Bank, Washington, D.C.

HEWETT, E.D.A. (1985), The Gross National Product of Hungary: Import issues for Comparative Research, *Staff Working Papers*, No. 775, World Bank, Washington, D.C.

HILL, P. (1982), *Multilateral Measurements of Purchasing Power and Real GDP*, Eurostat, Luxembourg.

HODGMAN, D.R. (1954), *Soviet Industrial Production, 1928-1951*, Cambridge, MA.

HOLLISTER, W.W. (1958), *China's Gross National Product and Social Accounts, 1950-1957*, Glencoe, Illinois.

HOUBEN, A. (1990), "An International Comparison of Real Output, Labour Productivity and Purchasing Power in the Mineral Industries in the United States, Brazil and Mexico for 1975", *Research Memorandum*, No. 368, Institute of Economic Research, Groningen.

INDUSTRY DIVISION, SSB OF HUNAN PROVINCE (1989), "The Issues on the Calculation of Industrial Production Index" (in Chinese: Ji Suan Gong Ye Sheng Chan Zhi Shu De Ruo Gan Wen Ti) *Journal of Statistical Studies.*

INTERNATIONAL MONETARY FUND (1993), *World Economic Outlook,* Washington, D.C.

INTERNATIONAL MONETARY FUND (1994), *International Financial Statistics,* Washington, D.C.

JACKSON, M.R. (1985), "National Accounts and the Estimation of Gross Domestic Product and Its Growth Rates for Romania", *Staff Working Papers*, No. 774, World Bank, Washington, D.C.

JASNY, N. (1951a), *The Soviet Economy During the Plan Era; The Soviet Price System; Soviet Prices of Producers' Goods*, Stanford University Food Research Institute, Miscellaneous Publication 11A, Stanford University Press, Stanford, CA.

JASNY, N. (1951b), *The Soviet Price System*, Stanford University Food Research Institute, Miscellaneous Publication 11B, Stanford University Press, Stanford, CA.

JASNY, N. (1952), *Soviet Prices of Producers' Goods*, Stanford University Food Research Institute, Miscellaneous Publication 11C, Stanford University Press, Stanford, CA.

JEFFERSON, J. (1992), "Growth and Productivity Change in Chinese Industry: Problems of Measurement", *in* M. DUTTA, (ed.) *Research in Asian Economic Studies*, Vol. 4.

KEIDEL, A. (1992), *How Badly Do China's National Accounts Underestimate China's GNP*, Rock Creek Research Inc., December.

KHAMIS, S.H. (1970), "Properties and Conditions for the Existence of A New Type of Index Number", *Sankhya*, 32.

KHAMIS, S.H. (1972), "A New System of Index Numbers for National and International Purposes", *Journal of the Royal Statistical Society*, 32.

KHAMIS, S.H. (1984), "On Aggregation Methods for International Comparisons", *Review of Income and Wealth*, Vol. 30, June.

KRAVIS, I.B. (1981), "An Approximation of the Relative Real Per Capita GDP of the People's Republic of China", *Journal of Comparative Economics*, 5.

KRAVIS, I.B. (1984), "Comparative Studies of National Income and Prices", *Journal of Economic Literature*, Vol. 22.

KRAVIS, I.B., I. KENESSEY, A. HESTON AND R. SUMMERS (1975), *A System of International Comparison of Gross Product and Purchasing Power*, Johns Hopkins University Press, Baltimore and London.

KRAVIS, I.B., A. HESTON, AND R. SUMMERS (1978), *International Comparisons of Real Product and Purchasing Power*, Johns Hopkins University Press, Baltimore and London.

KRAVIS, I.B., A. HESTON, AND R. SUMMERS (1982), *World Product and Income: International Comparisons of Real Gross Product*, Johns Hopkins University Press, Baltimore and London.

KRAVIS, I.B. AND R.E. LIPSEY (1983), *Towards an Explanation of National Price Levels*, Special Studies in International Finance, No. 52, Princeton University Press, Princeton NJ.

LEE, C.H. AND H. REISEN (eds.) (1994), *From Reform to Growth: China and Other Countries in Transition in Asia and Central and Eastern Europe*, OECD Development Centre, Paris.

LARDY, H.R. (1992), *Foreign Trade and Economic Reform in China, 1978-1990*, Cambridge University Press, Cambridge.

LI, K.W. (1994), *Financial Repression and Economic Reform in China*, Westport, Connecticut and London, Praeger.

LI, JINGWEN AND ASSOCIATES (1993), *Productivity and Economic Growth in China, USA and Japan, (in Chinese: Shen Chan Lu Yu Zhong Mei Ri Jing Ji Zheng Zhang Yan Jiu)*, Chinese Social Science Publishing House, Beijing.

LIU, L. (1989) "On the Calculation of Industrial Growth Rate" (in Chinese: "Lun Gong Ye Fa Zhan Su Du De Ji Suan"), *Journal of Statistical Studies*.

LIU, L. AND P. NIE, (1993), "On the Calculation of Industrial Growth Rate of Industrial Value Added", (in Chinese: "Gong Ye Zeng Jia Zhi Jie Suan Fa Zhan Su Du Yan Jiu"), *Journal of Statistical Studies*.

LIU, T.-C. (1946), *China's National Income, 1931-36: An Exploratory Study*, Brookings Institution, Washington, D.C.

LIU, T.-C. (1959), "Structural Changes in the Economy of the Chinese Mainland, 1933 to 1952-1957", *American Economic Review*, Vol. 49, No. 2, May.

LIU, T.-C. AND K.-C. YEH (1965), *The Economy of the Chinese Mainland: National Income and Economic Development, 1933-59*, Princeton University Press, Princeton, NJ.

LIU, T.-C. (1968), "Quantitative Trends in the Economy", in A. ECKSTEIN, W. GALENSON, AND T.-C. LIU (eds.), *Economic Trends in Communist China*, Aldine Publishing Company, Chicago.

LIU, T.C. AND K.-C. YEH (1973), "Chinese and Other Asian Economies: A Quantitative Evaluation", *American Economic Review*, Vol. 63, No. 2, May.

MA, G. AND R.GARNAUT (1992), "How Rich is China? Evidence from the Food Economy", Working Papers in Trade and Development No.92/4, Department of Economics and National Centre for Development Studies, Australian National University.

MADDISON, A. (1970), *Economic Progress and Policy in Developing Countries*, ALLEN AND UNWIN, London.

MADDISON, A. (1993), "Standardized Estimates of Fixed Capital Stock: A Six Country Comparison", *Innovazione e Materie Prime*, May.

MADDISON, A. (1995), *Monitoring the World Economy 1820-1992*, OECD Development Centre, Paris.

MADDISON, A. AND B. VAN ARK (1988), Comparisons of Real Output in Manufacturing, Policy, Planning and Research, Working Papers, WPS5, World Bank, Washington, D.C.

MADDISON, A. AND B. VAN ARK (1994a), *International Comparison of Real Product and Productivity*, Research Memorandum 567, Institute of Economic Research, Groningen.

MADDISON, A. AND B. VAN ARK (1994b), *An International Comparison of Real Product and Purchasing Power and Labour Productivity in Manufacturing Industries: Brazil, Mexico and the USA in 1975*, Research Memorandum 569, Institute of Economic Research, Groningen.

MADDISON, A. AND H. VAN OSTSTROOM (1993), *International Comparison of Value Added, Productivity and Purchasing Power Parities in Agriculture*, Research Memorandum 536 (GD-1), Institute of Economic Research, Groningen.

MANAGEMENT BUREAU OF HOUSING, (1985), *Regulation of Housing*, Beijing.

MARER, P. (1985), *Dollar GNPs of the U.S.S.R. and Eastern Europe*, The Johns Hopkins University Press, Baltimore.

MARK, J.A. (1982), "Measuring Productivity in Service Industries", *Monthly Labour Review,* June.

MAURICE, R. (ed.) (1968), *National Accounts Statistics: Sources and Methods,* Her Majesty's Stationery Office, London.

McKINSEY (1992), *Service Sector Productivity*, Washington, D.C.

McKINSEY (1994), *Latin American Productivity*, Washington, D.C.

McGUCKIN, R.H., V.N. SANG, J.R. TAYLOR AND C.A. WAITE (1992), "Post-Reform Productivity Performance and Sources of Growth in Chinese Industry: 1980-85", *Review of Income and Wealth,* Vol. 38, No. 3, September.

MESA-LAGO, C. (1985), *A Study of Cuba's Material Product System, Its Conversion to the System of National Accounts, and Estimation of Gross Domestic Product Per Capita and Growth Rates*, *Staff Working Papers*, No. 770, World Bank, Washington, D.C.

MINISTRY OF AGRICULTURE PLANNING BUREAU, (1989), *Comprehensive Book of China Rural Economic Statistics, 1949-1986 [in Chinese: Zhongguo Nongcun Jingji Tongji Ziliao Daquan, 1949-1986]*, Agriculture Press, Beijing.

MULDER, N. (1994a), *New Perspectives on Service Output and Productivity: A Comparison of French and US Productivity in Transport, Communications, Wholesale and Retail Trade*, Research Memorandum No. 575, Institute of Economic Research, Groningen.

MULDER, N. (1994b), *Output and Productivity in Brazilian Distribution: A Comparative View,* Research Memorandum, No. 578, Institute of Economic Research, Groningen.

MULDER, N. (1994c), *Transport and Communications in Mexico and the United States,* Research Memorandum, No. 579, Institute of Economic Research, Groningen.

MULDER, N. (1995a), *Transport and Communications Output and Productivity in Brazil and the USA, 1950-90,* Research Memorandum, No. 580, Institute of Economic Research, Groningen.

MULDER, N. (1995b), *Comparative Performance in Financial Services,* processed paper, Institute of Economic Research, Groningen.

MULDER, N. (1995c), *Productivity Performance of Mexican Health Care in Comparative Perspective,* processed paper, Institute of Economic Research, Groningen.

MULDER, N. (1995d), *The Performance of Mexican Education in a Comparative Perspective, 1950-90,* processed paper, Institute of Economic Research, Groningen.

MULDER, N. (1995e), *The International Comparison of Real Estate: Brazil, Mexico, and the United States,* processed paper, Institute of Economic Research, Groningen.

MULDER, N. (1995f), "Long-Term Growth and Performance of Mexican Health Care in International Perspective", in D. PAPOUSEK (ed.), *Mexico en Movimiento,* University of Groningen Press, Groningen.

MULDER, N. AND A. MADDISON (1993), *The International Comparison of Performance in Distribution,* Research Memorandum No. 537, Institute of Economic Research, Groningen.

OECD (1994), *National Accounts,* Paris.

OLG (citation abbreviation), (1987-88): Office of Leading Group of the National Industrial Census under the State Council, Peoples Republic of China, *Industrial Census, 1985,* Vol. I-X (in Chinese). Statistics Printing House of China, Beijing.

OLG (1988), Office of the Leading Group of the National Industrial Census under the State Council, People's Republic of China, *Industrial Census, 1985 (Large and Medium-Sized Enterprises),* (in English), Hong Kong, Economic Information Agency, June.

OOSTSTROOM, H. VAN AND A. MADDISON (1984), *An International Comparison of Levels of Real Output and Productivity in Agriculture in 1975,* Institute of Economic Research, Research Memorandum, No. 62, Groningen.

OU P.-S. *et al.* (1946), Industrial Production and Employment in Pre-War China", *The Economic Journal,* September.

OU, P.-S. (1946), "A New Estimate of China's National Income", *Journal of Political Economy.*

OU, P.-S. *et al.* (1947), *China's National Income, [in Chinese: Zhong Guo Guo Min Shou Ru],* 2 vols., Shanghai.

PAIGE, D. AND G. BOMBACH (1959), *A Comparison of National Output and Productivity,* OEEC, Paris.

PENEZOLA WEBB, T. (1985), "La Productividad de la Banca en Mexico", *Trimestre Economico,* Vol. 52.

PERKINS, D.H. (1975), "Growth and Changing Structure of China's Twentieth-Century Economy", in D.H. PERKINS (ed.), *China's Modern Economy in Historical Perspective* , Stanford University Press, Stanford, CA.

PERKINS, D.H. (1980), "Issues in the Estimation of China's National Product", *in* A. ECKSTEIN, (ed.), *Quantitative Measures of China's Economic Output*, University of Michigan Press, Ann Arbor.

PERKINS, D.H. (1988), "Reforming China's Economic System", *Journal of Economic Literature*.

PILAT, D. (1994), *The Economics of Rapid Growth, the Experience of Japan and Korea,* Edward Elgar, Aldershot.

PILAT, D. AND B. VAN ARK (1994), "Competitiveness in Manufacturing: A Comparison of Germany, Japan and the United States", *Banca Nazionale de Lavoro Quarterly Review,* Vol. 43, No. 89.

POSTLETHWAITE, T.N. AND D.E. WILEY (1992), *The IEA Study of Science II: Science Achievement in Twenty-Three Countries*, Oxford, Pergamon Press.

PRASADA RAO, D.S. (1993), *International Comparisons of Agricultural Output and Productivity*, FAO Economic and Social Development Paper No. 112, FAO, Rome.

REN, R. AND K. CHEN (1994), "An Expenditure-based Bilateral Comparison of Gross Domestic Product between China and the United States", *Review of Income and Wealth*, Vol. 40, No. 4, December.

REN, R. AND K. CHEN (1995), "China's GDP in U.S. Dollars Based on Purchasing Power Parity", World Bank Policy Research Working Paper, No. 1415, January.

ROSTAS, L. (1948), *Comparative Productivity in British and American Industry*, National Institute of Economic and Social Research, Cambridge University Press, London.

SMITH, A.D., D.M.W.N. HITCHENS AND D.W. DAVIES (1982), *International Industrial Productivity: A Comparison of Britain, America and Germany*, NIESR, Cambridge University Press, Cambridge.

SINGH, S. AND J. PARK (1985), "National Accounts Statistics and Exchange Rates for Bulgaria", *Staff Working Papers*, No. 771, World Bank, Washington, D.C.

SPEAGLE, E.S. AND E. KOHN (1958), "Employment and Output in Banking, 1919-55", *Review of Economics and Statistics*.

STATE STATISTICAL BUREAU (1960), *Ten Great Years*, People's Republic of China, Foreign Languages Publishing House, Beijing.

STATE STATISTICAL BUREAU (1986), *Statistical Yearbook of China, 1986*, People's Republic of China, Statistical Publishing House, Beijing.

STATE STATISTICAL BUREAU (1987*a*), *Price Statistics Yearbook of China*, People's Republic of China, Statistical Publishing House, Beijing.

STATE STATISTICAL BUREAU (1987*b*), *The Explanation on the Main Indicators in National Accounts,* 3 vols. (in Chinese), People's Republic of China, Statistical Publishing House, Beijing.

STATE STATISTICAL BUREAU (1988*a*), *Industrial Statistical Yearbook of China, 1988*, People's Republic of China, Statistical Publishing House, Beijing.

STATE STATISTICAL BUREAU (1988*b*), *Price Statistics Yearbook of China, 1988,* People's Republic of China, Statistical Publishing House, Beijing.

STATE STATISTICAL BUREAU (1989), *Statistical Yearbook of China, 1988,* People's Republic of China, Statistical Publishing House, Beijing.

STATE STATISTICAL BUREAU (1991), *Input-Output Tables of China, 1987*, People's Republic of China, Statistical Publishing House, Beijing.

STATE STATISTICAL BUREAU (1993*a*), *Industrial Statistical Yearbook of China, 1993*, People's Republic of China, Statistical Publishing House, Beijing.

STATE STATISTICAL BUREAU (1993*b*), *Explanation of Industrial Statistical Indicator*, processed, Beijing.

STATE STATISTICAL BUREAU (1993*c*), *Statistical Yearbook of China, 1993*, People's Republic of China, Statistical Publishing House, Beijing

STATE STATISTICAL BUREAU (1994), *Statistical Yearbook of China, 1994*, People's Republic of China, Statistical Publishing House, Beijing.

STATE STATISTICAL BUREAU (1995) *Statistical Yearbook of China, 1995*, People's Republic of China, Statistical Publishing House, Beijing.

SUMMERS, R AND A. HESTON (1984), "Improved International Comparisons of Real Product and Its Composition, 1950-80", *Review of Income and Wealth,* Vol. 30, No. 2, June.

SUMMERS, R AND A. HESTON (1988), "A New Set of International Comparisons of Real Product and Price Levels: Estimates for 130 Countries, 1950-1985", *Review of Income and Wealth*, Series 34, No. 1.

SUMMERS, R AND A. HESTON (1991), "The Penn World Table (Mark 5): An Expanded Set of International Comparisons, 1950-1988", *The Quarterly Journal of Economics,* Vol. 106, No. 2.

SWAMY, S. (1973), "Economic Growth in China and India, 1952-1970: A Comparative Appraisal", *Economic Development and Cultural Change*, Vol. 21, No. 4.

SZIRMAI, A. (1993), "Comparative Productivity in Manufacturing: A Case Study for Indonesia", *in* A. SZIRMAI, B. VAN ARK AND D. PILAT, (eds.), *Explaining Economic Growth, Essays in Honour of Angus Maddison*, Elsevier, North Holland.

SZIRMAI, A. (1994), "Real Output and Labour Productivity in Indonesian Manufacturing, 1975-90", *Bulletin of Indonesian Economic Studies,* Vol. 30, No. 2, August.

SZIRMAI, A. AND D. PILAT (1990), "Comparisons of Purchasing Power, Real Output and Labor Productivity in Manufacturing in Japan, South Korea and the USA, 1975-1985", *Review of Income and Wealth*, Series 26, No. 1.

SZIRMAI, A. AND R. REN (1995), "China's Manufacturing Performance in Comparative Perspective, 1980-1992", Research Memorandum No. 581, Institute of Economic Research, Groningen, June.

TAYLOR, J.R. (1986), "China's Price Structure in International Perspective", CIR Staff Paper, Washington, D.C.

TAYLOR, J.R. (1991), "Dollar GNP Estimates for China", CIR Staff Paper, Washington, D.C.

UNITED NATIONS (1968a) *A System of National Accounts,* Series F, No. 2, Rev. 3, New York.

UNITED NATIONS (1968b), *International Standard Classification of All Economic Activities (ISIC),* New York.

UNITED NATIONS *et al.* (1994) *World Comparisons of Real Gross Domestic Product and Purchasing Power,* Series F/64, New York.

UNITED NATIONS DEVELOPMENT PROGRAM (UNDP), (1990), *Human Development Report,* Oxford University Press, New York.

US CENTRAL INTELLIGENCE AGENCY, (1991). *The Chinese Economy in 1990 and 1991: Uncertain Recovery*, Directorate of Intelligence, Washington, D.C.

US CONGRESS, (1975), *China: A Reassessment of the Economy,* Joint Economic Committee (JEC), US Government Printing Office, Washington, D.C.

US DEPT. OF COMMERCE, (1986a), *National Income and Product Accounts, 1929-1982, Statistical Tables* , Bureau of Economic Analysis, Washington, D.C.

US DEPT. OF COMMERCE, (1986b), *Survey of Current Business*, various issues, Bureau of Economic Analysis, Washington, D.C.

US DEPT. OF COMMERCE (1987), *Statistical Abstract of the United States*, US Bureau of the Census, Washington, D.C.

US DEPT. OF COMMERCE (1988), *Statistical Abstract of the United States*, US Bureau of the Census, Washington, D.C.

US DEPT. OF COMMERCE (1989), *Statistical Abstract of the United States*, US Bureau of the Census, Washington, D.C.

US DEPT. OF COMMERCE (1989), *US Industrial Outlook*, Washington, D.C.

US DEPT. OF COMMERCE (1990), *US Census of Manufacturing, 1987, General Summary and Industry Series*, Washington, D.C.

US DEPT. OF COMMERCE (1992), *Statistical Abstract of the United States*, US Bureau of the Census, Washington, D.C.

US DEPT. OF COMMERCE, (1992), *National Income and Product Accounts, 1959-1988, Statistical Tables*, Bureau of Economic Analysis, Washington, D.C.

US DEPT. OF COMMERCE, (1993), *Survey of Current Business,* Bureau of Economic Analysis, May, Washington, D.C.

US DEPT. OF LABOR (1984), *Producer Prices and Price Indexes Data*, US Bureau of Labor Statistics, Washington, D.C.

US DEPT. OF LABOR (1985), *Producer Price Indexes Data*, US Bureau of Labor Statistics, Washington, D.C.

US DEPT. OF LABOR (1986a), *Producer Price Indexes Data*, US Bureau of Labor Statistics, Washington, D.C.

US Dept. of Labor(1986*b*), *CPI Detailed Report*, US Bureau of Labor Statistics, Washington, D.C.

US Dept. of Labor, (1992) "International Comparisons of Hourly Compensation Costs for Production Workers in Manufacturing, 1991", *BLS Report 825,* US Bureau of Labor Statistics, June, Washington, D.C.

WEFA: Wharton Econometric Forecasting Associates (1984), *China Macro-economic Data Bank*, Volume III: Foreign Trade. Prepared under contract number 1724-220-144 for the US Department of State, Washington, D.C.

Welch, J.H. (1992), *Capital Markets and the Development Process: The Case of Brazil*, Macmillan, London.

Wieringa, P. and A. Maddison (1985), "*An International Comparison of Levels of Real Output in Mining and Quarrying in 1975* ", processed, Faculty of Economics, University of Groningen.

Wolf, T.A. (1985). "Exchange Rates, Foreign Trade Accounting, and Purchasing Power Parity for Centrally Planned Economies", *Staff Working Papers*, No. 779, World Bank, Washington, D.C.

World Bank (1985), *China: Long-Term Development Issues and Options, Annex 5: China — Economic Structure in an International Perspective*, Washington, D.C.

World Bank, (1989), *Social Indicators of Development, 1989* , The Johns Hopkins University Press, Baltimore and London.

World Bank (1991), *World Tables 1991*, The Johns Hopkins University Press, Baltimore and London.

World Bank, (1992a), *World Development Report 1992*, Oxford University Press, New York.

World Bank (1992b), *China: Statistical System in Transition,* Report no 9557-CHA, Washington, D.C.

World Bank (1994), *World Tables 1994,* The Johns Hopkins University Press, Baltimore and London.

World Bank (1995), *World Tables 1995*, The Johns Hopkins University Press, Baltimore and London.

Wu, H.X. (1993), "The 'Real' Chinese Gross Domestic Product (GDP) for the Pre-Reform Period, 1955-1977", *Review of Income and Wealth*, Series 39, No. 1, March.

Yi, G. (1994), *Money, Banking and Financial Markets in China*, Boulder, San Francisco and Oxford, Westview Press.

MAIN SALES OUTLETS OF OECD PUBLICATIONS
PRINCIPAUX POINTS DE VENTE DES PUBLICATIONS DE L'OCDE

AUSTRALIA – AUSTRALIE
D.A. Information Services
648 Whitehorse Road, P.O.B 163
Mitcham, Victoria 3132   Tel. (03) 9210.7777
                                 Fax: (03) 9210.7788

AUSTRIA – AUTRICHE
Gerold & Co.
Graben 31
Wien I   Tel. (0222) 533.50.14
                                 Fax: (0222) 512.47.31.29

BELGIUM – BELGIQUE
Jean De Lannoy
Avenue du Roi, Koningslaan 202
B-1060 Bruxelles   Tel. (02) 538.51.69/538.08.41
                                 Fax: (02) 538.08.41

CANADA
Renouf Publishing Company Ltd.
1294 Algoma Road
Ottawa, ON K1B 3W8   Tel. (613) 741.4333
                                 Fax: (613) 741.5439
Stores:
61 Sparks Street
Ottawa, ON K1P 5R1   Tel. (613) 238.8985
12 Adelaide Street West
Toronto, ON M5H 1L6   Tel. (416) 363.3171
                                 Fax: (416)363.59.63

Les Éditions La Liberté Inc.
3020 Chemin Sainte-Foy
Sainte-Foy, PQ G1X 3V6   Tel. (418) 658.3763
                                 Fax: (418) 658.3763

Federal Publications Inc.
165 University Avenue, Suite 701
Toronto, ON M5H 3B8   Tel. (416) 860.1611
                                 Fax: (416) 860.1608

Les Publications Fédérales
1185 Université
Montréal, QC H3B 3A7   Tel. (514) 954.1633
                                 Fax: (514) 954.1635

CHINA – CHINE
China National Publications Import
Export Corporation (CNPIEC)
16 Gongti E. Road, Chaoyang District
P.O. Box 88 or 50
Beijing 100704 PR   Tel. (01) 506.6688
                                 Fax: (01) 506.3101

CHINESE TAIPEI – TAIPEI CHINOIS
Good Faith Worldwide Int'l. Co. Ltd.
9th Floor, No. 118, Sec. 2
Chung Hsiao E. Road
Taipei   Tel. (02) 391.7396/391.7397
                                 Fax: (02) 394.9176

DENMARK – DANEMARK
Munksgaard Book and Subscription Service
35, Nørre Søgade, P.O. Box 2148
DK-1016 København K   Tel. (33) 12.85.70
                                 Fax: (33) 12.93.87

J. H. Schultz Information A/S,
Herstedvang 12,
DK – 2620 Albertslung   Tel. 43 63 23 00
                                 Fax: 43 63 19 69
Internet: s-info@inet.uni-c.dk

EGYPT – ÉGYPTE
Middle East Observer
41 Sherif Street
Cairo   Tel. 392.6919
                                 Fax: 360-6804

FINLAND – FINLANDE
Akateeminen Kirjakauppa
Keskuskatu 1, P.O. Box 128
00100 Helsinki
Subscription Services/Agence d'abonnements :
P.O. Box 23
00371 Helsinki   Tel. (358 0) 121 4416
                                 Fax: (358 0) 121.4450

FRANCE
OECD/OCDE
Mail Orders/Commandes par correspondance :
2, rue André-Pascal
75775 Paris Cedex 16   Tel. (33-1) 45.24.82.00
                                 Fax: (33-1) 49.10.42.76
                                 Telex: 640048 OCDE
Internet: Compte.PUBSINQ@oecd.org

Orders via Minitel, France only/
Commandes par Minitel, France exclusivement :
36 15 OCDE

OECD Bookshop/Librairie de l'OCDE :
33, rue Octave-Feuillet
75016 Paris   Tél. (33-1) 45.24.81.81
                                      (33-1) 45.24.81.67
Dawson
B.P. 40
91121 Palaiseau Cedex   Tel. 69.10.47.00
                                 Fax: 64.54.83.26

Documentation Française
29, quai Voltaire
75007 Paris   Tel. 40.15.70.00

Economica
49, rue Héricart
75015 Paris   Tel. 45.75.05.67
                                 Fax: 40.58.15.70

Gibert Jeune (Droit-Économie)
6, place Saint-Michel
75006 Paris   Tel. 43.25.91.19

Librairie du Commerce International
10, avenue d'Iéna
75016 Paris   Tel. 40.73.34.60

Librairie Dunod
Université Paris-Dauphine
Place du Maréchal-de-Lattre-de-Tassigny
75016 Paris   Tel. 44.05.40.13

Librairie Lavoisier
11, rue Lavoisier
75008 Paris   Tel. 42.65.39.95

Librairie des Sciences Politiques
30, rue Saint-Guillaume
75007 Paris   Tel. 45.48.36.02

P.U.F.
49, boulevard Saint-Michel
75005 Paris   Tel. 43.25.83.40

Librairie de l'Université
12a, rue Nazareth
13100 Aix-en-Provence   Tel. (16) 42.26.18.08

Documentation Française
165, rue Garibaldi
69003 Lyon   Tel. (16) 78.63.32.23

Librairie Decitre
29, place Bellecour
69002 Lyon   Tel. (16) 72.40.54.54

Librairie Sauramps
Le Triangle
34967 Montpellier Cedex 2   Tel. (16) 67.58.85.15
                                 Fax: (16) 67.58.27.36

A la Sorbonne Actual
23, rue de l'Hôtel-des-Postes

06000 Nice   Tel. (16) 93.13.77.75
                                 Fax: (16) 93.80.75.69

GERMANY – ALLEMAGNE
OECD Bonn Centre
August-Bebel-Allee 6
D-53175 Bonn   Tel. (0228) 959.120
                                 Fax: (0228) 959.12.17

GREECE – GRÈCE
Librairie Kauffmann
Stadiou 28
10564 Athens   Tel. (01) 32.55.321
                                 Fax: (01) 32.30.320

HONG-KONG
Swindon Book Co. Ltd.
Astoria Bldg. 3F
34 Ashley Road, Tsimshatsui
Kowloon, Hong Kong   Tel. 2376.2062
                                 Fax: 2376.0685

HUNGARY – HONGRIE
Euro Info Service
Margitsziget, Európa Ház
1138 Budapest   Tel. (1) 111.62.16
                                 Fax: (1) 111.60.61

ICELAND – ISLANDE
Mál Mog Menning
Laugavegi 18, Pósthólf 392
121 Reykjavik   Tel. (1) 552.4240
                                 Fax: (1) 562.3523

INDIA – INDE
Oxford Book and Stationery Co.
Scindia House
New Delhi 110001   Tel. (11) 331.5896/5308
                                 Fax: (11) 332.5993
17 Park Street
Calcutta 700016   Tel. 240832

INDONESIA – INDONÉSIE
Pdii-Lipi
P.O. Box 4298
Jakarta 12042   Tel. (21) 573.34.67
                                 Fax: (21) 573.34.67

IRELAND – IRLANDE
Government Supplies Agency
Publications Section
4/5 Harcourt Road
Dublin 2   Tel. 661.31.11
                                 Fax: 475.27.60

ISRAEL – ISRAËL
Praedicta
5 Shatner Street
P.O. Box 34030
Jerusalem 91430   Tel. (2) 52.84.90/1/2
                                 Fax: (2) 52.84.93

R.O.Y. International
P.O. Box 13056
Tel Aviv 61130   Tel. (3) 546 1423
                                 Fax: (3) 546 1442

Palestinian Authority/Middle East:
INDEX Information Services
P.O.B. 19502
Jerusalem   Tel. (2) 27.12.19
                                 Fax: (2) 27.16.34

ITALY – ITALIE
Libreria Commissionaria Sansoni
Via Duca di Calabria 1/1
50125 Firenze   Tel. (055) 64.54.15
                                 Fax: (055) 64.12.57
Via Bartolini 29
20155 Milano   Tel. (02) 36.50.83

Editrice e Libreria Herder
Piazza Montecitorio 120
00186 Roma   Tel. 679.46.28
                                 Fax: 678.47.51

Libreria Hoepli
Via Hoepli 5
20121 Milano   Tel. (02) 86.54.46
   Fax: (02) 805.28.86

Libreria Scientifica
Dott. Lucio de Biasio 'Aeiou'
Via Coronelli, 6
20146 Milano   Tel. (02) 48.95.45.52
   Fax: (02) 48.95.45.48

JAPAN – JAPON
OECD Tokyo Centre
Landic Akasaka Building
2-3-4 Akasaka, Minato-ku
Tokyo 107   Tel. (81.3) 3586.2016
   Fax: (81.3) 3584.7929

KOREA – CORÉE
Kyobo Book Centre Co. Ltd.
P.O. Box 1658, Kwang Hwa Moon
Seoul   Tel. 730.78.91
   Fax: 735.00.30

MALAYSIA – MALAISIE
University of Malaya Bookshop
University of Malaya
P.O. Box 1127, Jalan Pantai Baru
59700 Kuala Lumpur
Malaysia   Tel. 756.5000/756.5425
   Fax: 756.3246

MEXICO – MEXIQUE
OECD Mexico Centre
Edificio INFOTEC
Av. San Fernando no. 37
Col. Toriello Guerra
Tlalpan C.P. 14050
Mexico D.F.   Tel. (525) 665 47 99
   Fax: (525) 606 13 07

Revistas y Periodicos Internacionales S.A. de C.V.
Florencia 57 - 1004
Mexico, D.F. 06600   Tel. 207.81.00
   Fax: 208.39.79

NETHERLANDS – PAYS-BAS
SDU Uitgeverij Plantijnstraat
Externe Fondsen
Postbus 20014
2500 EA's-Gravenhage   Tel. (070) 37.89.880
Voor bestellingen: Fax: (070) 34.75.778

**NEW ZEALAND –
NOUVELLE-ZÉLANDE**
GPLegislation Services
P.O. Box 12418
Thorndon, Wellington   Tel. (04) 496.5655
   Fax: (04) 496.5698

NORWAY – NORVÈGE
NIC INFO A/S
Bertrand Narvesens vei 2
P.O. Box 6512 Etterstad
0606 Oslo 6   Tel. (022) 57.33.00
   Fax: (022) 68.19.01

PAKISTAN
Mirza Book Agency
65 Shahrah Quaid-E-Azam
Lahore 54000   Tel. (42) 735.36.01
   Fax: (42) 576.37.14

PHILIPPINE – PHILIPPINES
International Booksource Center Inc.
Rm 179/920 Cityland 10 Condo Tower 2
HV dela Costa Ext cor Valero St.
Makati Metro Manila   Tel. (632) 817 9676
   Fax: (632) 817 1741

POLAND – POLOGNE
Ars Polona
00-950 Warszawa
Krakowskie Przedmieácie 7   Tel. (22) 264760
   Fax: (22) 268673

PORTUGAL
Livraria Portugal
Rua do Carmo 70-74
Apart. 2681
1200 Lisboa   Tel. (01) 347.49.82/5
   Fax: (01) 347.02.64

SINGAPORE – SINGAPOUR
Gower Asia Pacific Pte Ltd.
Golden Wheel Building
41, Kallang Pudding Road, No. 04-03
Singapore 1334   Tel. 741.5166
   Fax: 742.9356

SPAIN – ESPAGNE
Mundi-Prensa Libros S.A.
Castelló 37, Apartado 1223
Madrid 28001   Tel. (91) 431.33.99
   Fax: (91) 575.39.98

Mundi-Prensa Barcelona
Consell de Cent No. 391
08009 – Barcelona   Tel. (93) 488.34.92
   Fax: (93) 487.76.59

Llibreria de la Generalitat
Palau Moja
Rambla dels Estudis, 118
08002 – Barcelona
   (Subscripcions) Tel. (93) 318.80.12
   (Publicacions) Tel. (93) 302.67.23
   Fax: (93) 412.18.54

SRI LANKA
Centre for Policy Research
c/o Colombo Agencies Ltd.
No. 300-304, Galle Road
Colombo 3   Tel. (1) 574240, 573551-2
   Fax: (1) 575394, 510711

SWEDEN – SUÈDE
CE Fritzes AB
S–106 47 Stockholm   Tel. (08) 690.90.90
   Fax: (08) 20.50.21

Subscription Agency/Agence d'abonnements :
Wennergren-Williams Info AB
P.O. Box 1305
171 25 Solna   Tel. (08) 705.97.50
   Fax: (08) 27.00.71

SWITZERLAND – SUISSE
Maditec S.A. (Books and Periodicals - Livres
et périodiques)
Chemin des Palettes 4
Case postale 266
1020 Renens VD 1   Tel. (021) 635.08.65
   Fax: (021) 635.07.80

Librairie Payot S.A.
4, place Pépinet
CP 3212
1002 Lausanne   Tel. (021) 320.25.11
   Fax: (021) 320.25.14

Librairie Unilivres
6, rue de Candolle
1205 Genève   Tel. (022) 320.26.23
   Fax: (022) 329.73.18

Subscription Agency/Agence d'abonnements :
Dynapresse Marketing S.A.
38, avenue Vibert
1227 Carouge   Tel. (022) 308.07.89
   Fax: (022) 308.07.99

See also – Voir aussi :
OECD Bonn Centre
August-Bebel-Allee 6
D-53175 Bonn (Germany)   Tel. (0228) 959.120
   Fax: (0228) 959.12.17

THAILAND – THAÏLANDE
Suksit Siam Co. Ltd.
113, 115 Fuang Nakhon Rd.
Opp. Wat Rajbopith
Bangkok 10200   Tel. (662) 225.9531/2
   Fax: (662) 222.5188

TRINIDAD & TOBAGO
SSL Systematics Studies Limited
9 Watts Street
Curepe
Trinadad & Tobago, W.I.   Tel. (1809) 645.3475
   Fax: (1809) 662.5654

TUNISIA – TUNISIE
Grande Librairie Spécialisée
Fendri Ali
Avenue Haffouz Imm El-Intilaka
Bloc B 1 Sfax 3000   Tel. (216-4) 296 855
   Fax: (216-4) 298.270

TURKEY – TURQUIE
Kültür Yayinlari Is-Türk Ltd. Sti.
Atatürk Bulvari No. 191/Kat 13
Kavaklidere/Ankara
   Tel. (312) 428.11.40 Ext. 2458
   Fax: (312) 417 24 90
Dolmabahce Cad. No. 29
Besiktas/Istanbul   Tel. (212) 260 7188

UNITED KINGDOM – ROYAUME-UNI
HMSO
Gen. enquiries   Tel. (0171) 873 0011
Postal orders only:
P.O. Box 276, London SW8 5DT
Personal Callers HMSO Bookshop
49 High Holborn, London WC1V 6HB
   Fax: (0171) 873 8463
Branches at: Belfast, Birmingham, Bristol,
Edinburgh, Manchester

UNITED STATES – ÉTATS-UNIS
OECD Washington Center
2001 L Street N.W., Suite 650
Washington, D.C. 20036-4922   Tel. (202) 785.6323
   Fax: (202) 785.0350
Internet: washcont@oecd.org

Subscriptions to OECD periodicals may also be placed
through main subscription agencies.

Les abonnements aux publications périodiques de
l'OCDE peuvent être souscrits auprès des principales
agences d'abonnement.

Orders and inquiries from countries where Distributors
have not yet been appointed should be sent to: OECD
Publications, 2, rue André-Pascal, 75775 Paris Cedex
16, France.

Les commandes provenant de pays où l'OCDE n'a pas
encore désigné de distributeur peuvent être adressées
aux Éditions de l'OCDE, 2, rue André-Pascal, 75775
Paris Cedex 16, France.

5-1996

OECD PUBLICATIONS, 2, rue André-Pascal, 75775 PARIS CEDEX 16
PRINTED IN FRANCE
(41 97 10 1 P) ISBN 92-64-15581-3 – No. 49651 1997